Moche Art and Visual Culture in Ancient Peru

The Revolt of the Objects, rollout drawing of fineline bottle (drawing by Donna McClelland).

Moche Art and Visual Culture in Ancient Peru

Margaret A. Jackson

UNIVERSITY OF NEW MEXICO PRESS ❖ ALBUQUERQUE

© 2008 by the University of New Mexico Press
All rights reserved. Published 2008
Printed in the United States of America

LIBRARY OF CONGRESS CATALOGING-IN-PUBLICATION DATA
Jackson, Margaret A. (Margaret Ann)
  Moche art and visual culture in ancient Peru / Margaret A. Jackson.
    p. cm.
  Includes bibliographical references and index.
  ISBN 978-0-8263-4365-9 (HARDCOVER : ALK. PAPER)
  1. Mochica pottery—Themes, motives.
  2. Picture-writing—Peru.
  3. Peru—Antiquities.
  I. Title.

  F3430.1.M6J32 2008
  985'.101—dc22
                    2008036819

Book and cover design and type composition
by Kathleen Sparkes.
This book is typeset using Minion OT PRO 10/13.
Display type is Scala Sans OT.

THE LITTLE SPACES BETWEEN THE TWIGS AND THE AIR

SPEAK TO THE PLACES OF THE MIND

CONTENTS

List of Illustrations xi

Acknowledgments xv

PART I: Social and Cultural Contexts of Moche Art
(= Situation)

ONE: Introduction: Toward a Moche Epigraphy 3

TWO: Moche Art: Social Contexts, Functions, and Religious Underpinnings 13

THREE: The Production of Ceramic Imagery 49

PART II: Interpretation of Moche Iconographic Configurations
(= Extraction)

FOUR: Issues of Iconographic Analysis 79

FIVE: Mold Technology and the Formation of Semantic Units 93

SIX: Muchic and the Linguistic Analogy 115

SEVEN: Hybrid Presentational Syntax in Moche Iconography 133

EIGHT: Concluding Comments 151

APPENDIX A: Analysis and Cross-Tabulation of Ceramic Form and Image Frequencies (Cerro Mayal, 1992 Field Season) 159

APPENDIX B: Muchic Phonetics 163

Notes 169

Bibliography 191

Index 223

LIST OF ILLUSTRATIONS

FIGURES

1.1. Map of Peru's North Coast. 4
2.1. Illustration of the Sacrifice Scene. 18
2.2. Adobe bricks with makers' marks, Huaca de La Luna. 20
2.3. Diagram of the Huaca de La Luna site plan. 23
2.4. General view of Great Plaza (North Plaza), Huaca de La Luna. 24
2.5. The "Arraignment of Prisoners," rollout drawing of bottle. 25
2.6. Water Snake and Moon Animals and Warrior Procession detail, Huaca de La Luna. 28
2.7. Rocky outcropping, Plaza 3, Huaca de La Luna, adjacent Cerro Blanco. 30
2.8. Corner chamber, lower plaza, Huaca Cao Viejo. 32
2.9. "Complex Theme" friezes on the corner chamber, lower plaza, Huaca Cao Viejo. 33
2.10. Ceramic mace heads associated with architectural features. 34
2.11. Bat effigy bottle with funerary vessel depictions. 39
2.12. Examples of ceramic vessel forms typically found in Moche graves. 41
2.13. Whistles depicting a panpipe player and a ribbon dancer, Cerro Mayal. 43
2.14. Ceramic figurines, Cerro Mayal. 44
3.1. Photo of Cerro Mayal. 51
3.2. Fineware vessel fragment depicting a Warrior Procession, Cerro Mayal. 52
3.3. Examples of vessel forms common to Cerro Mayal. 56
3.4. Stylized motifs. 57
3.5. Human face appliqués. 57
3.6. Conventionalized animal imagery. 58
3.7. Animal appliqués and molds. 58
3.8. Snake motifs. 59
3.9. Figurines from Cerro Mayal. 60
3.10. Pendant beads. 61
3.11. Musical instruments and musicians. 63

3.12. Looped ceramic trumpet and drummer effigy bottle.   63
3.13. Plant motifs.   64
3.14. Miniature trumpets and cascabeles and clay mask fragments.   65
3.15. Ceramic tools.   66
3.16. Stone tools.   67
3.17. Measured clay lump.   67
3.18. The excavated floor of one of Cerro Mayal's kilns.   68
3.19. Small stamp mold.   70
3.20. Large stamp molds of the Mayal Mold Master.   70
3.21. Slip-glued appliqués.   72
3.22. Large Wrinkle-Face Whistler face mold.   74
3.23. "Prisoner Jar with Lizards."   75
4.1. Illustration of the rebus "I saw Aunt Rose."   82
4.2. Domain of images as an interlocking triad.   87
5.1. Pictorial alignment inscriptions on figurine and appliqué molds.   95
5.2. Pictorial alignment inscriptions on Wrinkle-Face Whistler mold.   96
5.3. Pictorial alignment inscriptions.   97
5.4. Edge register marks.   98
5.5. Rattle mold, rattle player inscription, and double-chamber rattle.   99
5.6. Rattle players.   100
5.7. Birth mold with rattle inscription and mold impression and "Birth Bowl."   101
5.8. Mold, exterior inscription, and drawing of rattle inscription from birth mold.   102
5.9. Molds with "ritual vessel assemblage" inscriptions.   103
5.10. Bottles with painted "vessel assemblages."   104
5.11. Face molds with exterior geometric "textile pattern" inscriptions.   104
5.12. Huaca de La Luna mold inscriptions.   106
5.13. Huaca de La Luna molds with inscribed signs.   107
5.14. Huaca de La Luna molds with inscriptions.   108
5.15. Huaca Sialupe molds with iconic tassel inscriptions.   109
5.16. Huaca Sialupe molds with iconic checked and chevron inscriptions.   110
6.1. Rollout drawing of animated helmet and prisoner bottle.   125
6.2. Mixtec place glyphs, Codex Muro.   126
6.3. Mixtec place glyphs with modifiers, Codex Muro.   126
6.4. Stirrup-spout bottle with stepped pyramid temple.   127

6.5. Moche Lord from the "Presentation of Plates" and detail of Mixtec Lord.   128
6.6. Xian crab.   130
7.1. Drawing of a Warrior Confrontation.   137
7.2. Seated Moche lord wearing step-crescent headdress.   139
7.3. The "Presentation of Plates," rollout drawing of fineline bottle.   140
7.4. Stirrup-spout bottle with gourd plates.   141
7.5. Drawing of a Prisoner Capture.   143
7.6. The Revolt of the Objects, rollout drawing of fineline bottle.   144
7.7. The Revolt of the Objects, details of narrative clusters.   145
7.8. Confrontation of Bean Warriors and Deer Warriors.   147

PLATES

1. Huaca de La Luna and Cerro Blanco, Moche Valley, Peru.
2. Grand Patio friezes, Platform 1, Huaca de La Luna.
3. North face friezes, lower registers, and corner chamber, Huaca de La Luna.
4. North face friezes, arachnid detail, Huaca de La Luna.
5. Complex Theme friezes, east wall, Plaza 1, Huaca de La Luna.
6. *Usnu*, Platform 1, Huaca de La Luna.
7. Polychrome friezes, Huaca Cao Viejo.
8. Upper Chamber, Huaca Cao Viejo.
9. Bottle depicting ribbon dancers.
10. Large portrait head bottle with bird appliqué headdress.
11. Headdress bottles.
12. Warrior Capture bottle.
13. Bottle painted with animated weapon bundles.
14. Anthropomorphized Deer Prisoner stirrup-spout effigy bottle.

TABLES

3.1. General Analysis of Cerro Mayal Form and Image Correlations   54
6.1. Muchic Consonant Sounds   119
6.2. Comparison of Moche Linguistic and Pictorial Domains   121
B.1. Muchic Vowel Sounds   164
B.2. Muchic Consonant Sounds   165

ACKNOWLEDGMENTS

Work on this project never could have gone forward without the goodwill and assistance of many people. I am grateful to Cecelia Klein, Joanne Pillsbury, and Carol Mackey for their unfailing support of my work; and to Ricardo Morales and Santiago Uceda of the Projecto Huaca de La Luna, and Andres Alvarez Calderon of the Museo Larco, for their generous support of all manner of Moche research, including the present study. Likewise, I owe thanks to the staff of the Museo Nacional de Sicán in Ferreñafe for their generous assistance. Several parts of the book stem from earlier research at Cerro Mayal. I am grateful to Glenn Russell, Banks Leonard, Jesus Briceño, Chris Attarian, Sally Donahue, and Tom Wake for their patience and hard work at Cerro Mayal. In its later stages, the work has benefited from the unstinting help of colleagues, including Tom Cummins, Jeffrey Quilter, and Luis Jaime Castillo. I especially appreciate the work of Donna McClelland. Many thanks are due to my editor, Lisa Pacheco. Most especially, I thank Elizabeth Benson, Michael Moseley, Christopher Donnan, Gary Urton, John Verano, and Elizabeth Boone for their own inspiring research, which has greatly influenced my own. Research on Moche iconography was made possible through financial support from the American Philosophical Society, University of Miami Max Orovitz Awards, and the American Council of Learned Societies Andrew W. Mellon Fellowship.

PART I

Social and Cultural Contexts of Moche Art (= Situation)

O N E

Introduction
Toward a Moche Epigraphy

In the absence of phonetic script, visual representation often works in concert with oral communication to simultaneously record and transmit a society's ideology and values. The Moche of the North Coast of Peru (ca. A.D. 100–800; see Figure 1.1) provide an excellent example of an ancient American culture that developed an elaborate, systematized pictorial code, whose symbols had well-understood meanings that were used to communicate particular narratives, sets of ideas, and ideological constructs. As a group, the Moche are well known for having produced artworks of impressive technical virtuosity and complex figural imagery, whose remains are still found throughout their Peruvian coastal homelands. Most notably these works include monumental pyramids and temple complexes extensively decorated with polychrome murals, elaborately modeled and painted ceramic vessels, sophisticated textiles, and metalwork. Among the distinctive aspects of Moche art are the recurrence and continuity of specific pictorial images throughout the culture's long history, despite diverse media and geographic locations.

Of all surviving media, Moche ceramic arts are perhaps the most popularly known. Because of their numbers, they provide the greatest consistency, the longest continuum, and the largest iconographic sample for study. The ceramics bear a distinct, recognizable style, forming the basis for the definition of a broad temporal and spatial distribution of a cultural complex that we today recognize as Moche.[1] They come as part of an extremely long-lived artistic tradition in northern Peru; most of the major motifs and forms familiar from Moche can be identified in earlier epochs, albeit in stylistically distinct manifestations, antedated in some cases by almost a millennium.[2]

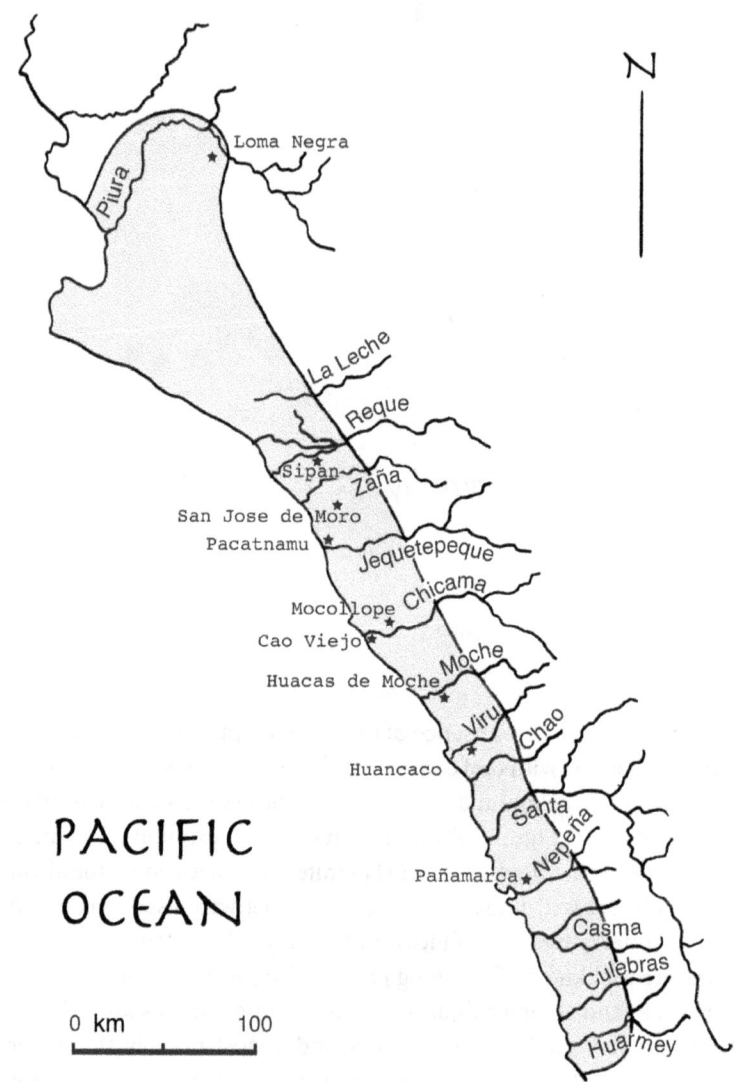

FIGURE 1.1. Map of Peru's North Coast indicating the extent of Moche cultural influence (after Castillo and Donnan 1994).

Lasting eight centuries or more, the Moche ceramic style was produced and maintained by very specific technological traditions. Objects and images played a dynamic role in the maintenance and stability of the culture's social fabric, constituting an integral element of the society's overall communication strategy. Moche representation generally followed well-established artistic conventions that changed very little over time. The stylistic changes that did occur are sometimes discussed in terms of sequential development, with iconographic standardization increasingly evident in later phases. Many familiar iconic motifs continued in widespread use on the North Coast well after the decline of the Moche polity, and some are still evident to this day.

By what means and for what reasons were those forms maintained? How best to characterize them? The mechanisms and motivations responsible for the development of iconography lead to larger questions surrounding the origins of writing and the uses of pictorial signs and systems of visual notation. The components of Moche visual language were more than generally symbolic; they functioned at the level of pictorial signs. Conventionalized images were combined, disassembled, and recombined to create nuance of meaning. Just as rhythm and repetition help the rememberer without recourse to written notes, an analogous link between repetitive clauses commonly used by mnemonists and the use of repetitive icons in Moche imagery is likely. Because the iconography was employed in art forms whose specialized uses were tied to ideologically bounded contexts, apparently intended to convey only certain kinds of information, the nexus of orality, memory, and the physical performance of ritual was indispensable to their function and meaning. Furthermore, the presence of various configurations of standardized signs suggests that some aspects of social or ideological imperatives were satisfied by the visual system in ways analogous to writing. A tendency toward consistency and reiteration in Moche iconography signals the presence of a widely understood system of visual imagery standardized to the point of codification. The existence of such a codified symbol system, the social mechanisms that produced it, and its workings are the subject of this book.

Iconographic Studies, Past and Present

Yet how best to reconstruct the social systems and technologies of a culture that is only known archaeologically? Studies to date have usually dealt with disparate elements, such as iconography, funeral practices, commodity exchange, craft technology, and political structures.[3] The Moche Style is so distinctive and easily recognizable that it is often cited as a diagnostic indicator of cultural presence or absence, social hierarchy, religious belief, and temporal phase. In lieu of stratigraphic evidence, past scholars used stylistic analysis to create ceramic seriations, and, although recent studies have dramatically increased what is known, such studies continue to be used extensively in formulating chronological accounts of Moche culture history.[4]

Interpretations of Moche art have tended to focus on what is perceived as pictorial veracity. Indeed, the last two decades of research affirm that Moche artists often did depict identifiable events that took place in real architectural space.[5] These advances bear direct consequences on the present interpretation of Moche imagery because they help to clarify, by default, what *is not* realistically depicted in Moche art. Moche depictions routinely incorporate pictorial elements that are obviously not mimetic. Such images are composed, instead, of what seem to be eccentric assemblages of incongruent parts that seem to function at the level of graphic signs. Often glossed as "symbolic," a designation that offers little in the way of true insight, the composition of such imagery remains underexplored.

It is recognized from the outset that Moche iconography shows little evidence of *alphabetic* characteristics. Based on what is known of indigenous Yunga (or Muchic) languages, the corpus of signs does not appear to bear direct correspondence to specific phonemes in an overtly systematized manner. Indeed, with the possible exception of the knotted string *khipu*, the idea that a system of phonetic writing existed in the Andes prior to the Spanish invasion in the sixteenth century runs contrary to what is historically believed.[6] Nor has any graphic script or numeric code allowed outsiders the kind of cultural access made possible, for example, by Mesoamerican hieroglyphs and pictorial texts. Yet recent reevaluations of the origins and definitions of written scripts in early complex societies, combined with new thinking on pictorialism and the construction of meaningful iconography, point toward important paradigmatic shifts in how nonphonetic, phonetic, and partially phonetic notational systems should be regarded.[7] In relation to studies of Moche visual culture, such shifts suggest that the case for Moche is more complex than the simple presence or absence of phonetic script.

On Writing, Notation, and Pictures

Questions related to the ways in which visual imagery may or may not have been systematized typically hinge on one's definition of writing. There are at least two schools of thought on the issue. One commonly expressed view emphasizes the reconstruction of vocal messages. As Michael Coe puts it in *Breaking the Maya Code*, "Writing is speech put in visible form, in such a way that any reader instructed in its conventions can reconstruct the vocal message."[8] Thus, only script forms, such as phonetic alphabets or syllabaries, that closely reproduce human speech qualify as "true writing" under Coe's definition.

An important drawback of the definition is its seeming neglect of the myriad other visual forms whose formats evince notational or script-like characteristics but whose elements do not necessarily directly reflect speech sounds. Musical and mathematical notations are perhaps the most widely recognized modern examples of notational forms used to communicate complex spatial relationships without direct links to particular spoken languages (a subject to which we will return at length). Greater flexibility is allowed by Gary Urton, who, after Boone and Sampson, proposes to define writing as "the communication of specific ideas in a highly conventionalized, standardized manner by means of permanent, visible signs."[9] The focus of this expanded definition is on communication rather than on the reconstruction of speech, per se.

Most certainly, Moche iconography conforms to this latter definition. Yet neither definition fully recognizes the kind of mixed notational systems that developed in the ancient Americas; nor do they address the complex relationships between textual inscriptions that are pictorial and pictorial imagery embedded with textual signs. Such areas belong to what scholars of visual culture would regard as the "domain of images."[10] In the ancient Americas, these were the rule rather than the exception. Therefore, rather than addressing iconographic systems like Moche in terms of diametrically opposed concepts—directly representational marks ("pictures") versus glottographic scripts ("writing")—the reader is invited to consider them against a triadic framework of iconographic forms, one whose third pier can be conceived of as systematized "notation." Here, greater or lesser degrees of verbal or representational elements translate into systems of graphic coding or alternative notation, pictographic orthographies perhaps mixed with occasional word signs and other devices.

Methodological Approach

Graphic scripts, either phonetic or mixed, generally evolved in ancient societies in response to active social demands—most often in conjunction with or as by-products of other technologies. Stephen Houston notes that writing came into existence in various places in the world, including the Americas, because there was some kind of "compelling local need" for it to exist; such needs included religious or ceremonial practices, kingly display, public assertion of status, and monetary or administrative functions.[11] Additionally, in most cases a preexisting system of orderly representation existed. Thus, Houston notes that, because of the presence of specific, long-standing artistic traditions, groups that developed notational scripts generally had an iconographic preadaptation toward visual signing. Perhaps not surprisingly, systems of counting tend to be consistently among the earliest technological developments, though not necessarily coupled with narrative or iconic visual forms.[12]

Houston's research on communication technology in archaeological context provides a useful framework in which to proceed. He suggests two primary means of deriving ancient meaning and sound from graphic notations: a reasoned reconstruction of "situation" combined with the "extraction" of meaning via scholarly processes.[13] The situation of a notational form is inherently sociological, referring to its context, participants, and relationships between the various social and environmental factors. It includes how the notational form was used, in what social and cultural setting it functioned, and, of course, the physical form of the message and the code in which it is communicated. Human agency also falls within this designation. The status and roles of participants and the settings in which the messages were encoded and decoded are considered as situational factors. Processes of extraction, although informed by studies of social context, essentially refer to the hermeneutic scholarship of decoding particular graphic forms. These, Houston suggests, involve three main techniques: What he terms "informed methods" draw directly on information and methods supplied by the makers themselves. Absent those, Houston notes that researchers must devise other formal methods of analysis based on their own ingenuity and the particular circumstance. He points to analogies drawn from comparable settings in other parts of the world as a source of useful models.

Loosely adopting that model, the present work is conceived as two complementary areas. The first investigates the social milieu in which Moche art existed, its social functions, its religious base, and the political atmosphere that sustained it. Monumental temple complexes are explored as the epicenters whence radiated the political and ideological currents informing Moche imagery. The Moche ceramic production workshop at Cerro Mayal, in the Chicama Valley, serves as the primary case study for articulating forms and technologies by which symbolically loaded imageries were disseminated.[14] Data from the site additionally provide a solid basis for comparison with similar workshops elsewhere. In subsequent chapters, the analysis turns inward, toward hermeneutic considerations of the internal ordering of the symbolic system and examination of discursive models. Ceramic mold inscriptions highlight the role of technology and human agency in the development of discreet iconographic units, and an investigation of linguistic sources serves as the basis for exploration of possible interfaces between archaic Yunga (Muchic) languages and graphic signs. Further analyses of structural and canonic organization address the semiotic arrangement of Moche pictorial notation. Each thread of discussion contributes in some way to a larger understanding of the ways in which Moche pictography functioned and the manner of its internal logic.

Organization of the Book

Part I focuses on the social contexts that gave rise to Moche art. Particular emphasis is given to monumental and ceramic arts, on the hypothesis that imagery created in monumental scale broadcast ideological programs in ways that differed substantially from that seen in small-scale artworks, both in terms of internal agency and in composition. A range of social needs was satisfied by the differing manifestations of visual culture. Spectacular murals at religious centers, like Huaca de La Luna or Huaca Cao Viejo, and small portable arts in burials, such as found at Sipán, San José de Moro, and other, more modest sites, make it very clear that imagery served elite agendas as well as wider functions in middle-level society. The murals' clear iconography leaves little doubt about a Moche predisposition to pictorial communication and its social applications. What emerges from these studies is an overall synthesis, placing elite Moche monuments as the central foci of key political and religious activities on which the iconography of portable arts was based.

As Moche imagery became increasingly codified, it lent itself ever more readily to conscription by those in power, and with conscription came increased motivation toward standardization. The evidence suggests that elites controlled certain kinds of specialized knowledge and were patrons of selected aspects of artistic production, the ritual use fineware ceramics in particular. What seems to have been a system of embedded patronage is exemplified by the ceramic workshop at Cerro Mayal.[15] An examination of the production output of the workshop is useful to the present study for what it suggests about artistic agency in the production of standardized pictorial iconography.

Lying immediately adjacent to the Moche civic-ceremonial center of Mocollope in the Lower Chicama Valley, Cerro Mayal was clearly the site of large-scale manufacture of ceramics, with an artistic product closely aligned to Larco Hoyle's description of Moche Phase IV style.[16] Its ceramic imagery shows a great variety of animals, male and female figurines, zoomorphic supernatural beings, and low-relief narrative scenes. A significant portion of ceramic molds and technological implements, including firing kilns, were also documented. Carbon 14 dates show that the workshop produced a very large number of ceramics for several centuries, from A.D. 570 to 990.[17] Statistical tabulation of formal characteristics, incidence of particular motifs, and incidence of particular vessel forms intimates what is known about how such objects were used.

Yet, perhaps most significantly, the technology at the site makes clear the use of molds as a key mechanism in the transfer and control of information. For the Moche, molds may have been important, not so much because of any resultant increase in production speed but because of the standardization that occurred through mold use. A typology based on the Cerro Mayal data set reveals a far greater flexibility and modular character than previously suspected. Mold use is seen here as the principal technological mechanism aiding in the standardization of imagery, a tool of ultimate importance in the widespread dissemination of religious ideology and the construction of memory in an oral society, and highly illustrative of the manner in which images become well-understood visual phrases.

A series of short chapters in part II focus on internal organization of Moche visual arts, with particular emphasis on discovering mechanisms of iconic meaning, syntax, and semiotic arrangement. Charles Sanders Peirce's notion that a *sign* is something that conveys an idea about a thing and his now-famous tripart categorization of signs as *icons*, *indexes*, and *symbols* serve as foundations for these chapters.[18] The study builds also on the ideas of Ferdinand de Saussure, whose later work served to recast Peirce's terminology, linking it in no uncertain terms to his concept of the *linguistic sign* and contesting the basic meanings assigned by Peirce in several key regards.[19] In the Saussurian view, *signs* reflect highly arbitrary relationships between signifiers and that which is signified (language as a reflection of ideation serves as his prime example). Along this line, and generally applied across disciplines, *sign* has come to mean those signifiers retaining no vestige of any "natural" relationship to their source, lying in contrast to *symbols*, which may retain some likeness to their subject and carry more generalized associations of meaning. In the present research, Peirce's fundamental tripart relationships among *icon*, *index*, and *symbol* are retained. As a designation, *sign* is used in its limited sense, to mean conventionalized forms whose traces arise from arbitrary or abstract relationships between signifier and signified. When intended in any broader sense, *sign* is qualified here by the addition of modifying adjectives. *Symbol* is meant to suggest those forms with relatively generalized bases for conventionalization and interpretation, and *icon* and *index* retain essentially imagistic, relational connotations.

A brief review of discursive models and terminology initiates this segment. Subsequent chapters address specific bodies of evidence to clarify the internal ordering of the pictorial system. Abstract inscriptions and ceramic mold technology are explored as a means of understanding the parsing and dissemination of information in Moche society. The study adopts the position that ceramic specialists, as part of a textual community, were the most likely to provide the agency needed to become producers of script forms. Again, ceramic molds prove invaluable to an understanding of Moche imagery as a specialized notational form.

Muchic, Quignam, and Sec are known to have been the major North Coast languages of pre-Hispanic times, members of a larger family known as Yunga—a linguistic group distinct from highland Quechua neighbors. These native languages have a highly agglutinative internal structure, utilizing a system of root words and appended modifiers. A brief summary of the internal structure of the Muchic language serves as a basis for analysis of visual syntax, supporting the idea that Moche iconography echoed linguistic forms in certain respects. The linguistic analysis suggests a likelihood of logographic signs integrated into the larger pictorial repertory and offers tantalizing support for that hypothesis. Further investigations of pictographic narrative structures, iconic abbreviation, and indexing complete the analysis of Moche semiotic ordering. A pattern of ideographic clustering, combined with frequently repeated signs and symbols, points to important similarities with other ancient American script forms.

The title of the book, *Moche Art and Visual Culture in Ancient Peru*, suggests a fundamentally dynamic relationship. The present work asserts that Moche art was systematized to the point of constituting a limited notational form, bringing to bear recent advances in empirical evidence and integrating contemporary discourses surrounding pictures, writing, and mixed notational forms. Such a finding challenges conventional opinions, which hold that no coherent system of visual signs was operative in this region at the time. It further tests operative paradigms about what constitutes incipient writing and mixed notational forms as they most often developed in the New World.

As a whole, the study articulates the dynamic versatility of Moche imagery, noting the presence of elements requisite to mixed notational forms and exploring how Moche's pictorial corpus can be seen as such an iconographic system. It addresses the various ways in which Moche imagery was integrally tied to esoteric knowledge and religious practice, seeking to clarify the manner in which the canonic rules governing Moche imagery effectively translated the larger ideology into codified form.

The findings suggest that, although the graphic system was not a reiteration of spoken language, it was capable of communicating relatively specific information to those trained in esoteric matters. To the larger population, the imagery doubtless held a mnemonic component keyed to prevalent social metanarratives. It possessed an internal logic and specificity that ordered and governed its use, while its iconographic vocabulary was framed by encompassing, pervasive ideological conventions and social habits. Although many of its internal structures are analogous to the patterns typically displayed in oral rhetoric, such as rhythm, repetition, and use of set phrases, Moche iconography constituted an independent visual language that operated in a separate symbolic register.

TWO

Moche Art
*Social Contexts, Functions,
and Religious Underpinnings*

The consistency of cultural manifestations throughout the Moche realm, over the span of many centuries, gives testament to a considerable level of social cohesion. Although stylistic changes over time are evident and local variations of major forms also exist, the prevailing configurations of art, architecture, and settlement patterns bespeak a coastal tradition with long-established customs that were conservatively kept. These commonly held values allowed disparate coastal groups to understand, replicate, and propagate the major communicative forms. Consistent among them are monumental structures, complemented by a range of portable arts. What we perceive as status items, carefully fabricated in metal, textile, and ceramics, share a common iconography. It is this iconography that unites objects made of diverse media. Rather than suggesting distinct conceptions for various classes of artifacts, the commonality hints at a unity of design and an underlying function somehow related to the larger community.

Monumental arts, in the form of imposing architecture with oversized murals and friezes, and portable arts, best exemplified by ritual-use ceramics, played critical parts in the society's communication strategy. Intensive development of those arts came as a result of larger environmental and cultural factors. The present chapter investigates the connections among the cultural milieu, Moche ideology, and monumental architecture as foundational elements to which systems of visual communication were keyed. In briefly reviewing key elements, it calls attention to the conditions under which the artistic programs operated and provides a logical framework against which to evaluate a proposition of iconographic standardization.

The Social and Physical Environment

Moche culture becomes distinctly recognizable in the archaeological record from its Gallinazo predecessors by roughly A.D. 1–100. At the height of its power, the Moche cultural sphere extended hundreds of miles, from the Nepeña River Valley in the south as far north as Piura. Although the exact sequence of cultural development is far from clear, within a few centuries, it appears that most of the people of the North Coast valleys, including those of the Moche and Chicama, came to share fundamental religious and political ideologies. Not a united state, Moche polities formed a system of culturally related, semiautonomous confederacies, loosely banded together into two primary clusters.[1] The northern groups had political and cultural focus in the Lambayeque area, and the southern polities centered on the Moche/Chicama region.[2]

Environmental instability and physical geography worked against political unity on a large scale; however, at local levels, long-standing social strategies offset ill effects. Particular artistic vocabularies aided people in the mediation of political and social relationships, with negotiations ranging from the public assertion of office on a monumental scale in urban capitals to the maintenance of political and religious structures in more peripheral social venues. In each context, visual vocabularies consistently point to the same social constructs and ideological narratives underpinning the basic power structures.

Temples, murals, and pyramids marked the loci of religious practice at the highest social levels, serving as landmarks, both physically and psychologically. Fancy ceramics, made for ritual or liturgical purposes, referencing the monuments and activities associated with them, promoted social affirmation of shared religious beliefs at the local or middle levels of society. Meanwhile, modest talismans and miniature figurines signal an integration of religious ideology at society's most humble levels. Such ritualized objects, portable and iconographically charged, were among the primary physical instruments aiding in the maintenance of social interdependencies.

Settlements along the coast are characterized by two main geoclimactic zones—a series of fertile river valleys, whose crops vary somewhat between the upper and lower microclimes, and maritime zones, found in immediate association with beaches, waterfronts, and saltwater estuaries. Habitable areas are separated by uninhabitable desert, which, over time, caused local areas to develop much like islands or oases in an archipelago.[3] Rainfall along the coast is minimal and unpredictable. Agriculture within each valley is entirely dependent on canal irrigation, deriving from the continued flow of rivers originating in the highlands. Thus, political control of upper-valley water canal intakes was of crucial importance, as was the apportionment of the water itself, once into the lower valleys. Flora, fauna, and elements of geophysical space are represented to varying degrees in the artistic corpus. Much imagery focuses on riparian environments, where watery courses are symbolized by dragon-like Water Snakes and various depictions suggest ritual activities to propitiate divine sources of water.

Differences in geographic features and natural resources created inequities among valleys, allowing some valleys to become stronger than others, opening the way for political domination.[4] Inequality doubtless encouraged intervalley predation between neighboring coastal polities. Simultaneously, the critical water supply and irrigation canal intakes in the upper valleys were vulnerable to highlander incursions.[5] As recurrent militaristic themes in the artwork suggest, military prowess was surely an important requisite for political leadership. The dynamic created by these semiautonomous habitation zones encouraged self-sufficiency on the part of individual communities and created obstacles to strongly unified political organization. Competition appears to have been endemic and, at times, ferocious.

Ironically, however, many of the same factors that encouraged social differentiation and division compelled people toward cooperation as they struggled to develop strategies to offset environmental hardship. It seems that complex, hierarchical sociopolitical organizations, centering on reciprocal kinship and long-standing clan alliances, probably counterbalanced the forces of social fragmentation. Although Moche rulers may have been an elite hereditary class of "warrior priests," as some scholars suggest, Moche stratified society was considerably more multifaceted than such labels imply.[6] Several distinct social roles or offices apart from warriors and priests are recognizable, including at least one extremely high-status office held by women.[7] Society was well defined in terms of labor specializations that included healers, administrators, and craftspersons, as well as transporters, farmers, and fishermen.[8]

The precise nature of Moche social organization remains nonetheless speculative. Given that collective survival absolutely depended on corporate works projects, such as canal maintenance, local communities had no option but to develop and maintain working relationships with neighboring communities. Such interdependencies were prevalent throughout the Andes, manifested through reciprocal obligations between members of extended clans. An interdependent model of leadership, where relationships were arranged in terms of extended clans, somewhat analogous to highland *allyus*, was very likely.[9]

It would thus follow that families of elites ruled specific territories by well-established custom and tradition.[10] At the time of the conquest, clan lineages controlled the valleys in a pyramidal hierarchy somewhat resembling feudalism, in the sense that farmers were obligated to make tribute payments to a local *curaca* (chieftain), who in turn owed tribute to a higher-level lord, who himself usually owed tribute to an even higher-status ruler.[11] A pattern of fealty and tribute payments, possibly similar, has been posited as the most likely means by which Moche lords supported the construction of monuments and other large-scale projects.[12] Social ties were forged in response to environmental stress and an overriding need for periodic cooperation for the renewal of water sources, and reciprocal obligations between clans or social classes counteracted the forces of social fragmentation.

Such relationships took several important forms; among the most relevant to the present discussion are shared religious practices, artistic patronage, and the distribution of goods based on kinship or other social obligations—precisely those that would facilitate and foster the development of a cohesive artistic corpus. Symbols of hierarchy and political domination were consistently presented within a framework of religious ideology, regardless of social station or context. Portable artworks carried common meanings from one valley outpost to another, helping to create social ties across physical barriers.

The Chicama–Moche Valley relationship is a notable example of one such ancient alliance. The longevity of the political bond between these two adjacent valleys is signaled in the archaeological record by what appears to have been a relative absence of warfare throughout the Moche period, suggesting that political equilibrium was achieved in the centuries immediately preceding the first millennium.[13] Rafael Larco Hoyle is among those who assert that the original Moche polity consisted of both the Moche and Chicama valleys, going so far as to suggest that the Moche culture actually first arose in the Chicama Valley.[14] The southern Moche region later grew to include Viru, Chao, Santa, and Nepeña valleys.[15]

Evidence concerning the long history of alliance and political interdependence is couched in human terms. According to Antonio de la Calancha (in 1638), in each valley, the founding ancestors were venerated in perpetuity and each faction or political entity had its own "creator." As part of that veneration, each valley was named in honor of the deified ancestor who was the founder of that clan.[16] Pablo Arriaga (in 1641) affirmed that each Indian faction or clan had its own separate origin, writing that the Indian's idols "are images representing . . . their progenitors and forebears, whom they invoke and worship as their creators."[17] Rulers traced their lineage and hereditary right to rule from these ancestors.

Political bonds may well have been based on marriages between ruling families, as exemplified by the legend of Chimor and Chacmac.[18] Although it refers to the Moche's Chimu descendants living in the Moche and Chicama valleys (ca. A.D. 950), the identification of the ruling elite with the dynastic creators is evident in the use of titles that were recorded for rulers. The male ruler of the Chimu people was referred to by the title Chimo (Chimu).[19] Thus, the word *Chimo* was his title, the name of his home valley, and the designation of the people he ruled. His wife, the queen, was referred to as Chacmac, which was both an honorific title and a reference to her own home valley, which today we call the Chicama Valley.[20] The queen's place of birth, her gender, and her title bear reference to a long-standing political alliance that cast the Chicama Valley in the role of "wife" to Chimor (Moche Valley). Although the Chicama Valley's conceptual designation as wife may have shifted over time in accordance with prevailing orders of political ascendancy in either valley, the fact that the relationship is couched in kinship terms within the mythological space of the founding ancestors lends credence to the idea of a strong interdependence from ancient times.

Religion

Droughts, floods, tidal waves, encroachment by desert dunes, and the constant battle to keep freshwater sources viable have always plagued the North Coast.[21] Among native people, the capriciousness and harshness of the natural environment figured into the overall cosmological view and was not viewed as a separate external feature operating independently from human life. The closeness of that connection was ostensibly a key factor in how religion developed and in how religious practice became inextricably entwined with political leadership.

Little is known conclusively about Moche religion; however, many separate threads of evidence build a composite image of a society whose beliefs centered around ancestor worship and the veneration of earth, water, and sky deities.[22] Dialogue between the living and the dead was a central tenet of indigenous Andean beliefs. Certain birds and animals were seen as spirit messengers, and on some occasions, humans were thought to transcend the earthly plane through transcendental practices. Supernatural beings might be physically manifested as rocks, springs, and other geographic features. Sacred rocks representing ancestors sometimes served as territorial boundary markers for lands traditionally divided along lines of kinship.[23] Such ideological constructs seem to have been well established by a very early date, perhaps as early as 1000 B.C., when elements of Chavín influence spread throughout the Andean area.[24]

Ideology and ritual practice lay at the heart of the Moche artistic corpus, even though other political and social agendas were simultaneously served. In conceptually linking spirits, living humans, and the physical environment, the land was transformed into a sacred landscape whose iconic value translated readily into artistic imagery. Certain details of ritual practice are easily seen in the artistic corpus. Consistency and reiteration of visual themes, often structured as pictorial narratives, help to identify particular individuals and events. Specific characters populate the art, recognizable by their various costumes and accoutrements. Several distinct individuals participate in more than one kind of event or ritual. It seems likely that at least some portion of the images represent actual portraits of high-status people. Various themes are so often repeated that modern scholars recognize an array of distinct ritual events, giving them titles such as "Mountain Sacrifice" and "Dance of the Dead."[25]

All evidence confirms the idea that human sacrifice was a central part of Moche religious belief. The now well-known "Warrior Narrative" and "Sacrifice Scene" provide key entry points into the lexicon of Moche visual vocabulary because of the extent to which their characters are correlative to archaeologically known figures.[26] These scenes indicate that leadership involved the procurement of prisoners for ritual sacrifice.[27] The basic sequence of events surrounding human sacrifice, according to the visual narratives, included a prelude to sacrifice that involved battle between warriors. The warriors are generally shown equally matched, that is, each is equipped with comparable weapons, shield, helmet, and costume. These battles, while energetic, are also highly stylized. Most are shown in one-on-one confrontation, never as part of large armies. It is unclear if the Moche deliberately staged ritualized battles,

FIGURE 2.1. Illustration of the Sacrifice Scene (drawing by Donna McClelland).

as did, for example, the Aztecs of Mexico, or if prisoners were taken during military conflicts triggered by less ideologically based motives. But regardless of how combatants came to participate, if we are to believe the illustrations, battles were followed by capture, public humiliation, and, eventually, the deaths of the prisoners.

In the artwork, a group of priests and priestesses, each with particular identifying elements and varying combinations of supernatural attributes, subsequently conduct a ritual whereby bound captives have their throats cut (see Figure 2.1). In one of the most celebrated versions of this event, the protagonists collect what appear to be blood droplets into large goblets, which are then celebrated as sacrificial offerings.[28] Some depictions indicate that skeletons may have been subsequently disarticulated. Essential participants in the warrior and sacrifice sequence include the rayed and helmeted "Warrior Priest," a central recipient of a goblet delivered by either an anthropomorphic Bird Priest or a Priestess with long braids. A second officiating Priest appears to pray; he wears an elaborate half-circle headdress, while a semihuman figure cuts the throat and collects the blood of one or more bound nude prisoners. Also pictured are assorted secondary figures including a spotted dog, a rayed sedan chair (a litter), various zoomorphic warriors, and an *ulluchu* fruit, whose juice is thought to have been used as an anticoagulant.[29]

It is not known at what intervals the sacrifices took place; perhaps they marked important events, such as ascension to the throne, or were conducted in response to natural disasters, like El Niño floods. They may well have been part of a cyclical ritual calendar keyed to agricultural or celestial events, as several scholars suggest.[30] There is some evidence to suggest that the annual reappearance of the Pleiades constellation, which signaled the start of the new agricultural year (in roughly May or June), may have been the occasion. Sacrifices may have been keyed to festivals surrounding the annual cleaning of the irrigation canals. It is also possible that the frequency and trigger events shifted over time.

At least one major sacrificial event is believed to have occurred during an El Niño event, a weather phenomenon that typically occurs sometime around the month of December.[31] It is questionable that sacrificial victims, who were most often male, were taken from the general population. Instead, it seems likely that combat resulting in the capture of sacrificial victims was the sole province of a specialized warrior class.[32] Regardless of these uncertainties, it is clear that sacrifice was an event of critical social and political importance in Moche religious practice, for it is heavily represented in the artistic corpus and underlies most, if not all, ideologically related artwork. Variants and isolated elements of imagery depicting sacrifice and offerings have been found in virtually every type of artistic media known to Moche, throughout centuries of depositional history and in conjunction with every major Moche site along the North Coast.

Archaeological data clarify the extent to which the imagery matched real-world people and places. A series of opulent royal tombs, excavated in the 1980s and 1990s, the famous tombs at Sipán and San José de Moro, in the Lambayeque and Jequetepeque valleys, demonstrate that, to a significant degree, artistic depictions accurately represent the religious practices underlying political legitimation within Moche hierarchy. The occupant of Tomb 1 at Sipán, for example, was arrayed with accouterments associated with the principal figure of the Sacrifice Scene, equating him to the Warrior Priest.[33] Tomb 2 at Sipán appears to have contained the remains of a second important figure, the Bird Priest.[34] Likewise, a high-status tomb at San José de Moro contained an individual whose paraphernalia identify her as the Moche High Priestess; osteological data confirm her sex.[35] Their socially defined identities, given meaning by the iconography of each one's costume and associated art objects, signal a cohesive ideology shared among otherwise fractious polities.[36]

The dates of the tombs, as early as A.D. 250 at Sipán through A.D. 550 at San José de Moro, illustrate that the ideology was long lived. All societies change and evolve over time, yet the tremendous programmatic consistency, both in imagery and in costuming of elite protagonists, attests to a widely held ideological commitment on the part of artists, practitioners of the religion, and the general population. Blood sacrifice was of central importance to Moche theocratic power. Its prevalence in art reflects its key role as part of a vitally important social narrative, or metanarrative, to which symbolic picturing was keyed.

Monumental Art at Temples and Huacas

Moche pyramids and temples were covered with dramatic, oversized murals glorifying the dominant ideology and its human agents. For most of the first millennium, each North Coast valley had at least one major center featuring monumental pyramids or platforms.[37] The structures tended to be associated with particular landmarks, signaling their importance within the sacred landscape. As the locus of ritual events, the architecture and its associated artistic programs symbolized elite fulfillment of critical social obligations mandated

FIGURE 2.2. Adobe bricks with makers' marks, Huaca de La Luna, 2004.

by ideological tenets. In both form and function, they served as the religious and political foci of each community or polity, simultaneously broadcasting a common ideological base and making public assertions of elite status.

The architecture was typically made of adobe brick, laid out in a square or rectangular configuration, often with two or more steplike platforms, terminating in large flat spaces on top; these served as foundations for clusters of buildings.[38] Courses of bricks with distinctive markings suggest that particular groups contributed to the building effort, as seen, for example, at the Huaca de La Luna. Crudely inscribed, the maker marks suggest that those responsible wanted their brick production efforts to be somehow recognized, possibly as part of a labor taxation obligation to the polity (see Figure 2.2). It seems likely that the builders of the pyramids were requisitioning all manner of construction materials from surrounding constituent communities. The upper platforms were accessible by earthen ramps. Many also had large, attached, rectangular enclosures at their bases and clusters of smaller habitations surrounding them.[39]

The use and reuse of these special sites, or *huacas*, seems to have been both desirable and socially obligatory.[40] Visually echoing and psychologically conjuring the notion of mountains, temple pyramids were obvious analogues to mountain *apus*, or living mountain peaks, representing the incarnation of powerful ancestors and the sources of water and fertility. In that regard, the monuments carried iconic value in and of themselves. Larger monuments tend to conceal older edifices covered by sequential building episodes. Over time, many pyramids came to include elaborate burials of elite people, whose remains were often intrusive to earlier architectural structures, a pattern consistent with the overall habit of reusing and overbuilding sacred locations. Pyramids were multifunctional—multiple buildings and the remains of the dead all combined to increase the psychic power permeating a monument.

Originally, the exterior walls of these enormous structures were entirely plastered and painted. The distinct platform levels were, in a number of instances, washed with terra-cotta red or light yellow, creating vast horizontal stripes of color.[41] Several noteworthy examples of more elaborate mural programs still remain. Moche mural cycles depict a range of prisoners, warriors, supernatural creatures, and visual references to a fearsome, fanged deity, known in earlier literature as Ai-Apaec and more recently as the Decapitator.[42]

These enormous artworks proclaimed a common ideological base in monumental terms. They did so through visual reiteration of iconic phrases referential to specific rituals performed at the huacas. The general organization of the imagery was not sequentially narrative in the way that is seen, for example, in fineline bottle painting. Rather, the iconographic program can be read as a series of emblematic or episodic images, independently meaningful yet linked by common reference to the larger ideological narrative and tied to the architectural purposes of the monument itself. The colossal murals and friezes emphasized the ritual events conducted at the temples, metonymically signaling particular events through iconographic abbreviation, that is, through the use of pictorial modes compressing and distilling events into compact signifiers (a subject to which we return in part II). The signifiers themselves were apt to be laden with additive symbolic elements, intended to enhance meaning. It is to be assumed that viewers were already familiar with the principal narrative and the purpose to which the architecture was dedicated. Thus, Moche monumental imagery is visually intelligible in two primary modes; it is interpretable programmatically, as an integrated whole whose parts were carefully synchronous with their architectural placement, or register by register, with individual images keyed to the larger conceptual base and with greater or lesser degrees of symbolic compression.

As the paramount manifestations of the ideological matrix, the temple monuments represented places where personal acts of faith, enactments of public ritual, and larger concepts of sacrality met. Of the major huaca complexes in the southern Moche area, the Huaca de La Luna (Moche Valley) illustrates very well the architectural juncture of ideology, pictorial representation, and ritualized performance. Artistic programs at Huaca Cao Viejo (Chicama Valley) and Pañamarca (Nepeña Valley) further demonstrate a commonality of civic and religious context for the iconographic corpus throughout the Moche region. The social narrative underlying and informing the artistic corpus was generated and reiterated within these built environments. Whatever ideologically based narratives were repeated elsewhere surely arose from the performative experience of seeing and sensing the liturgical affirmations of mutual belief expressed within the temple surroundings.

Procession, chant, dance, and sacrificial offerings all would have combined to create a sensory, synesthetic experience for those who participated.

Huaca de La Luna

Considered by many to have been the foremost of all Moche temples, Huaca de La Luna is certainly the most extensively studied. The Huaca de La Luna complex is nestled into the side of a small conical peak known as Cerro Blanco, in the Lower Moche Valley, adjacent the modern city of Trujillo. The site is paired with the Huaca del Sol, an immense stepped pyramid, located across what was once a densely settled urban area. Extensive excavations and significant conservation efforts in the last decade have revealed several large mural programs in distinct areas of the temple.

The Huaca de La Luna assumes a long-standing relationship to the rocky outcroppings of Cerro Blanco (Plate 1). Judging by the many burials scattered around its base, Cerro Blanco was considered an important locale, even prior to Moche times, and its importance continued well after the Moche period, into the Chimu era. The attraction of this conically shaped peak was perhaps tied to the presence of a distinctive black andesite arch embedded in the living stone, which may have served as a reference to long-standing beliefs concerning mountains as the source of water. This black arch, a geologic feature unique to Cerro Blanco and visible for several miles against the mountain's generally light beige color, has been associated with the "bicephalic arch" icon, a rainbow reference with obvious water connotations, and the "Mountain Sacrifice Scene," a frequent ceramic theme depicting a human sacrifice atop a mountain peak.[43]

Like other major ceremonial centers, Huaca de La Luna grew by accretion over time. By the late Moche period the structure had experienced at least five major expansions, reached a height of approximately 32 meters above the plain below, and had grown to include three main platforms, four main plazas, and numerous smaller chambers and enclosures (Figure 2.3). Early structures were overbuilt and expanded both vertically and horizontally.[44] Each architectural phase shows evidence of having been decorated with plaster and paint. Earlier murals were colorfully painted onto flat surfaces, whereas later images were executed as friezes in low relief.[45] A brief review of particular imagery and mural cycles in relation to its architectural configuration gives form to the sequences of ritualism suggested in smaller arts, making evident the temple's role as social and religious nexus.

The principal deity of Huaca de La Luna is strikingly depicted in a series of repetitive registers constructed on the interior walls of what is today known as the Great Patio of Platform 1.[46] This large patio, at the southwest corner on the pyramid's main platform, was accessible from the more public plaza below via an imposing ramp and various adjacent auxiliary corridors. The patio seems to have retained its basic configuration throughout the centuries of rebuilding. Its walls were once completely covered by extensive polychrome murals and friezes; phases B, C, and D, dating to roughly A.D. 400–610

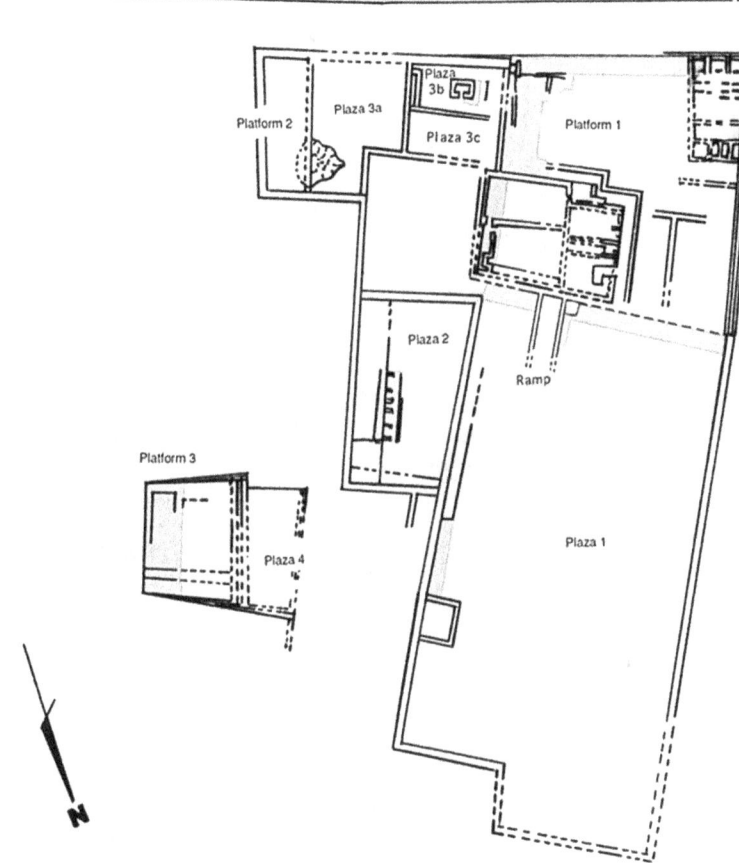

FIGURE 2.3. Diagram of the Huaca de La Luna site plan (based on Uceda et al. 1997: figure 1).

(Moche Phase III–IV), are presently visible (Plate 2). The imagery is dominated by friezes of carved adobe, approximately 1.37 to 2 meters in height, which run continuously around the structure's interior walls.[47] A repetitive geometric pattern of large rhomboids and triangles frames the face of an intimidating creature with bulging eyes, double earspools, and a feline mouth with large crossed fangs.

Twelve wavelike spirals surround the head of the Platform 1 deity, suggesting an association with marine and water concepts.[48] In terms of iconographic attributes, the association of wave motifs with this deity was well defined as early as the Cupisnique period, although specific details can be expected to have shifted over time.[49] Wave motifs, like those associated with the Decapitator deity, are also related to bicephalic arches (signs for sky or rainbow).[50] In recent years, modern scholars have variously called the deity Ai-Apaec, the Serpent

FIGURE 2.4. General view of Great Plaza (North Plaza), showing ramp and facade friezes, Huaca de La Luna, 2005.

Demon, the Fanged God, and the Mountain Deity, among others.[51] All refer to the same godlike Moche supernatural being associated with blood sacrifice, agricultural bounty, and water.

To the north, Platform 1 overlooked the Great Plaza (Plaza 1), an enormous walled enclosure perfectly configured for public participation in rituals and pageantry, a space large enough to hold sizable crowds and with good visibility for events that may have transpired on the platforms above (Figure 2.4). An immense earthen ramp, perpendicular to the platform's northeast face, dominates the space and leads to the upper levels of the structure.

Particular details of the architecture seem to have been dictated by the structures' role in ritual practice. The arrangement suggests that public ceremonies begun below ascended the pyramid against a grandiose and imposing backdrop and that events staged above would have been discernable to some degree from the plaza below. Moche fineline painting gives a visual record of what some of those ceremonies may have involved. In one example, four painted registers depict the arraignment and sacrifice of captives (Figure 2.5). All the captives are nude males, but nonetheless three high-status captives ride in litters, conveyed up the ramp of a stylized, stepped pyramid. At the top, upon a small raised platform, a seated lord presides. As he holds a goblet,

FIGURE 2.5. The "Arraignment of Prisoners," rollout drawing of bottle (drawing by Donna McClelland).

his subordinate faces him, standing beneath an emblematic weapons bundle. In the lowest register scenes of sacrifice occur; the temple servants, shown as vulture-headed, draw blood and perform other activities. A decapitated head is featured there. Meanwhile, the top register includes a very abbreviated version of the Sacrifice Scene, with a single prisoner whose throat is cut, an owl messenger, and a warrior who hoists a goblet within a separate architectural space, identifiable by its mace-head roof emblems.

At each level of the Huaca de La Luna, the monument's vertical surfaces were covered in gigantic, sculpted adobe friezes, which read much like registers (Plate 3). The imagery of the lower murals suggests procession and pageantry, whereas the upper friezes become increasingly esoteric (Figure 2.6). At ground level, the cycle of murals features a long series of warriors leading prisoners. They march from right to left, around what remains of the North Patio, toward the ramp leading upward. There is an aspect of self-aggrandizement implicit to the images, as if the depictions commemorate actual events. Yet none of the individuals is depicted in a directly mimetic way, and these are not realistic portraits of specific individuals. Although several warriors are shown with distinguishing costume attributes, which could perhaps serve as identifiers, the main thrust of the image is on the actions taking place.

In a row over the prisoner procession, larger-than-life human figures are shown possibly dancing, or chanting, and holding hands. Sculpted of adobe, plastered, and painted in multiple colors, they wear headdresses, large round earspools, and red tunics with yellow dots and triangular fringes at the bottom. The significance of ritual song and dance may well have been related to agricultural cycles, as previously mentioned. Evidence from Huaca Cao Viejo suggests that performance expressions may have been more than passive celebrations of ritual events; music, chanting, and dance seem to have been key elements in ritual experience.[52]

Above, a stunning row of arachnid images puts forward a clear reference to bloodletting (Plate 4). Blood sacrifice references are made explicit in these friezes by the addition of hand appendages grasping sacrificial knives. The motif fits closely with a character whom Cordy-Collins calls the "Spider Decapitator."[53] The sequence continues at the fourth level, with a procession of seemingly human figures walking toward the primary ramp. The figures have several curious elements strongly reminiscent of Chavín style, including feet terminating in fanged creature mouths, suggesting that the use of deliberate archaisms may have had specific iconographic value useful to the overall message. Such distinctive elements seem to serve as pictorial modifiers, perhaps identifying these particular characters as religious practitioners or shamans. As a group, the lower four registers allude to the performance of rituals related to prisoner sacrifice.

Punctuating the frieze registers at the juncture of wall and ramp, a small ground-level chamber functions to draw visual focus from the grandiose to the immediate. This dual chamber features stylized depictions of ritualized combat and a most remarkable Complex Theme frieze, executed in sculpted polychrome adobe plaster (Plate 5). The Complex Theme images manifest some of the *horror vacua* for which later Moche fineline paintings are known. Very little of the background is left unoccupied, and very few organizing elements serve to guide the viewer's eye in any particular sequence. Numerous small clusters of figures engage in activities whose meanings are not entirely clear. Smaller complex elements appear to function as iconic modifiers floating in proximal association throughout the picture plane.

Fishermen cast square nets, men brandish staves and orbs, and a few headless bodies lie prone; foxes, scorpions, snakes, and starbursts abound. Numerous pictorial elements have yet to be identified, and several seem unique to these friezes. The images could only have been fully discernable to viewers at relatively close range. Although they are extraordinarily busy, a sense of balance is introduced to the composition by the presence of three figures casting long ropes. The sinewy forms overarch the myriad of individual iconic clusters, guiding the eye from one image cluster to another. A very richly detailed narrative is being recounted here, yet the pictorial structure is not linear.

It seems likely that some portion of Moche myth-history relevant to the religious function of the architecture is being recounted at length in this mural, thus making explicit to the viewer the connection between the capture and parade of prisoners and the ideology that mandated their capture. Curiously, although the preservation of the friezes is generally excellent, several areas show large patches of heavy deterioration. The patches were repeatedly splattered with some type of liquid, and the damage was apparently deliberately inflicted, as if libations were thrown there. The most likely libations would have been *chicha* or blood (or both). Although it awaits further testing, the presence of human blood spatters on key parts of the Complex Theme mural would leave little doubt about the fate of the captive warriors pictured at the Huaca de La Luna.[54]

On the west side of the chamber, twenty-four pairs of warriors arranged in four horizontal registers face each other, engaged in what seems to be ritualized combat rendered in highly stylized artistic convention (Plate 3). The numerical repetition hints at purposeful selection, but the meaning remains unclear. Each pair faces each other, war clubs and shields raised. The gesture of the contest is emphasized, not the outcome; none of the pairs gives any indication of who is the victor or who is the vanquished, and the identity of these warriors is ambiguous.

As one moves up the pyramid, the imagery becomes more abstract, even though the architectural configuration remains steady in its assertion of ritualized function. At the fifth level, enormous images make explicit reference to decapitation, featuring a series of crouching, bicephalic Moon Animals; these clutch trophy heads in their pawlike grasp.[55] At roughly the same height, a lateral ramp connects the primary access ramp to the uppermost level of Platform 1. The face of this oblique ramp boldly features a gigantic water serpent, whose undulating body traverses the entire length of the ramp (Figure 2.6a). To one side of the serpent, a row of warriors with clubs and shields marches toward the ramp, and opposite, rows of snarling, Janus-headed creatures stand upon great, clawed feet.

At the seventh level, a repetitive series of Standing Decapitator figures glare ferociously outward. Suffering heavy erosional damage, these figures have multiple curving appendages, terminating in animal heads. An earlier iteration of the figures (building phase C) shows a huge, fanged anthropomorphic figure holding a *tumi* knife in one hand and a decapitated head in the other; his serpent-like belts curve outward, terminating in bird heads. These Decapitator images would be among the highest visible friezes available to onlookers below. From this point onward, processions of celebrants would pass into the interior space of the upper buildings.

At these higher levels, smaller, more inconspicuous ramps diverged toward various patios. Fineline imagery and the flow pattern of the architecture suggest that the next stop for processions might well have been the altar room of the Garrido sector, located in the northeast area of Platform 1. Adjacent the Great Patio, this intimate space is unique in several regards, not the least of which is the presence of a small raised platform, or *usnu*, reminiscent of a throne or altar (Plate 6). Whoever was seated there would have been framed by an interlocking series of delicately intricate murals. Though considerably scaled down, their motifs continue the Decapitator theme through at least three superimposed repainting cycles.[56] Mackey and Hastings identify the central deity with the ancient Andean "Staff God" seen in Chavín and Cupisnique arts, thus reiterating the longevity of the icon.[57] Perched at the summit of the north face friezes, located at the visual apex of the main ramp leading up the pyramid, the usnu platform is suggested as a likely stage for the culmination of various kinds of ceremonial activities.[58]

FIGURE 2.6. (a) Water Snake and Moon Animals, upper registers, north face, Huaca de La Luna; **(b)** Warrior Procession detail, east wall, Great Plaza, Huaca de La Luna.

28

Whereas the Great Patio and the altar chamber of Platform 1 seem to have been the loci of great pomp and ceremony, smaller chambers adjacent, in Plaza 3, were almost certainly places where the more private rituals occurred and where victims were actually dispatched. And in fact, one of the less conspicuous corridors leading off the north plaza led to this inner area. Over time, these structures were overbuilt and reconfigured; parts of later Platform 2 covered some of the earlier plaza areas. Archaeological nomenclature distinguishes the various sections of the plaza as parts a, b, and c. In general, the structures of Plaza 3 had only modest adornments; most were finished with a simple coat of white paint and in some cases small amounts of red detailing.[59] An exception, however, was a chamber inside of Plaza 3b that had bas-relief images of a rampant feline atop a reclining figure, suggesting a link to religious practice.[60] The imagery's exact significance is debatable. It is possible to view the reclining figure as female, leading to the suggestion that images refer to ritualized copulation sometimes seen in Moche art. It is also possible to interpret the feline as violently mauling or killing the woman, an outcome that would not be inconsistent with the sacrificial function of these chambers.

There is little doubt that the adjoining Plazas 3a and 3b were the sites of human sacrifice and ritual dismemberment. Numerous skeletons showing cut marks to the throat, ribs, vertebrae, arms, and legs attest to this. Plaza 3b demonstrates prolonged use and multiple layers of mutilated bodies that were accumulated gradually and covered with layers of eolian sand. In several instances, remains of rope were associated with victims, supporting the idea that these were captives.[61]

Skeletal remains of at least seventy individuals have been unearthed to date in Plaza 3a (Figure 2.7).[62] Verano's osteological analysis suggests that all the victims were adult males, between the ages of fifteen and thirty-nine, and many had signs of previously healed injuries consistent with injuries common to warriors. Several victims had injuries in the beginning stages of healing, a fact that Verano notes would point to a significant amount of time between capture and death.[63] The stratigraphic evidence indicates at least five discreet episodes of sacrifice and at least one instance when the sacrifices corresponded to the incidence of a major El Niño rain event. Additionally, over fifty shattered, unfired clay effigies of seated male prisoners were found among the bodies.[64] Most of the skeletons show evidence of mutilation, with some body manipulations seemingly quite bizarre.

One the more intriguing features of Plaza 3a is the presence of a conically shaped outcrop of living stone. The majority of the sacrificial victims were clustered in the patio to the north of this rock. Seen against the backdrop of Cerro Blanco, the rocky outcrop creates an almost sculptural echoing of the mountain behind. As a conceptually mirrored form, the rock becomes an iconic substitute for the larger, more intangible substance of the parent mountain, Cerro Blanco. On a human scale, this conceptual echoing generates a performance space within the walls of Plaza 3. Participants acted out predetermined rites in a relatively intimate space, one that could accommodate very few spectators. The function of art

FIGURE 2.7. Rocky outcropping, Plaza 3, Huaca de La Luna, adjacent Cerro Blanco.

in this space, and the demands placed on it, differed substantially from that of art in the more public areas and larger plazas.

The absence of showy, overwhelming mural programs in Plaza 3 supports the notion that such imagery was not designed for the benefit of the sacrificial victims or for the edification of the temple's inner staff. The most intense and lavish mural cycles, which appear in the larger ceremonial spaces and are emphasized on the pyramid facades, seem to have been directed from the highest temple elites across the social hierarchy toward middle-level participants and those members of the public who presumably gathered at the temple on significant occasions.

The placement and iconography at the Huaca de La Luna support the idea that well-established liturgical practices were conducted at the site over a very long period of time and that these included periodic sacrifices. The architecture was made to conform to particular functionalist demands, while simultaneously, its physical form helped individual participants to shape and reaffirm social narratives engendered by recurrent ritualized performances.

Huaca Cao Viejo, El Brujo

Close parallels between Huaca de La Luna and other monumental Moche temple sites are unlikely to have been coincidental. Numerous strong similarities signal the existence of a generally accepted liturgical sequence, widely practiced within spatially particular and symbolically meaningful architectural environments. Huaca Cao Viejo, in the El Brujo complex (Chicama Valley), for example, uses familiar iconographic themes, stylistic conventions, and architectural configurations to aggrandize blood sacrifice ideology and the activities associated with it. As is the case at Huaca de La Luna, the imagery of Huaca Cao Viejo's lower plaza emphasizes aspects of the Warrior Narrative and makes extensive references to the Decapitator deity. Though they are not identical, the close similarity of the mural cycles and their architectural placement is significant. Artists and practitioners in contiguous valleys were surely referencing a common ideology using a shared artistic canon and visual vocabulary (Figure 2.8).

Constructed in at least seven phases, the monument dates from around the first century to the seventh century A.D.[65] A substantial portion of the pyramid's north face has been excavated, with additional explorations on the south face, the top platforms, and the pyramid's west face. The north face frieze sequence begins at ground level, with a procession of warriors and nude male prisoners with ropes around their necks. On the second register, a row of figures with joined hands appear to dance, or perhaps chant, in celebration of the procession below (Plate 7).[66] Just above, Huaca Cao Viejo's third level once featured a series of enormous black spiders, although remnants of only two remain. The creatures are anthropomorphic—one clearly shows a human arm and hand holding a tumi (ceremonial knife). Little else remains of the upper registers, but even in its incomplete state, enough survives to allow a clear impression of strong thematic equivalence to the Huaca de La Luna.

Huaca Cao Viejo's dance figures are especially enigmatic because of their construction method. At least one of the frieze figures was found to have both llama and human leg bones imbedded in its feet.[67] Analysis by Verano, Anderson, and colleagues establishes that at least one human bone belonged to an adult male and had cut marks and points of breakage consistent with the disarticulation of a fresh body. Given the evidence of active dismemberment and the relatively immediate manner in which adobe plaster murals are constructed, it is reasonable to propose that the bones were placed into the wall within the short span of time that the adobe friezes were still wet.

The finding establishes human dismemberment and sacrificial rituals as having played a part in the consecration of the murals. It supports the idea that the second-level performers represent not only a passive commemoration of the ceremonial activities but also a participatory aspect consecrated in

FIGURE 2.8. Corner chamber, lower plaza, Huaca Cao Viejo.

blood.⁶⁸ The presence of sacrificial offerings, embedded as part of a monumental art program, suggests that the images themselves were vested with spiritual power. It also lends credence to the notion that the creators of the murals, the artists, held a level of status integrally connected to ritual practice and esoteric knowledge, which underlay the creation of special imagery.

Huaca Cao Viejo's north patio also included a small corner chamber, situated on a modestly raised platform. Its exterior was densely covered with imagery highly similar, but not identical, to the Complex Theme and the Warrior Pair friezes at Huaca de La Luna (Figure 2.9). Many of the same characters are found in both cycles of friezes; however, numerous instances of unique iconographic choices also exist.⁶⁹ For example, an enigmatic crowned figure, whose showy headdress features points terminating in small orbs, recurs several times in both compositions.⁷⁰ The repetition suggests that the character holds central importance to the image and implies that the composition refers to his activities at multiple points in time. It also suggests that both friezes refer to the same essential narrative. Variation of artistic emphasis is also evident between the two huacas; for example, the figures prominently holding the long sinewy ropes at Huaca de La Luna are shown in the Huaca Cao Viejo friezes in much smaller version. It has been suggested that the imagery bears calendrical significance, perhaps relating cultural narratives about ritual and agricultural cycles.⁷¹

The chamber was surely the staging point for whatever ritual activities were conducted on the adjacent platform. Remnants of plaster, paint, postholes,

FIGURE 2.9. "Complex Theme" friezes on the corner chamber, lower plaza, Huaca Cao Viejo.

and roof debris show that the small platform itself was covered with an unusually ornate roof. The underside of the roof, in fragmentary form, shows signs of having had elaborate mural decoration. Ceramic mace heads retrieved among rubble indicate that the roof was adorned with hollow ceramic *porras* (war clubs).[72] Similar ceramic elements were also recovered among the architecture at the Huaca de La Luna (Figure 2.10). Their presence demonstrates that the identifying architectural emblems shown in fineline paintings, such as the Arraignment of Prisoners scene (Figure 2.5), existed in reality as well as in visual vocabulary.

Architecture on the summit of the monument provides additional and highly convincing evidence of an ideological correlation from one valley to another. As at the Huaca de La Luna, the Huaca Cao Viejo featured large, decorated upper patios. The iconography of one patio is a complex pattern of interlocking volutes and *life* catfish. These are executed as deeply carved, polychrome friezes. The patio also featured a small chamber in the southeast corner, whose iconography unmistakably evokes the familiar Decapitator (Plate 8). Dramatically alternating in yellow and blue, the figures grimace with huge fanged mouths and hold highly detailed severed human heads, much like those on the upper levels of Huaca de La Luna.[73]

At the highest levels of the monument, made legible through painstaking reconstruction of fallen mural fragments, a fragile cluster of murals at the Huaca Cao Viejo's principal platform reveal a faded, fragmentary image of the Decapitator face, as seen in the Great Patio atop the Huaca de La Luna. With his

FIGURE 2.10. Ceramic mace heads (*porras*) associated with architectural features: **(a)** elaborately painted porra (Projecto Huaca de La Luna, 2006); **(b)** porra with spiral modeled top (Projecto Huaca de La Luna, 1997).

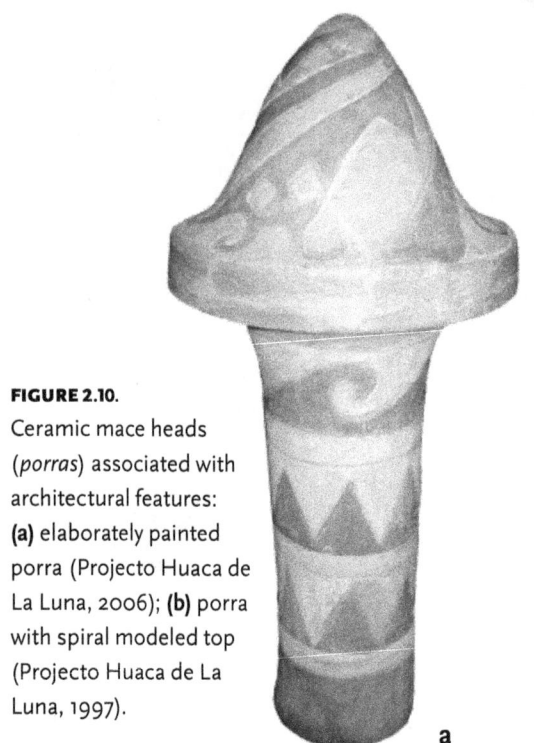

ferocious countenance, goggle eyes, fanged mouth, and wavelike hair, framed by heavy rhomboid borders, the image was executed during the temple's late phase observing identical stylistic conventions.[74] It is an echoing that cannot be coincidental. Though the two monuments display unique personalities, perhaps related to their physical proximity to important geographic features or sacred geography, such strong similarities speak to a shared worldview.

Pañamarca

If Moche religion found expression as far north as the royal tombs of Sipán and San José de Moro, physical evidence of the same belief system can be seen as far south as the Nepeña Valley, at the monumental site of Pañamarca. Located in one of the southernmost areas of the Moche sphere of influence, the site includes a series of platforms and walled plazas, typical of Moche architecture.[75] Sections of murals uncovered in various parts of the complex, although fragmentary, focus on ritual events, warfare, and human sacrifice. Of particular interest are monumental variants of the Warrior Procession, dancers, and Sacrifice Scene comparable to those found elsewhere.[76]

One sizable plaza, located beneath the structure's most imposing platform, included remains of a 30-foot-long series of larger-than-life figures engaged in ritual dance. First discovered by Richard Schaedel in 1951, the figures are recognizable as warriors by their back flaps, tassel belts, and blackened lower legs. Although the upper portion of the mural was missing, enough remained to see that the figures grasp what appears to be a long woven band of fabric. Its presence signals that the scene depicts a Moche ritual sometimes called the Ribbon Dance, or *baile con soga*.[77]

The purpose of the Ribbon Dance in Moche society is uncertain. Yet a similar dance, documented among the Inca at the time of conquest, associates it with agricultural fertility, water, and irrigation. Citing Molina, Anne Marie Hocquenghem draws a parallel between the Moche and the Inca, noting that in the highlands the dance corresponded to the end of a ritual combat, known as *camay*, and the beginning of the planting season, roughly starting with the first new moon after the late December summer solstice and lasting through approximately mid-January.[78] Although direct comparisons between Moche and Inca are problematic, the dance, and its association with ritual combat and a particular time of year, is distinctive enough to support Hocquenghem's conjecture that a ritual of widespread importance relating to planting and fertility was being represented.

Another panel, a small fragment of a larger scene, depicts two warriors, both wearing tunics and serpent belts, engaged in face-to-face combat, clearly attempting to capture each other by grasping each other's hair. At its most basic level, it constitutes an overt reference to warrior combat, and it is also a pictorial reference to the larger sequence of prisoner capture and sacrifice.

The mural most directly linking the monument to human sacrifice, however, was located in a smaller enclosure high on the upper platform.[79] In this panel, a great Priestess, dressed in her signature costume, with its long tunic and floppy tassel headdress, leads a procession that includes two lesser-status anthropomorphic warriors, three bound prisoners, a human guard, a bowl with goblets, a weapons bundle, and a Water Snake.[80] As the mural is fragmentary, there is no way of knowing how much more of the scene was originally portrayed; however, this remarkable mural is generally agreed to be a clear reiteration of the Sacrifice Scene.[81] Based on that identification, we can surmise that the Priestess shown here was an officiant at the sacrifice of the nude bound prisoners (shown seated toward the right side of the image) and that the goblet she holds would likely have been presented to a Warrior Priest.

Pañamarca's murals remain only in bits and pieces. Yet enough survives to insinuate a comprehensive artistic program in keeping with what is becoming apparent at other Moche monumental sites. The general ideas of blood sacrifice, the propitiation of deity (presumably in exchange for water and fertility), and the glorification of people associated with those activities, such as warriors and religious practitioners, come across as the iconography's primary message. Their presence here substantiates the notion of a belief system common to more than one valley, going far toward establishing something more than a loosely shared ideology.

The Function of Muralism

Elite architecture, emblazoned with enormous murals and friezes, broadcast messages that recalled religious obligations as well as the fulfillment of those obligations. They did so through the visual reiteration of iconic phrases referential to specific rituals performed at the huacas, reinforcing the interface between what can be termed liturgical ceremonies and architectural functions. Human sacrifice was part of a larger series of religious observations for which these monuments were fitted. The celebration of the prisoner capture carried obvious political overtones, a factor that surely made it a popular choice as a subject for artistic patronage. But the deeper meaning behind it seems to have related to an ongoing, unrelieved anxiety about water and fertility. Water, semen, blood, chicha—the symbolic substances of life, fertility, and rejuvenation—find ready expression in visual metaphor.[82] They also play out in the context of ceremony and ritual, as symbols of the underlying concerns of religious practice.

Artists and engineers, who were responsible for the creation and maintenance of the monuments, performed a highly specialized task, one requiring particular knowledge of ritual and artistic canon. It is unlikely, for example, that the groups of people responsible for brick making were the same population as the artists; the simple maker marks display no evidence of skilled pictorial literacy. The demands of Moche religion shaped the particular details of the art and architecture. In this regard, form and function were integrated. The end results were architectural arenas that provided the perfect staging areas for the dramatic enactment of pageantry and ritual. The forms and images generated there, by both architecture and actions, were translated into iconic representations that celebrated and recounted those events throughout the Moche realm. A correspondence of mural themes and material remains at platform sites in multiple valleys confirms the existence of closely related religious ideology shared by North Coast communities.

These monuments were not haphazardly designed. Although they grew by accretion over time, their basic configurations remained constant. It is clear that Moche architects (and patrons) had a cohesive plan dictated by the structures' role in ritual practice. Mural architects understood which programmatic components were correct and how they were to be ordered. Essential architectural information may actually have been planned at miniature scale and transmitted via ceramic or stone maquettes—a number of examples of such architectural models are known—yet, because the imagery was concept driven, variations in detail and technique exist from site to site.[83]

The commonality demonstrated in the temple imagery strongly supports the idea that the themes and characters populating the gigantic paintings were well-understood icons referring to the events that occurred there. Moche pyramids were conceptual points of connection, to which other meaningful visual forms were keyed.[84] They were the location where many of the primary actions by which the society defined itself happened—the sites of rituals, pageants, and sacrificial deaths. In this regard, they generated social motivation for the creation and maintenance of an iconographic lexicon specifically referential to the ideology and performance of religious obligation. They stood, simultaneously, as monuments to the fundamental ideology joining the society, as venues for the generation of a cohesive social narrative, and, self-referentially, as visually symbolic icons for all that occurred within those walls.

Itinerate Affirmations: Ceramic Arts

Moche fineware ceramics differed from monumental arts substantially in their mechanism of communication. They constituted a primary vehicle for the transmission of ideology between various social levels and geographic locations. Self-referential and more modest in scale, portable arts conceptually bridged the gap between elite temple activities and ritual enactments at the personal or community level. Ceramic arts were obviously highly mobile, circulating widely, and fulfilled various functions to reiterate shared beliefs and foster political cohesion throughout Moche society.

Ceramic motifs index themes like the Ribbon Dance, the Warrior Narrative, Ai-Apaec as the Decapitator, and the Sacrifice/Presentation Scene. Yet they also make pictorial references to activities and subjects not commonly seen in mural imagery, including portraits of individuals, animals, fishing, and erotic themes and scenes like Ritual Badminton, the Marsh Scene, the Burial Theme, and the Tule Boat Theme.[85] It is worth noting the absence of certain themes in monumental contexts, for it signals fundamental differences in use and function.

Ceramics, by their plasticity, ubiquity, and wider function, had a greater range of expression than the self-reflexive iconography of temple environments. Even though both were keyed to the same core belief system, ceramic arts tapped into larger structures and mythologies, what some authors propose as a larger cosmological narrative of gods and culture heroes.[86] For middle-level elites and ordinary people at the community level, ritual-use ceramics recalled the religious ideology by which they lived and reinforced social integration under the auspices of diverse religious observances carried out at various levels of the social hierarchy. As liturgical objects, fineware ceramics were activated by human performance while also actively contributing to the creation of ritual performances. In contrast to the built environment, where the human viewer experienced a sense of place through interactions with the architectural structures of that place (complete with all aspects of scale, ambience, and physical subordination), portable objects, and specifically ritual-use ceramics, elicited more internalized kinds of responses and interactions.

Specialized ceramics were meant to be seen at close range, handled, and passed hand to hand. Their scale and form made an element of human agency implicit in terms of how information was packaged and transferred. Without architectural structures to reinforce the contextual meanings of particular icons, comprehension of symbolic codes required an increased level of esoteric knowledge. Those who were in command of essential information became the performative social links, supplying the religious narrative structures necessary to allow the average participant, who may not have had the same level of esoteric knowledge or visual literacy, to understand the meaning of the ceremonies and their relevance away from the temple setting.

The functional aspect of the ceramics proves essential in understanding how they occupied the nexus between ideological dissemination and social cohesion. An analysis of the formal characteristics of the objects themselves, and an understanding of archaeological contexts, sheds light on how they were used. Chief among their applications were widespread use as funerary offerings, service in relation to diverse public and private rituals, and employment as units of economic patronage exchange.

Funerary Contexts

Most high-quality Moche ceramics known today were encountered in funerary contexts. Obviously, this fact is influenced by factors of preservation, but it also indicates the special regard in which such objects were held. Fineware vessels were not common household containers, although ceramic assemblages in tombs do sometimes include ordinary wares. Within the sphere of daily Moche life, plain utilitarian vessels outnumbered ceremonial ceramics by an inestimable proportion, yet such wares rarely had complex imagery. The incidence of what can be thought of as special fineware or fancy ceramics, those with complex imagery or recognizable motifs or those made of fine orange paste with slip paint decoration or polish, is largely limited to certain vessel forms and contexts that bear distinct connections to certain kinds of ritual or liturgical practices.

Evidence suggests that, prior to inclusion in burials, fineware ceramics functioned in various facets of ritual life. Such ceramics usually show some signs of relatively light wear or occasional use. Scarcity in contexts other than religious or funerary attests to a dedicated purpose, even though fragments of fineware ceramics are sometimes discovered in household midden and other locations.

Fineware ceramics were usually included in tombs as part of a larger suite of burial items. The circumstances of particular burials make it clear that certain kinds of messages were being transmitted about wealth status and, most likely, the social affiliation of the deceased person. Artwork featured on the vessels is sometimes self-referential, alluding to specific kinds of vessels as part of a burial cluster (see Figure 2.11). Just as tombs ranged in complexity from simple pits to elaborate stone and adobe-lined chambers fitted with numerous niches and attendant burials, the items included in burials ranged from humble to grandiose. Burials of less wealthy Moche individuals may have included one or two ceramic or gourd vessels, small talismans, spindle whorls, reed mats, and simple garments or shroudlike textile wrappings.[87] Burials of middle-level elites, such as those found in the floodplain between the Huaca del Sol and the Huaca de La Luna, tended to have more and finer ceramics,

FIGURE 2.11.
Bat effigy bottle with funerary vessel depictions (C-01225, Museo Nacional de Antropología y Arqueología, Lima).

along with limited amounts of precious metal and textiles.[88] Very complex tombs of extremely high-status individuals, like those at Sipán and San José de Moro, included literally hundreds, or even thousands, of ceramic vessels, human and animal sacrifices, fine jewelry, and ornate textiles.[89]

Moche burials show a definite preference for a particular suite of vessel types. Ceramic assemblages are generally consistent with set forms: stirrup-spout bottles, straight-necked bottles, jars, lids, and flaring vases (*floreros*) are among the most common. Yet individual tombs did not always contain examples of every vessel type; nor does it appear that tombs had any set ratios of vessel variety or quantity. Presumably, the vessels were conceived as traveling with the deceased to a new life in the spirit world, and, once there, the vessels' intended functions may not have been much different than in the world of the living.

The particulars of Moche funerary rituals are uncertain, although painted vessels depicting interments of very high-status individuals and elaborate funerary processions depicted in sculptural form by Chimu successors indicate that elite burials probably included a sizable number of participants.[90] Such people would surely have seen (and helped to carry) the grave offerings.

The vessels doubtless communicated something to the living who participated in the burial services. Once they were assembled and installed in a tomb, it is unclear if the vessels were intended to be read as individual statements or as a comprehensive suite. Grouping and positioning within the tomb are likely to have been meaningful elements.[91] Particular vessel forms seem to have conveyed meaning by virtue of long association of form and ritual, apart from any iconographic content. As instruments of ritual, the objects became indexes in their own right; their physical form referred to ideological complexes enacted during their use. This is how, for example, a stirrup-spout bottle might be shaped in the form of a lidded jar (Figure 2.12h)—the false jar neck was in itself symbolically referential, as was the shape of the stirrup-spout bottle—resulting in a compound icon.[92]

In general, a community's beliefs concerning the soul and afterlife are reflected in burial patterns.[93] The number and quality of grave furnishings give strong notions about the wealth and status of the deceased. In cases where tombs contained hundreds of vessels, very fine-quality unique pieces were mixed with mass-produced ceramics. In some burials, the presence of duplicate "moldmates" (identical objects produced from the same mold) substantially increased the tomb's content. Mass quantities of relatively poor-quality vessels in many tombs appear to have had no purpose other than providing large numbers of goods, probably as part of a display of status and wealth.[94] In a few cases, ceramics were not even fired before being included in tombs, implying that their physical presence and the messages carried by their visual appearance were more important than actual functionality.[95]

Selection of grave offerings clearly hinged on symbolic elements whose form and content were at least as important as other considerations. An implicit assumption is that the deceased would need certain kinds of things in the afterlife. As burial offerings, the vessels often held perishable materials. Traces of foodstuffs are occasionally detected, which most researchers interpret as symbolic nourishment for the dead.[96] Yet the vessels sometimes held other, far more enigmatic materials. In at least one case, evidence of human blood has been found inside pedestal goblets, a specific vessel form closely associated with the Sacrifice Ceremony and Moche priestesses.[97] Given what we know about sacrificial rituals and their depictions in ceramic media, the liturgical uses of particular objects before their inclusion as grave goods seem undeniable. Yet, apart from the example above, surprisingly few direct correlations can be made between social position and the particular imagery of any given vessel, a finding that may be related, in large part, to a preponderance of unprovenanced artworks and inconclusive evidence.

Ceramic vessels of all degrees of quality occur in burials of widely differing social status, discounting the idea that fineware ceramics were limited only to members of the high elite. Although status differentiation in terms of access to quality and quantity of the finest wares is obvious, it nonetheless follows that people at most levels of Moche society had at least some degree of access to the basic ideological concepts expressed by ceramic forms and images. The

FIGURE 2.12. Examples of ceramic vessel forms typically found in Moche graves: (a) jar (olla); (b) flaring vase (florero); (c) strap-handle bottle; (d) pedestal goblet; (e) small bowl/cup; (f–g) stirrup-spout bottles with modeled elements; (h) tall-neck jar; (i) stirrup-spout bottle effigy figure; (j) portrait head bottle (from "Cultural Stratigraphy in the Viru Valley, Northern Peru," by William Strong and Clifford Evans, © 1951, Columbia University Press; reprinted with the permission of the publisher).

finer aspects of iconographic complexity and detailed understanding of their nuances, however, were controlled by specialists. The mechanisms by which lesser-status persons might come to acquire elite objects were most likely related to the social institutions of political reciprocation and gift exchange.

Ritual Functions

Pottery was ubiquitous in all social contexts; ceramic media were used for a wide array of tools, implements, and activities. This included ritual cycles embedded within Moche society, which required appropriate paraphernalia. Entire suites of ceramic objects were made specifically to fulfill the needs of liturgical practices, of which funerary rites were but one aspect. Ritual practices, typically, engender telltale characteristics in objects linked to various activities, even though many objects might be appropriate for more than one type of ritual. Of those ceramics bearing complex pictorial elements, certain form typologies emerge, creating broad outlines of at least three main areas of devotional practice where symbolically laden ceramic arts can be identified as having a significant role. Although these are discussed at greater length in later chapters, a summary of ritual-use ceramics includes musical instruments (flutes, whistles, drums, rattles), figurines and talismans, and ritual serving vessels (bowls, bottles, jars, floreros, *cancheros*).[98] In each case, the formal and ergonomic qualities of the object suggest the kinds of activities in which the users were engaged and, by extension, the kinds of interactions that necessarily accompanied the actions.

Musical instruments bear an obvious link to ritual events. Representations of individuals engaged with various instruments give a good understanding of how the instruments were played and in what ceremonial contexts they were used. Music and dancing were, and continue to be, important aspects of Andean ritual life, particularly in connection with planting and harvesting. The Ribbon Dance, referenced in murals and ceramic representations, provides at least one clear instance of a Moche dance performance event, although there were surely others (Plate 9).[99] Conch shell trumpets are still considered to be useful in calling the attention of the gods, as they were, presumably, in Moche times. Making music was part of the performance of ritual. Images of processions and ritual events frequently include people playing rattles, whistles, trumpets, flutes, horns, and drums. Stand-alone images of musicians are also relatively common.

When instruments appear in the art, they function as referents to human participation in ritual observance or as functional objects integrated into an overall synesthetic experience. Ceramic musical instruments were symbolic objects only insofar as they referred to the larger activity, signaling the participation of individuals in corporate activity. Fancy ceramic whistles are good examples of pieces whose musical functions were signaled by imagery suggesting how they were used (Figure 2.13). To fulfill an object's purpose required an intimate interaction on the part of individuals playing it, regardless of

FIGURE 2.13. Whistles depicting an elaborately dressed panpipe player and a ribbon dancer, Cerro Mayal.

particular details of performance. Meanwhile, the signification of the object was evident to all who experienced it.

In contrast, figurines and pendants are less overtly functional and more inherently symbolic. Their conceptual value and performative functions cannot be divorced from iconographic content. Figurines are among the earliest ceramic artworks known in the Andean region, dating as early as 3000–2500 B.C.[100] It has been speculated that they were used as part of healing practices, fertility petitions, or puberty rites.[101]

Moche figurines were generally made of humble ceramic materials. They most often depict clothed or nude females; lesser numbers show male warriors, bound prisoners, or other human characters (Figure 2.14). They read as singular figures and have not been found arranged in interactive groupings or poses. Some figurines are extremely small—the tiniest often had holes punched in them, making them into pendants.

The contexts and patterns of wear suggest that the figurines were actively used as agents of social transaction. Most often, they are found in domestic contexts, as part of the household midden, and in nontemple environments. They most likely functioned as talismans for individual petitions for protection, fertility, or health. Most seem to have been deliberately broken. It may

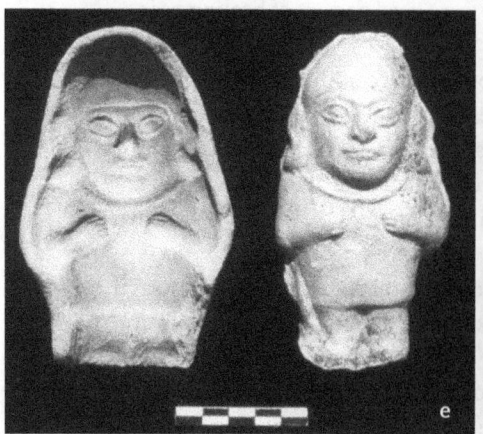

FIGURE 2.14. Ceramic figurines, Cerro Mayal: **(a)** large hollow figurine; **(b)** small solid female figurines; **(c)** warrior figurine; **(d)** nude female figurine; **(e)** mold for hollow figurine; **(f)** "Lambayeque"-style female figurines.

well be that small figurines and pendants functioned in ways analogous to how modern indigenous Andean groups use private talismans. Catherine Allen notes that contemporary people often possess special power objects that are referred to as *kawsaqkuna* or "living ones." Kept in the household, the objects are repositories of family health and fertility. They are brought out on special occasions to refresh the relationship between the members of the household and the local sacred places. Small blessings, offerings to the earth or sacred places, known as *despachos*, occur frequently.[102] The diminutive scale of Moche figurines precludes them having a showy function as an element of large-scale pageantry or public display. Their modest form suggests that they were intended for ritual use at an individual level.

The significance of figurines seems to have changed according to social context. Comparable artworks produced by later cultures take on an aspect of miniature figural sculpture, with the associated implications of more formalized iconographic signification. For example, small figures and figurines made of wood and included as part of Chimu high-status burials, often arranged as tableaux depicting specific ritual activities, seem to act as surrogates for the characters they represent.[103] Inca figurines, made of finely worked shell or precious metal and elaborately clothed, are generally associated with offerings made at sacred Inca shrines.[104] Use of figurines continued into the Late Horizon and early colonial period, with Spanish chroniclers suggesting that the figures were considered as substitutes for the things they represented, that some may have represented deities, or that others represented members of the royal elite.[105]

By far the most common ritual-use ceramics are Moche fineware serving and consumption vessels. Feasting in the Andes has a long, well-documented history; examples can be found in archaeological, ethnohistoric, and contemporary contexts.[106] All types of rituals, funerary or otherwise, seem to have routinely involved libation and feasting, for which, of course, appropriate vessels were necessary. Large quantities of such vessels would have been needed. Many of the same vessels found in funerary contexts were surely used for special feasts.

Certain vessel types constituted the primary suite. Medium- and tall-necked jars were the most universal. Generally, these had modest convex lids, presumably to conserve the jars' liquid contents. *Keros* were used in drinking and toasting, and the food-service utility of open jars and bowls is self-evident. Whereas some vessels served for feasting, it is significant that several recurrent forms were not particularly well shaped for purposes of eating or drinking. Instead, their functions may have been primarily liturgical and, hence, symbolic. Vessels like floreros or stirrup-spout bottles are impractical for ordinary use—floreros are top heavy and tip easily because of their exaggerated flare, and stirrup-spout bottles are slow to pour because of the shape of the spout. The requirements of ritual use, which dictated vessel shapes suitable for serving, feasting, toasting, and the like, remained important and constant elements in the objects' overall design for centuries.

Feast occasions are moments of social negotiation, and though there is much to distinguish between secular and sacred occasions, all such gatherings involve some level of ritualized behavior.[107] In oral societies, these are also the occasions when public recounting of important narratives tends to occur. Such narratives may well have been cued or evoked by small-scale imagery presented on ceramic vessels. Such moments of active agency would have been key elements in the formation of shared overarching social memory.

Ritual toasting, making libations to deities, and providing large quantities of food at a public gathering carried a range of social, political, and economic ramifications. These would have been opportunities for the satisfaction of clan obligations and reaffirmation of social identity. Participating in these events gave local leaders a forum where they might appear generous and powerful, as well as allowing middle-level people the opportunity to assert all kinds of other social positions.

Feasts provide opportunities for sponsors to enhance their status through display of goods and through gift giving. A well-known ethnographic example of the relationship between gifting and status enhancement is the North American Northwest Coast potlatch tradition. There, potlatches were highly political venues of status display, where social prestige was obtained and enhanced. Ritualized tellings of communal history, giving gifts, and sharing feasts cemented relationships and fostered strong feelings of self-identity.[108]

If the same were true among the Moche, then it would provide ample motivation for the patronage of specialized ceramic production, which, in fact, seems to have been the case at the Cerro Mayal workshop. Specialized ceramic production there was almost entirely geared to creating a particular suite of vessels suited to feasting: a corpus of ceramics embellished with a specific range of iconographic elements. A fair assertion is that Moche feasting vessels propagated ideology through the nexus of orality and participation, what Cummins calls synesthesia, resulting in the fixation of a cultural narrative in the memory of participants.[109]

Patronage and the Propagation of Iconography

The distribution of special-use ceramics, with their ideologically charged iconography, may well have been linked to complex patterns of social organization. It is hypothesized that social patterns documented in the colonial period might serve as indicators of traditional social arrangements. At the time of conquest, for example, the Chicama Valley (where Cerro Mayal is located) was subdivided along a complex pattern of dominant and lesser moieties (paired social units).[110] The moieties were composed of small, relatively stable political units (later known as *parcialidades*) tied to specific geographic areas. Reflective of long-standing territorial divisions, boundaries were most often defined by the irrigation canals. Tribute taxation took the form of labor or goods; contributions were reciprocated in the form of protection and redistribution of goods. Parcialidades were grouped by economic activity; most were made up of farmers, but occupational specialists such as fishermen and artisans were grouped apart, under their own local leaders.[111] Workshops producing specialized products, like ceramics, had complex social and economic obligations to neighboring lords of greater and lesser status. Rulers, as patrons, had a responsibility to provide subsistence goods to those under their protection. As clients, the farmers and craftspersons produced whatever goods were required for the fulfillment of community obligations.

Under this arrangement, a workshop of ceramic specialists might apply a portion of their output toward maintenance of the group's social relations with other groups holding similar rank. Part of the group leader's responsibility would include giving over a portion of the workshop production to the next higher-level lord in response to established patronage relationships. That lord, in turn, would redistribute the ceramics according to his own reciprocal obligations with others of his status level. Thus, specialized ceramics could be distributed throughout various levels of society both horizontally and vertically. This type of social organization created hierarchies of semiautonomous polities and valley-wide networks, engaged in a system of embedded patronage.[112]

Patron–client relationships created a situation where "master" artisans could arise. It seems likely that master artisans, bound by clan obligations, would necessarily have remained attached to specific patrons and territories, and the products of their clientage would have been available to the principal patron for redistribution. Although they were not "landed," and therefore not geographically "bound" as agriculturists were, groups of specialists were apparently strictly endogamous, marrying only those of their own kind.[113] Some scholars suggest that individuals self-identified with their particular specialty groups to the point of considering them as separate ethnicities.[114] A system of embedded patronage would, therefore, have encouraged two social factors important to the development of systematized iconography: a social vehicle by which specialized imagery could be disseminated throughout various parts of the community and an arrangement that fostered and encouraged cohesion among a group of specialists who, over time, generated, maintained, and propagated a highly conventionalized iconographic system.

Commentary

Hierarchic social structures generated an intrinsic need for widespread reiteration of ideology, which iconographically laden artwork helped to fulfill. Members of the elite residing at the highest level of Moche society, engaged in endemic competition among themselves, harvested the fruits of production from all those under their protection, while elite patronage, in the form of socially embedded systems of fealty and obligation, shaped the production and distribution of particular types of artwork, such as fineware ceramics. At multiple levels, art served to communicate political legitimation and maintain Moche social fabric.

Moche monuments represent the foci of religious and political power—the core areas of shared cultural practices. Smaller portable arts, often carried to areas of peripheral social control, became the loci of social and ideological negotiation. Because the structure of Moche polities was loosely held, relationships between high elites and local lords, that is to say, core and periphery, required continuous renegotiation. The built environment and portable arts were related elements of an integrated mode of communication. Pictorially coded artworks served as catalyst for oral and performative recanting of legends and events while affirming the membership, knowledge, and authority of the participants. Visual signs and symbols derived from monumental contexts were often the principal subjects of smaller arts.

Moche's ancestral artistic traditions were such that, as a group, they seem clearly to have possessed a cultural predisposition toward visual notation. They were the heirs to Cupisnique tradition, a coastal manifestation of Early Horizon Chavín, whose visual corpus was heavily laden with visual synecdoche, structures of abbreviation, and iconic modification; patterns of communication that are also seen in Moche art. Although the fundamental patterns of ritual practice shifted significantly from one epoch to the next, with Moche showing a markedly increased imperative toward showy monumentalism, the appearance of archaism in Moche art suggests that artists were well aware of the earlier tradition's forms and meanings.[115] By at least the mid Moche period, elite architecture emblazoned with colossal murals broadcast messages recalling the basic precepts of Moche theology. As the primary sites of ritual events, the architecture and its associated artistic programs simultaneously sent public messages declaring the elite fulfillment of social obligations mandated by ideological tenets. Meanwhile, in the context of religious or ceremonial events, smaller art objects reiterated the central narratives on which the social structure was built. In this regard, religion, esoteric knowledge, and art were pressed into the service of political legitimation and the maintenance of Moche social fabric.

CHAPTER 3

The Production of Ceramic Imagery

The present study operates on the premise that certain kinds of cultural vestiges, particularly those sharing discreet iconographic vocabularies, are related to a larger ideology, once central to Moche society. It additionally assumes that the primary function of the iconography was to communicate or reiterate key aspects of belief and practice and that its propagation and maintenance were somehow integral to the well-being of society. The range and quality of Moche visual arts, across diverse media, support the assertion. For the purpose of analysis, ceramic arts occupy a privileged position among this array because of the sheer numbers that have survived and the iconographic richness of their composition. Evidence from the workshop at Cerro Mayal sheds light on the range and variation of a particular cohort of manufacture.

Perhaps more significantly, the evidence makes it very apparent that orderly symbolic production was occurring on a large scale at this workshop. The types of imagery, range of forms, and manufacture techniques from Cerro Mayal underscore the degree to which ideologically charged imagery was standardized in Moche ceramic arts. Production techniques, especially mold use, signal the junctures where discreet pictorial units are recognizable. Specific forms can be roughly associated with certain kinds of activities, and the statistical incidence of particular motifs within those categories gives interpretive clues about the meanings that may have been associated with them. The data quantify proportional demands for specific forms, which, in turn, help us to gauge the functional and conceptual emphases of the artists and their patrons. Because Moche fineware ceramics very often included mold-made parts, along with hand-built elements, the information is illuminating for what it suggests about the parameters of image construction within a specialized workshop environment.

The present chapter briefly summarizes the relationships between particular iconographic motifs and distinct ceramic forms, proposing ways in which those art forms were keyed to specific social activities, and articulates the critical role of mold technology in the standardization of certain kinds of ritually keyed objects. The evidence of specific technologies related to the use of molds and complex joinery supports the idea that Moche artists did not move toward standardization of iconic elements accidentally but, rather, that certain kinds of visual signs and symbols became fixed units of meaning because of the modularization of familiar visual phrases encouraged by the use of molds.

The Workshop at Cerro Mayal

Situated on a rocky outcrop approximately four kilometers from the Chicama River, Cerro Mayal lies in the center of the lower valley amid fields watered by a complex system of canal irrigation (Figure 3.1). It was the site of large-scale manufacture of ritually important Moche ceramics, adjacent to the enormous civic-ceremonial center at Mocollope. The remains of earlier settlements scattered around Cerro Mocollope indicate that this particular geographic feature enjoyed a very long history of habitation.[1] Cerro Mocollope undoubtedly held religious meanings, visible as it is for miles across the fertile floodplain of the Chicama Valley. Yet carbon 14 samples from Cerro Mayal indicate that the ceramic workshop itself was in use only during the mid to late Moche period, from roughly A.D. 550 to 800.[2] At the time of the workshop's occupation, Mocollope is estimated to have been a sprawling urban or semi-urban center with an impressive sector of monumental architecture, temples, and palaces and a large residential area, with the ceramic workshop located near its periphery.

Cerro Mayal's artists were apparently employed in full-time ceramic production; no evidence of any other kind of craft production has been found.[3] Excavations revealed that the locale was generally divided into zones of intensive production, what appear to be production support areas, and sectors of habitation. The artists and their families both lived and worked there. Distinct areas where various activities took place, such as raw clay mixing, pottery firing, and community hearths, were found. Kilns were distributed across the site, interspersed with various domestic features and evidence of ephemeral structures made of adobe brick footings and *quincha* (woven mat) walls. The arrangement of the workshop, combined with the presence of a domestic component, clearly indicates that Cerro Mayal was home to a very specialized enclave of people.[4]

The ceramists seem to have enjoyed a form of patronage support—in all likelihood, support offered by the ruling hierarchy at Mocollope.[5] Analysis of botanical remains supports the idea of artistic patronage at Cerro Mayal. It seems that the bulk of agricultural products consumed consisted of maize and beans, both high-value, storable foods.[6] In addition, preliminary analysis of faunal remains suggests that camelid meat, a protein source generally associated with wealthier groups, was also a significant component of the diet.[7] The

FIGURE 3.1. Photo of Cerro Mayal, Chicama Valley, Peru: ceramic production areas (*right*) and habitation zones (*left*).

kinds of seasonal foods associated with part-time opportunistic harvesting are not readily present.

A patron–client relationship between Mocollope and Cerro Mayal implies that certain kinds of social imperatives were in action. The workshop economy, for example, would have been supported by other groups' fulfillment of taxation and reciprocal obligations to the lord(s) of Mocollope. Such a relationship presupposes that the needs of the patrons were addressed by workshop production, specifically the need for ritual-use ceramic wares. Patronage also implies a particular social status for those persons supported by special economic arrangements. Provisioning such a large workshop surely represented a sizable economic burden. One might conjecture that, in exchange for a heavy level of economic patronage, a sizable portion, if not all, of the finished ceramics were given over to the wealthy elites at Mocollope.[8]

Production of Ceramic Form and Image

Although all ceramic arts begin with raw clay, ceramic technology varies tremendously from one part of the world to another. Pottery formation can include modeling, molding, throwing, and casting, although Moche ceramists employed only techniques involving modeling and molding.[9] Cerro Mayal's ceramists were heirs to a long coastal tradition. Apart from tools, most or all of the items produced at Cerro Mayal appear to have been intended for use in special events, in ritual activities, and, eventually, as grave goods. These wares were hand modeled, mold made, or combined elements of both.[10]

Workshop ceramics are best described as being mostly of middle quality, that is, well made with various iconographic elements but lacking exquisitely

FIGURE 3.2. Fineware vessel fragment depicting a Warrior Procession, Cerro Mayal.

detailed painting, ultrahigh polish, or inlay. All of the ceramics manufactured at Cerro Mayal were typically made from very fine tempered orange paste. There was little or no apparent production of coarse tempered cooking or large storage vessels, although remnants of several large storage vessels were found in some of the domestic areas. The pieces were usually smoothed on the surface and sometimes polished or burnished. Often a plain coat of slip paint was added, which then served as a background for contrasting painted motifs. Slip paint colors fell into two main groups, white or cream and red or brown.[11] Stylistically, all conform to what Rafael Larco Hoyle's well-known typology would categorize as Moche IV.[12]

The workshop's artists did not employ the fineline painting technique to any large degree, relying instead on molding and modeling techniques. With the notable exception of *floreros* (flaring vases), ceramic forms that were entirely hand built had very little iconographic content.[13] Ceramic pieces entirely or partially created with molds tended to have the most frequent occurrence of complex imagery. Painted elements on workshop ceramics were most often simple and decorative, with repetitive motifs.

A small number of ceramics produced at the workshop could be considered among the very finest of Moche ceramic arts. These were made of fine paste, with delicate attention to finishing details, and designs were impressed, polished, and painted with different shades of white and red slip and occasionally, fugitive black paint (Figure 3.2). Their presence signals that Cerro Mayal artists were capable of, and did produce, artworks of superlative quality, confirming that at least some of the artists in residence were master ceramists and insinuating that the workshop's patrons probably included upper-level elites.

Excavations at Cerro Mayal during the 1990s recovered a formidable sample of materials. Some 139,240 sherds were analyzed in detail, along with large samples of botanic, shell, lithic, and other artifacts. Many of the resulting analyses have been published in detail elsewhere.[14] Of the ceramic sample, some 11,793 sherds had recognizable characteristics, such as a rim or handle, allowing them to be identified as bottles, jars, floreros, *crisoles* (miniature jars), figurines, and other distinct forms. All are strongly consistent with other North Coast typologies and, in particular, correlative to that published by Strong and Evans, whose original catalog serves as a point of reference for Cerro Mayal's vessel assemblage.[15] Of these, a large group of pieces, numbering 1,474, composed mostly of molds, modeled elements, and painted pieces, was drawn from the larger excavation lots for additional iconographic study.[16] This cohort, categorized according to form type and image, is the basis of the present discussion. (See Appendix A.)

Ceramic Form, Function, and Imagery

Considering that the workshop was in use for over two centuries, the artistic corpus is remarkably consistent within a range of forms and variations. What emerges is a visual vocabulary of iconic clusters and themes, operating at a level divorced from purely formalist or aesthetic restrictions. The artistic freedom represented by this disjuncture endorses the idea that these were understood as pictorial signs, independent from the forms upon which they were impressed or painted. Nonetheless, the placement of imagery seems to have maintained a close relationship to the functional ends for which the objects were intended. For example, the portrait-like faces so common to jar necks and bottles are not seen on floreros or figurines.

Particular kinds of events, both public and private, dictated the need for distinct ceramic forms. The ceramics themselves—their form, imagery, function, and scale—provide clues as to what some of those activities may have been. Quantitative analyses suggest that they fall generally into four main categories correlative to different aspects of ritual practice: ritual serving vessels, figurines and pendant beads, musical instruments and musicians, and ceramic tools and technology (Table 3.1).

RITUAL SERVING VESSELS

If most public events were accompanied by feasting and gift exchange, local leaders would require an appropriate assemblage of specialized vessels. These likely included basins, bottles, jars, cups, and plates, useful for drinking, eating, passing substances from one person to another, or making ceremonial toasts. Such feasting would require food service–type vessels, whereas burial rituals conceivably might call for more complex, and perhaps more symbolic, ceramic

Table 3.1. General Analysis of Cerro Mayal Form and Image Correlations

Sherd Form	Subgroup Total	Percent of Subgroup	Total No. Sherds	Percent of Sample
Ritual Serving Vessels				
Basin	1,479	16.50		
Bottle	310	3.46		
Dipper/*canchero*	6	0.07		
Florero/flaring vase	337	3.76		
Jar/bottle—body fragment	868	9.68		
Jar/bottle/florero base	1,171	13.06		
Jar/olla	4,357	48.59		
Jar neck appliqué	95	7.70		
Jar/bottle appliqué element	103	8.35		
Kero/cylinder with straight sides	18	0.20		
Lid	175	1.95		
Oval cup (no handle)	31	0.35		
Plate	16	0.18		
Subtotal			8,966	76
Figurines and Pendant Beads				
Bead	39	27.27		
Figurine—hollow	714	57.91		
Figurine—solid	480	38.93		
Subtotal			1,233	11
Musical Instruments				
Rattle handle	117	81.82		
Rattle pod (chamber)	16	11.19		
Whistle	10	6.99		
Subtotal			143	1
Tools and Other				
Clay—baked lump	22	1.52		
Clay—raw	2	0.14		
Grater	32	2.21		
Mold—whole or fragment	1,271	87.59		
Spindle whorl	21	1.45		
Spoon	103	7.10		
Other	215	14.82		
Subtotal			1,451	12
Total			11,793	100

assemblages. The fact that elaborate food dishes appear alongside more elaborate vessels in burial contexts supports the idea that these were considered to be somehow special. With political authority integrally linked to religious efficacy, such specialized objects generally carry iconographic elements invoking larger, commonly held beliefs. What might otherwise be plain food vessels were thus differentiated by virtue of the special circumstance of their manufacture, what we assume was the context of their use, and their imagery.

Such vessels were created in a range of sizes and shapes, each variously suited for liquid or solid substances (see Figure 3.3; also Figure 2.12). The most elaborate jars had both necks and bodies created of mold-made sections. The most humble vessels, small neckless jars (or ollas), rarely had any decoration beyond simple stripes and repetitive motifs, such as dots or scallops. Specialized vessels of moderate labor investment, floreros especially, were often neatly finished with well-known painted motifs, such as the rolling wave or step-fret *escalonado* (Figure 3.4)—designs ubiquitous and long lived throughout Moche territory in all media, believed to be iconic references to monumental stepped platform pyramids.[17]

Among the jars and bottles, two artistic trends are evident. One involves the addition of single iconic elements (usually faces) that serve to metaphorically animate the vessel using minimal symbolism. The other utilizes more complex symbolic aggregations, whereby the entire vessel is modeled or somehow manipulated. Straight-neck jars, for example, most frequently have single, iconic images of humans or animals, shown as a simple face molded onto the vessel's neck. The addition of the face serves to conceptually animate the vessel, giving it a specific identity, by creating an obvious analogy between the vessel body and the human or animal body. If one considers that such vessels commonly held water and are also associated with *chicha* (the ubiquitous ceremonial beverage), an analogy among blood, water, chicha, and the contents of a living body is insinuated.[18]

Why particular faces were chosen for such vessels is unclear. Several distinctive characters are often repeated in the Cerro Mayal sample. The two most frequent were dubbed the "Angry Moche Man" and the "Wrinkle-Face Whistler" (Figure 3.5).[19] The Angry Moche Man appears almost exclusively on single-spout, strap-handle bottles. The Wrinkle-Face Whistler, the distinctive "Cachetón," and several others are found on straight-neck jars. Such faces were typically mold made, using a simple thumb-press technique or a more complex appliqué process. In each case, it seems clear that the globular body of the jar stands in metaphoric relationship to the human body implied by the face.

Animal representations were molded or appliquéd directly to jar necks in the same way. Animal imagery was limited to a very small number of species, with three animals predominating: "owls/Fanged Owls," "Fanged Lizards," and "felines" (Figures 3.6–3.7).[20] Other frequent animals include birds and snakes (Figure 3.8). Animal imagery was almost entirely mold made and very often highly conventionalized. Fanged Owls and Lizards, for example, show a range of stylized graphic modifiers contributing little to realism, serving

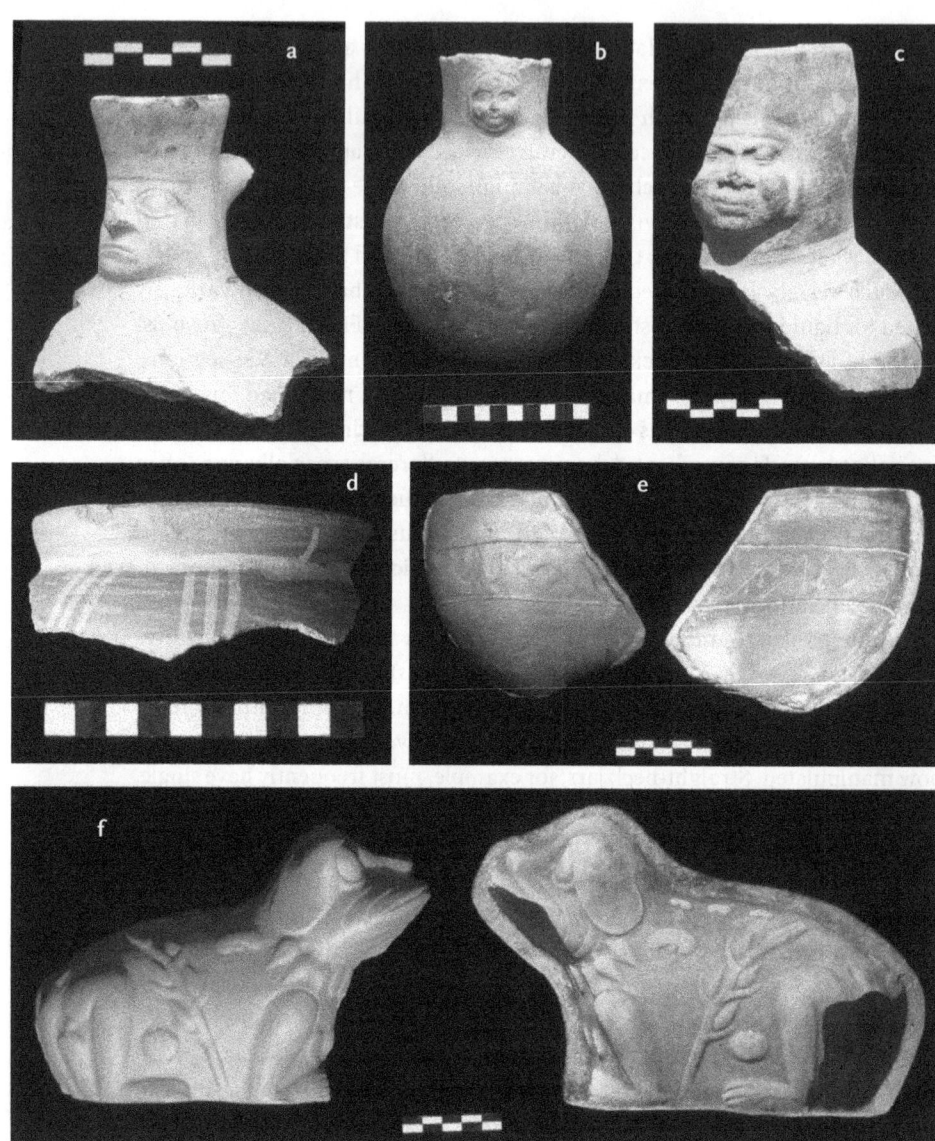

FIGURE 3.3. Examples of vessel forms common to Cerro Mayal: **(a)** straight-neck bottle with strap handle and impressed face; **(b)** small globular jar; **(c)** tall-neck jar with impressed face; **(d)** short everted-neck jar; **(e)** oval cup; **(f)** molds for various vessels and vessel parts (large frog vessel mold shown).

FIGURE 3.4. *Facing page, top:* Stylized motifs: **(a)** step-fret wave; **(b)** flower/marsh/heron; **(c)** escalonado; **(d)** zigzag and triangle.

FIGURE 3.5. *Facing page, bottom:* Six human face appliqués.

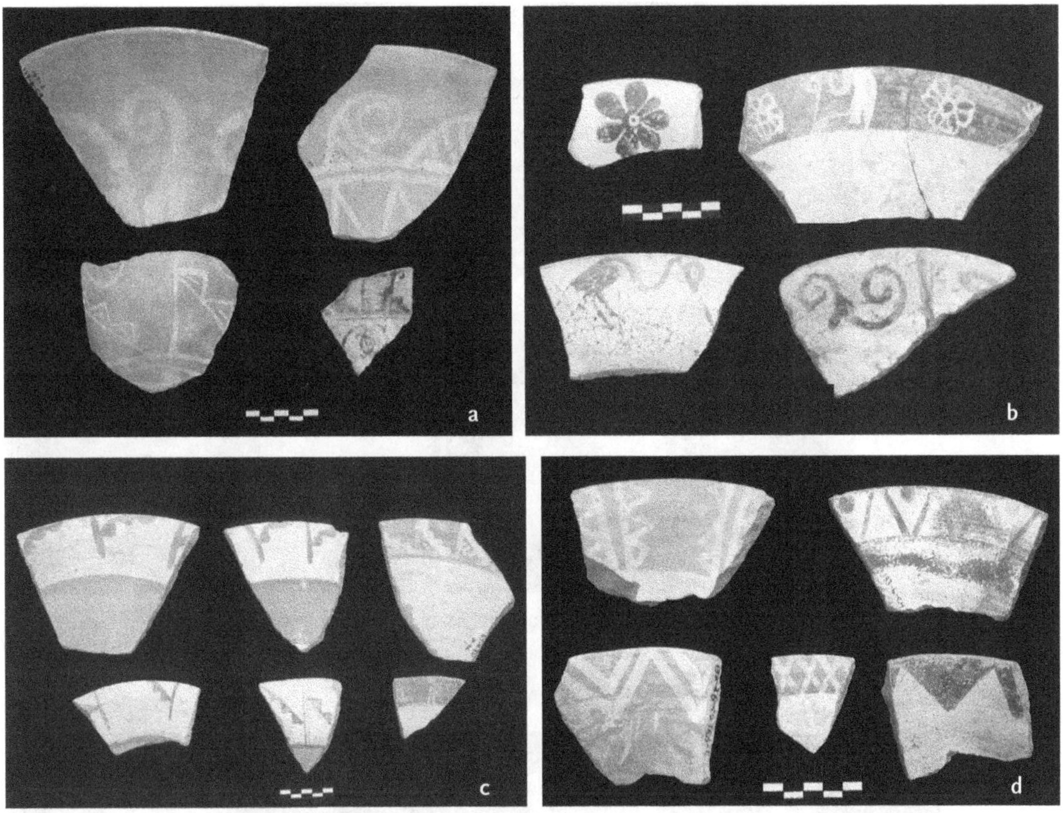

The Production of Ceramic Imagery

57

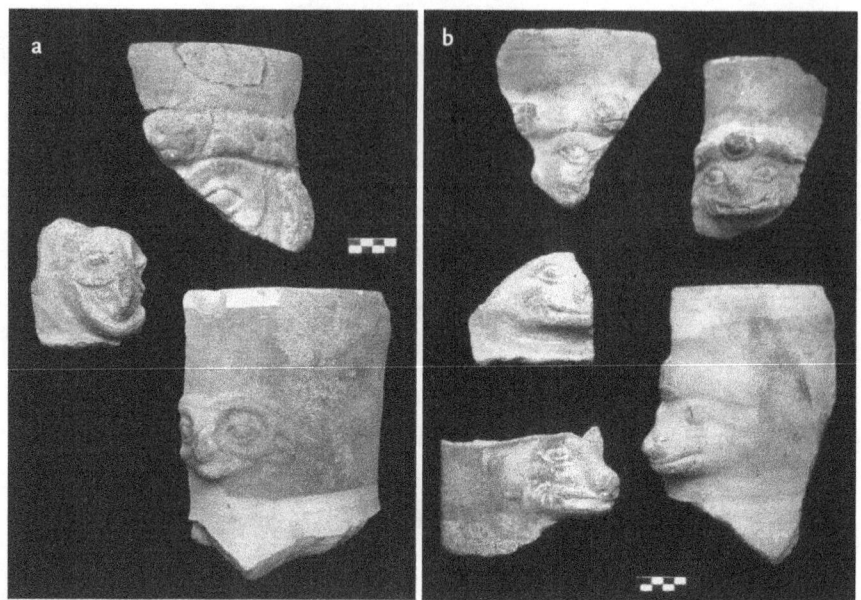

FIGURE 3.6. Conventionalized animal imagery: **(a)** Fanged Owl; **(b)** Fanged Lizard.

FIGURE 3.7. Animal appliqués and molds: **(a)** felines; **(b)** snarling foxes; **(c)** molds of parrot, bird, and llama; **(d)** monkey.

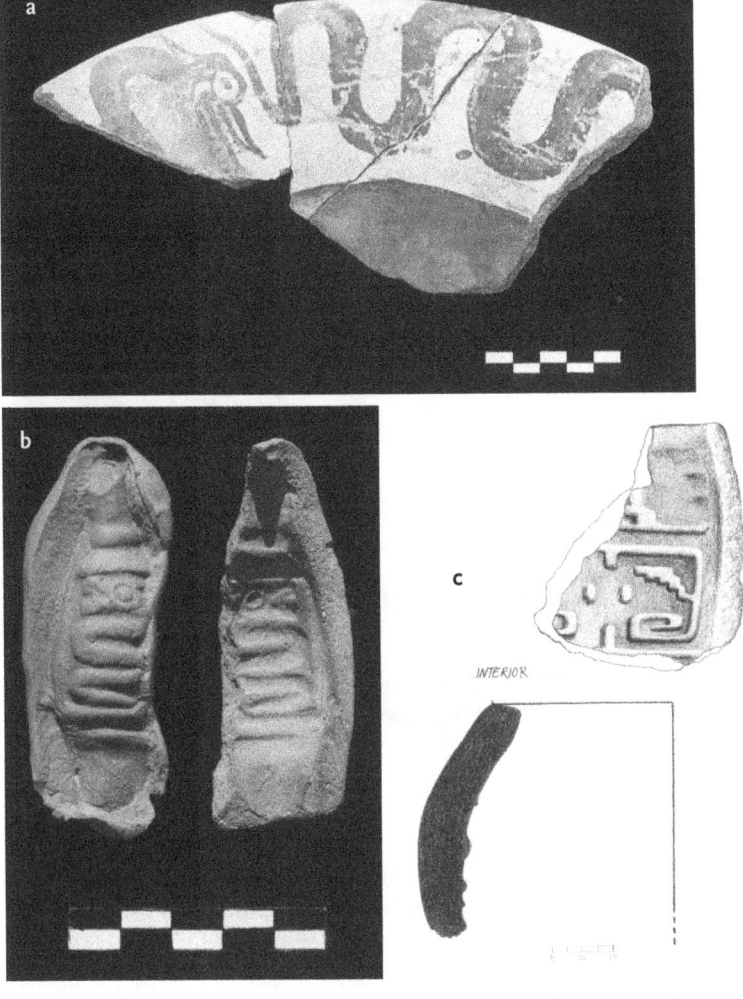

FIGURE 3.8. Snake motifs: **(a)** painted florero rim; **(b–c)** mold-impressed geometric serpents on rattle and globular jar mold.

instead to reference larger narrative structures. Highly stylized, such characters have naturalistic beaks or snouts modified with humanesque eyes, ears, headdresses, and other distinctive clothing. Each one's specific iconographic elements function within a larger symbolic vocabulary, signaling that the character is not to be read as an ordinary animal but, rather, as an icon or sign for some larger concept. Both the Fanged Lizard and the Fanged Owl—identified in other contexts as Iguana and Owl Warrior—correlate to larger thematic contexts, functioning here as references to key ritual scenes, such as the Sacrifice Scene and the Mountain Sacrifice.[21]

FIGURE 3.9.
Figurines from Cerro Mayal: (a) solid figurines, nude females; (b) solid figurines, females with tunics and braids; (c) mold for hollow female figurine.

FIGURINES AND PENDANT BEADS

Figurines and pendant beads probably enjoyed a ritual life apart from feasting. Although their actual meaning is open to interpretation, their form strongly suggests that they were not viewed in the same way as serving vessels. Laden with imagery but with no readily apparent utilitarian capacity, they appear as inherently symbolic objects, made to fulfill a purely conceptual role. The small scale of figurines and pendants most readily suggests intimate contact between object and viewer. Such artworks, even when placed out for display, sewn to a garment or presented publicly, by necessity required very close proximity to see the iconographic details. It is certainly possible that, given their ubiquity and relatively consistent iconography, most people would recognize the intent of the object even without close inspection. Yet, intuitively, we suspect that they were made to be handled up close and that they may well have circulated from one individual to another.

Cerro Mayal's artists produced large numbers of figurines, both hollow and solid (Figure 3.9). Ranging in size from about 3 centimeters up to 18 centimeters, figurines often have a somewhat generic look, unlike the distinctive portraits found on jars and bottles. A small number of figurines depict male characters, such as warriors with a war club and crescent headdress, or standing figures with their arms behind their backs, as if they are prisoners. By far, however, females are the most commonly depicted. Women are typically

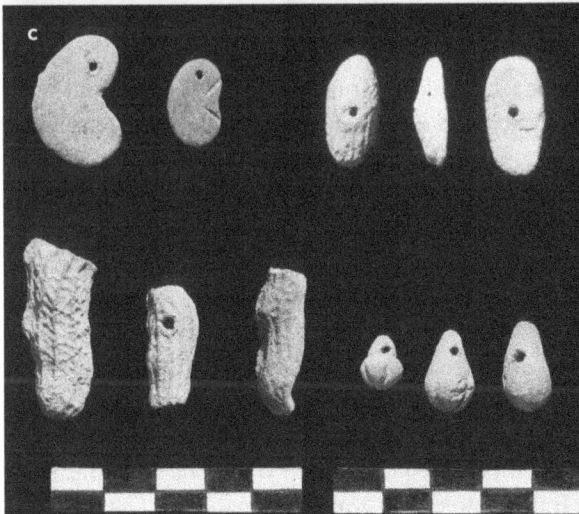
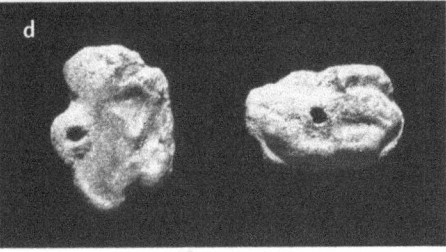

FIGURE 3.10.
Pendant beads: **(a)** human;
(b) abbreviated human;
(c) botanical (beans, *nectandra* seeds, miniature peanuts, gourds);
(d) animal (feline, deer).

shown in a frontal standing pose, either nude or wearing a tunic. A characteristic gesture places the hands on the stomach or chest. In the case of the nudes, the genitalia are always clearly shown but with minimal emphasis given to the breasts. Nude figures are sometimes shown with a round collar-style necklace, with the necklace beads articulated, and pendant earrings. Clothed figures have a fairly conventionalized set of attributes: knee-length tunic, pendant earrings, round neck collar or necklace, no headdress per se (although the horizontal line across the forehead may indicate a head covering of some kind). Women's hair is occasionally shown with double braids hanging down.

Tiny pendant beads echo the gesture and costume of figurines. The pendants' diminutive scale and single perforation suggest that they were intended to be worn by individuals, perhaps sewn onto garments or as jewelry. Like figurines, they seem to have functioned in some way as talismans. And as with figurines, these were mold made, using tiny, shallow, miniature molds (Figure 3.10). These miniscule ornaments sometimes depict deer, felines, peanuts, or beans, and even the tiniest mold-made objects faithfully reproduce elements found in larger ceramics, albeit in designs distilled to their most abbreviated iconographic level. Though the Moche tendency toward standardization and the distillation of salient iconographic details is discussed at length in the second part of this book, it bears mention at this juncture. These diminutive pendants remarkably demonstrate that certain pictorial elements had critical importance, regardless of scale, implying that even small adornments may have had ritual importance when conveying ideologically loaded symbols. Pictorial imagery, when distilled to its most minimal or abbreviated form, seems particularly akin to the kinds of graphic conventions we expect to find in conjunction with pictographic notational forms.

MUSICAL INSTRUMENTS AND MUSICIANS

Musical instruments and images of musicians form a conceptually linked cluster. Although the Moche did make instruments of metal, bone, and shell, within the ceramic production context at Cerro Mayal, the most frequently found instruments are percussive. These are ceramic rattles, *cascabeles* (jingle bells), and drums. Other instruments include fancy whistles and trumpets, sometimes embellished with images of people playing those instruments (Figures 3.11–3.12).

Rattles consisted of one or two hollow ceramic pods with loose pellets inside. These were relatively small, usually about the size of the palm of one's hand. The bulbous chambers were made using two-piece molds, with low-relief geometric patterns impressed into them. Handmade, solid handles were attached at bottom, sealing pea-sized clay pellets inside (Figure 3.8b). Rattles in the shape of *chirimoya* fruit are frequent, as are Water Snake motifs. Such configurations suggest links between musical performance and agricultural fertility and a connection between form and function (Figure 3.13). Depictions of rattles in use, on figurines, for example, show that the instruments often had a ribbon or cord attached to the handle, although no such example has yet been archaeologically retrieved.

Although the iconographic components of rattle pods were mold formed, cascabeles, in contrast, rarely carry mold-impressed imagery. These hollow, semicircular ceramic forms with pellets inside were used percussively, as clusters attached to poles or sewn onto garments around the lower hem of a tunic (Figure 3.14). Drum cylinders, of circular ceramic rims, to which, presumably, resonant membranes were later attached, complete the percussive group.

Wind instruments, whistles, and trumpets often carried complex iconography. Fancy ceramic whistles were created with molded front sides attached

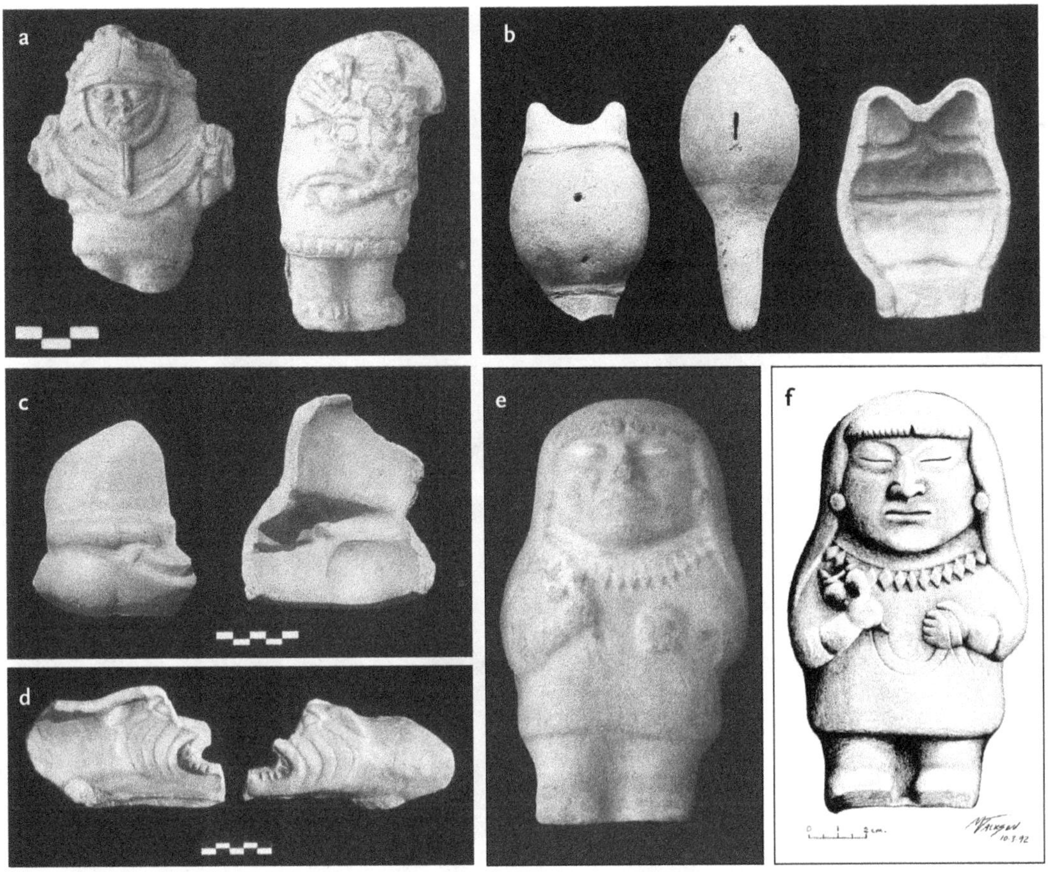

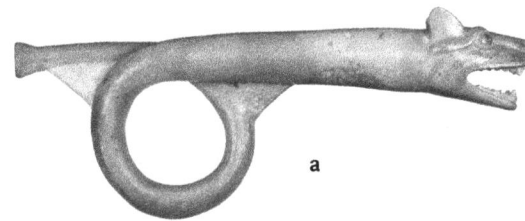

FIGURE 3.11.
Musical instruments and musicians: **(a)** fancy whistles; **(b)** hollow rattles and rattle mold; **(c)** mold for drum player effigy bottle; **(d)** trumpet mold; **(e)** hollow figurine; **(f)** woman playing rattle (CM177-10).

FIGURE 3.12.
(a) Looped ceramic trumpet (X86-3937, University of California, Los Angeles, Fowler Museum of Culture History); **(b)** drummer effigy bottle (894.100058, Collection of the Field Museum, Chicago).

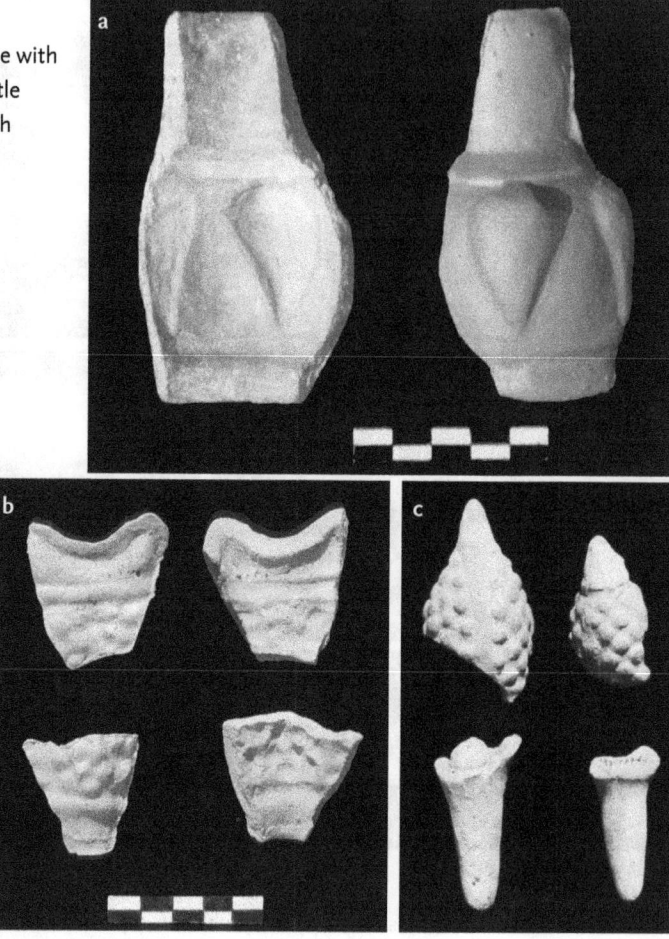

FIGURE 3.13.
Plant motifs: **(a)** bottle with *ají* peppers; **(b–c)** rattle molds and rattles with chirimoya motifs.

to hand-modeled hollows on the back sides. Cerro Mayal's whistles feature some of the most finely detailed imagery produced at the workshop. Likewise, Moche ceramic trumpets, made of a single long tube, either straight or looped once in the center, were usually finished with elaborate mold-made imagery at the larger terminus (Figure 3.12a). Such elaborately detailed images are often supernatural creatures, Water Snakes, or other fanged beasts. In these, the trumpet sound would equate with a voice issuing from the creature's mouth. Because these were produced using multiple molds—the central loop was fashioned with a two-part mold, and the large, decorated terminus was made with a separate mold or pair of molds—the artist was free to attach any desirable imagery to a relatively standardized trumpet body.

Additionally, trumpets seem to have carried well-understood meanings in and of themselves. Solid clay loops, sometimes called *fideos*, appear to have been miniature versions (Figure 3.14). Often with a crudely incised face on the terminating end, these were produced at Cerro Mayal and have been found at numerous other sites around the valley.[22] At first hypothesized to be children's

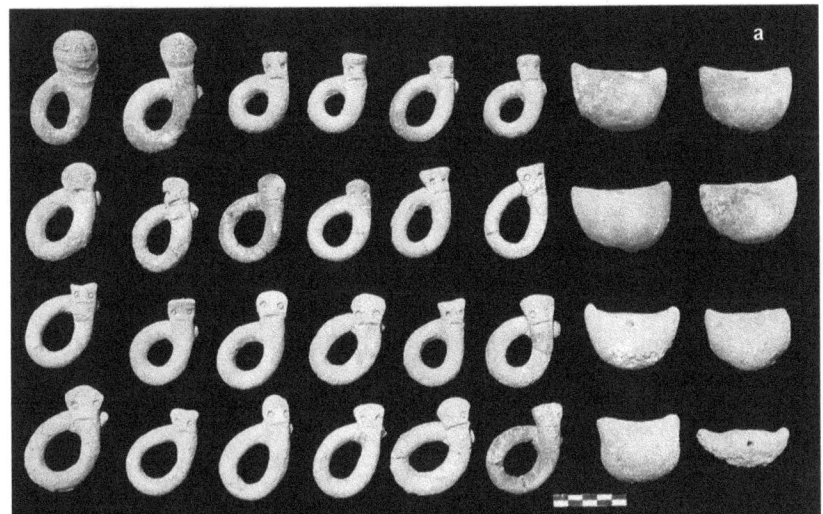

FIGURE 3.14.
(a) miniature trumpets and cascabeles;
(b) clay mask fragments.

toys or textile weights, they are remarkably consistent, most resembling miniature ceramic trumpets. As such, they perhaps reference a generalized concept of "calling to the gods," functioning at the level of personal talismans.

Moche narrative imagery gives a strong indication that these instruments may have formed musical ensembles. When shown in complex scenes, they most often coincide with themes like the Dance of the Dead and the Ribbon Dance. In such scenes, musicians are usually shown as members of a procession, and the instruments are in active use; they were an integral part of ritual practice, becoming grave goods only at some later time. Ethnohistoric evidence from both coast and highlands supports the idea that music was played at all kinds of ritual events. Music and dancing were, and are, important aspects of Andean rituals related to planting and fertility.

The ethnohistoric parallel serves as a reminder that a much larger cycle of ritual events, requiring appropriate paraphernalia (such as musical instruments), was surely being supplied by workshop production. The fact that artists created instruments and various self-referential images showing those same instruments signals a level of self-awareness on their part, intimating an understanding of the symbolic value of performance, the function of the ceramic instruments, and their independent symbolic value as specialized liturgical or ritual-use objects.

FIGURE 3.15.
Ceramic tools:
(a) turnette (turning plate);
(b) vessel modified to become a scoop;
(c) baked clay cone.

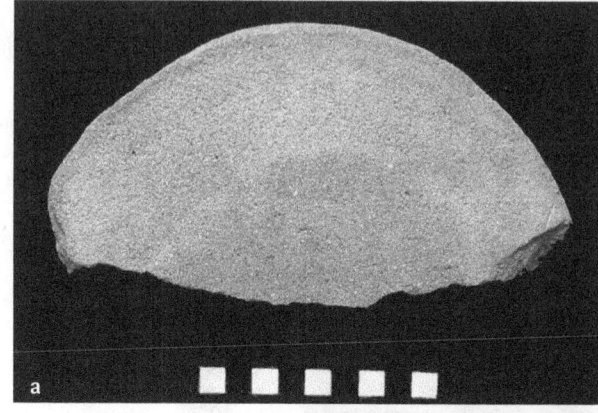
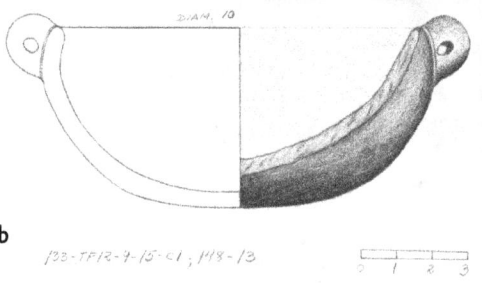

CERAMIC TOOLS AND TECHNOLOGY

Tools tell a different kind of tale. The kinds of information they carry speak less about the ultimate use for finished ceramic pieces, less about the communication of particular thoughts, and more about the internal dynamics of how forms and iconographic content were assembled. All the implements for basic pottery production are seen at Cerro Mayal, including a variety of hand tools, raw clay mixing areas, and kilns. Additionally, an extraordinarily high number of molds and mold fragments were present, attesting to a high level of production and sophisticated craftsmanship.

In lieu of a potter's wheel (which the Moche did not use), "turnettes," also called bats or turning plates, were commonly used as movable surfaces on which to build a vessel (Figure 3.15a). Some implements were created from cast-off or recycled items, as, for example, with an ordinary cooking pot whose cut edge was ground flat, modified to become a scoop (Figure 3.15b). Other tools are more enigmatic, a fired conical wedge of clay, for example, perhaps used for burnishing or polishing (Figure 3.15c). A number of well-worn stones also appear to have served as tools for polishing and burnishing (Figure 3.16). Perhaps most intriguing, an unfired lump of clay (Figure 3.17) suggests that craftspeople were measuring clay portions, possibly in standardized measures, using a scoop lined with finely woven cloth. A close inspection of the impressions visible on the lump's surface shows what appear to be a delicately sewn seam down the center and fabric puckers around the sides.

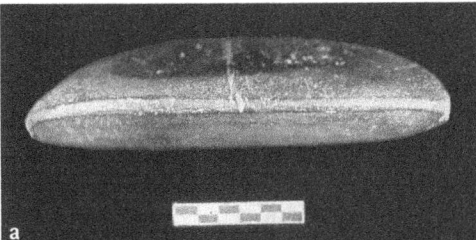
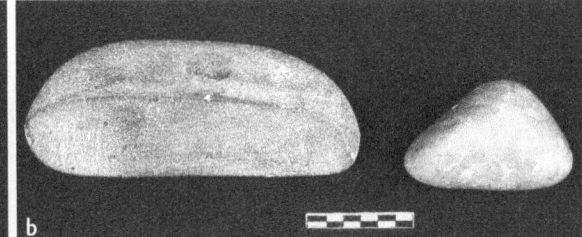
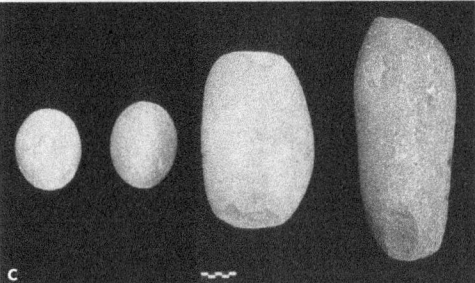

FIGURE 3.16.
Stone tools: **(a–b)** polishing stones; **(c)** hammer stones.

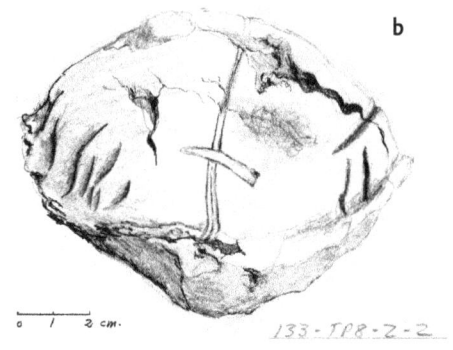

FIGURE 3.17.
Measured clay lump: **(a)** photo; **(b)** drawing.

The clay would have been scooped in a measure, with the fabric serving to release the clay from the scoop.

Clusters of kilns indicate that at Cerro Mayal certain locations within the site were preferred for firing. Located in the central area of the workshop, the kilns were deliberately positioned to take advantage of the wind, which funneled through the small *quebrada*. The small promontory upon which the workshop was located opens out toward the sea. In normal weather conditions, the wind intensifies in velocity every afternoon, channeling a steady stream of increased air pressure into the kiln area. A relatively predictable air stream allowed kilns to fire at a hotter, steadier temperature. The kilns were primarily of the open-pit type, intentionally transitory in construction (Figure 3.18).[23] Some show evidence of surrounding walls of two or three courses of adobe brick, with multiple vessels stacked inside, one atop another. Firing fuel consisted of tall grass

FIGURE 3.18. The excavated floor of one of Cerro Mayal's kilns.

(*cola de caballo*), dung, or wood, placed around the ceramics. The mound was then covered with large broken sherds, which served as a refractory material to conserve and distribute heat more evenly. A final layer of dung would have been added to the exterior of the kiln to give additional longevity to the kiln's internal fire. After firing, the mound was easily disassembled.

Variability in Ceramic Molds

Molds are by far the most numerous and, for our purposes, most significant tools recovered from Cerro Mayal.[24] It has long been known that molds were used to produce certain kinds of Moche vessels; such molds are generally assumed to be two pieces, basically producing the front and back sides of a vessel's main chamber.[25] Yet the evidence from Cerro Mayal makes it clear that, in addition to these, Moche artists were combining a variety of other molding and hand-modeling techniques to achieve an impressively high degree of artistry. Mold types included small thumb-press seals and stamps, figurine molds, multiple-part appliqué, and body molds. Complex mold construction played an important part in how iconographic clusters were composed, conserved, and transmitted. Furthermore, it appears that molds themselves may have been important products in their own right.

In general, any ceramic object may be composed of any number of parts that have been shaped by any combination of techniques, as long as the consistency and moisture of the clay allow for successful joining and subsequent firing. Workshop molds were concave; the soft clay was pressed into the mold (press molded), regardless of any subsequent applications or manipulations. Cerro Mayal's molds fall into one of three main types: stamp molds, one-piece press molds, and multiple-part press molds. From the craftsperson's point of view, the most difficult aspect of complex mold usage would not have been the actual mold pressing of clay. Rather, because of a tendency toward cracking and breaking in the jointed areas, the most challenging aspect of multiple-part mold technology would be the joining of the various parts (known as "luting" or "sprigging").[26] For a firm joint, the clay bodies must be the same consistency.[27] A higher level of skill was required for complex joinery involving mold-made parts than for simple hand-built pottery, and it was accompanied by higher investment of labor and risk of loss should the joining fail.

The use and function of molds are not necessarily self-evident. In the present case, mold variability was not simply a means of producing multiple images quickly; it also served to transmit fixed iconographic phrases efficiently. Complex variability of mold types suggests that artists clearly understood the usefulness of fixed unit signs and symbols.

STAMP MOLDS (SEALS)

Stamps are generally small, shallow molds used to impress a design into a soft surface.[28] At Cerro Mayal two basic types of stamp molds are identified: intaglio stamps (those whose shallow designs are impressed in a planar manner at or below the main surface of the vessel) and low-relief stamps (which create an impressed design in which some part projects above the main surface of the vessel).[29] Intaglio stamps and low-relief stamps are similar in form and method of application; however, they differ in the depth or height of the finished impression. Both could be applied freely to almost any surface that was sufficiently plastic. No extra clay was added to the vessel when using this type of mold.

Low-relief stamps depicting the faces of various beings common to Moche art were commonly used on the necks of jars and bottles. Simple, straight-necked bottles with faces (Figure 3.19) exemplify the products of these small (4 to 6 square centimeters) low-relief stamps. The stamp mold was applied directly to the neck (or spout) of an already formed vessel using a thumb-press technique. Larger, medallion-sized stamp molds were also used to impress shallow, low-relief images onto vessel bodies. Ovoid, square, or rectangular, about the size of one's palm, their edges are somewhat rounded, not precisely cut or angled (as is seen in molds intended to fit with mates). Among the most exceptional of these are a group of molds with a distinctive artistic style, apparently all created by the same hand, the Mayal Mold Master (Figure 3.20). This artist's personal style is recognizable for its persistent curvilinear gesture and reductive stylization of detail, distinctive from others seen at Cerro Mayal.

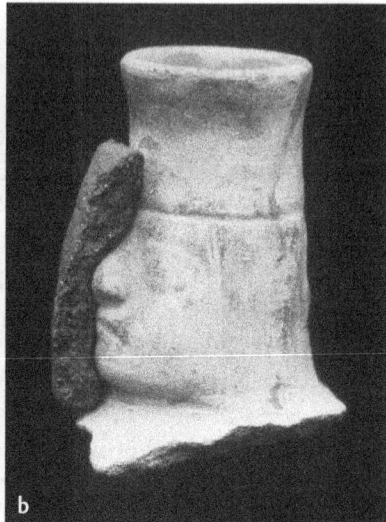

FIGURE 3.19. Small stamp mold: **(a)** apart; **(b)** applied to bottle neck.

FIGURE 3.20. Large stamp molds of the Mayal Mold Master.

ONE-PIECE PRESS MOLDS

One-piece press molds were also commonly used at Cerro Mayal. These are among the simplest of technologies, and the action involved in using this type of mold differs from that of the stamp molds, in the sense that one-piece press molds were not applied to already complete vessels. Rather, they were the essential forming mechanism used to create finished ceramic items. Each mold was essentially a single concave piece into which soft clay was pressed. Any excess clay was trimmed from around the edges of the mold. After the clay began to dry, because of shrinkage, the finished item was easily removed from the mold. The process yielded an object whose "front side" details were mold formed and whose "back side" was left to be hand finished.

Figurines were the most frequent objects made at Cerro Mayal using this type of mold. Scale was the main factor affecting whether or not a figurine was hollow; larger items were hollow. Pendant ornaments were made in much the same way but with very tiny molds that included, as part of their design, provision of a "hole" where a thread might have passed. Figurines were inevitably front side only; back sides were hand finished. Mold edges tend to be cut at a slightly acute angle away from the mold interior, a feature that allows for a neater edge on the finished piece.

MULTIPLE-PART MOLDS

When artists sought to convey unusually complex visual messages, low-relief stamping or single-mold fabrication may have presented technical limitations. Shapes with heavy undercutting were impossible to make using single-piece molds.[30] Very intricate sculptural forms needed more clay with a wetter consistency. These very complex Moche constructions were the product of multiple-part molds and multiple-part joinery.[31] Entire vessel bodies could be transformed into sculptural forms by using multiple-part molds. The technique allowed artists the freedom to build extremely asymmetrical three-dimensional compositions or use traditional vessel forms as backdrops for narrative scenes, intaglio impressions, and painted motifs. Whereas some compositions carefully integrated form and imagery, others treated the vessel body as a convenient surface upon which to attach appliqués in veritable "tableaux" of modeled imagery.[32] Variations of complex, multiple-mold techniques found their most masterly expression in appliqué processes, sculpted vessel bodies, and multiple-part compositions.

APPLIQUÉS

Medium- or high-relief iconographic elements were added to already-formed vessels as appliqués.[33] Appliqués could be applied almost anywhere on a vessel, to create sculptural appendages, additional chambers, or compositional elements. Appliqués were attached to jar necks (as faces or heads on straight-neck jars), or they were used as modeled appliqué elements (more commonly associated with vessel bodies and deck figures).[34] Appliqué elements tended to have some of the finest detail. Artists paid careful attention to minute aspects

FIGURE 3.21.
Slip-glued appliqués:
(a) joinery detail;
(b) appliqué variants.

of pose and expression, allowing them a tremendous range of character and plasticity. The high caliber of artistic skill and added labor investment suggest something unusually important about appliqué pieces, a conceptualization of meaning apart from the larger production process.

Timing played an important part in the successful joining process. Appliqué pieces were essentially finished prior to any attempt at joining with a larger composition. The appliqué had to be removed from the mold while still relatively plastic and joined before becoming too dry. In joining, the area where the piece was to be applied was scored (to roughen the surface), as was the open edge of the appliqué piece. A coating of slip was then applied to both surfaces to help glue the two parts together (Figure 3.21). A vent hole was then cut into the vessel behind the appliqué to allow for air expansion during firing.[35] In many cases, the applied piece not only was sprigged into place (a comparatively superficial joining) but was in fact integrally joined, or luted, by cutting away a section of the main vessel where the molded element was substituted, with edges slipped and pinched together.

The Technology of Multiple-Part Compositions

Complex joinery techniques can be found on the entire spectrum of Moche ritual-use ceramics. The most iconographically significant elements (signs, icons, motifs) tended to be mold made. Yet, technologically speaking, the most important differences between the various mold types are not found in the molds themselves—the basic press molding technique is inherently similar in all. Rather, the differences lie in the way in which the molds were handled. Press molds could be used in the most simple and minimal manner, as with single-piece stamp molds, to add small iconographic elements. Yet they were also used in increasingly complex ways, to construct elaborate compositions with compound iconography and multiple parts.

Sometimes, entire vessels became sculptural forms or narrative tableaux, created by means of multiple-part body molds. Such molds were generally large and finely made, displaying the entire range of the Moche iconography, everything from portrait heads and fantastic zoomorphic creatures to architectural forms and mountain landscapes. In many cases, the only reference to functionality was through the addition of a spout or handle, which seems, by later Moche times, to have been little more than artistic convention signaling ritual function.

Ceramists exercised a measure of freedom in choosing vessel forms and compositions to create a range of messages operating within well-understood social parameters. Such variability played out in terms of finishing techniques, which could dramatically affect the final form of the product without substantially altering the iconographic program. This is true, for example, for one of the more striking human images found at Cerro Mayal, a very large mold depicting the Wrinkle-Face Whistler (Figure 3.22a). In this version, the distinctive face was created at a scale large enough to become a singular portrait head vessel or to be used as part of a larger construction. An example of such a construction is found in a large double-chambered jar originally published by Julio C. Tello; one of the jar faces was almost certainly created with the mold retrieved from Cerro Mayal (Figure 3.22b).[36] Although whistling humans may be associated with shamanism and the custom of whistling to call the spirits, the present example pairs the whistler with an image of a skeletal head on the vessel's second chamber. The precise meaning of the pairing is unclear; however, it is significant that the use of multiple molds allowed the artist a degree of conceptual liberty in how such visual phrases could be constructed. Likewise, the large Wrinkle-Face Whistler mold, whose top and bottom are purposely left open, created a portrait "head" that could be attached to a larger vessel body or simply be closed at the bottom to form, with the addition of an appropriate spout, a portrait jar or bottle. Ultimately, there is little appreciable technological difference between molds used to create a "head" for attachment to a vessel "body" and molds used to create the "head" of a portrait bottle.

Analysis of molds and complete vessels makes clear the ways in which mold-made parts were mixed and matched with great flexibility. The "Prisoner Jar with Lizards" (Figure 3.23), in the collection of the Museo de Arqueología

FIGURE 3.22.
Large Wrinkle-Face Whistler face mold: **(a)** mold and impression, Cerro Mayal; **(b)** identical face on finished jar (Tello 1924).

(Trujillo), is an excellent example of multiple icons nested within the same vessel. Here, the vessel is a stirrup-spout bottle (although the spout that was once attached to the back side of the vessel body's upper shoulder has broken off and is not visible). Although it is a stirrup-spout bottle, the vessel represents a tall-neck jar topped by a small, permanently attached convex lid (a "false jar" neck)—the very type of tall-neck jar and lid so often shown in scenes of ritual events. That this is no ordinary jar is made clear by the addition of a rope around the vessel's neck, indicating that the jar is a prisoner, probably destined for sacrifice.[37] The foot of the vessel suggests that the vessel body may have been at least partially mold made, and the lizard motifs along the vessel shoulder were mold formed in a separate molding episode with a low-relief press mold like those identified with the Mayal Mold Master (Figure 3.19).[38] Through the addition of a stirrup spout and fine attention to paint and surface polish, the artist visually signals the special offertory nature of the image.

FIGURE 3.23. "Prisoner Jar with Lizards" (Universidad Nacional de Trujillo Museo de Arqueología; photo by Christopher B. Donnan).

Commentary

The ceramists living and working at Cerro Mayal engaged in large-scale production of middle-level fineware ceramics for more than two hundred years. It was a community that appears to have enjoyed a patronage relationship with the monumental civic-ceremonial center at adjacent Mocollope. Feasts and ceremonies at Mocollope, we can assume, were supplied with appropriate ceramic wares made by workshop artisans. Most of the ceramics produced at the workshop had basic decoration, such as slip coat paint or simple motifs; a modest proportion had complex imagery; and a small percentage was made in the very finest fashion. Such a variable range of quality makes it likely that the workshop's artisans possessed differing levels of skill and that perhaps their wares ultimately went to different segments of society. The high level of esoteric knowledge displayed in the finer ceramics and the technical skill evident in complex ceramic constructions make it probable that artists' skills translated into an elevated degree of social status.

Formal and statistical analyses of the Cerro Mayal iconographic sample allow for some generalizations about how the ceramics may have been used in Moche society. The functional life of specialized ceramics, in the context of feasting and burials and as personal talismans, surely affected the finished forms of each. Humans interfaced with symbolically loaded objects in very specific ways; certain imagery was appropriate for certain kinds of activities. Strongly standardized forms and images suggest that there were accepted norms for different rituals and events. Feasting vessels generally had only minimal ideological references. Vessel forms that became recognizably iconic over time, such as floreros and stirrup-spout bottles, often had more complex religious indexes (possibly signaling a higher level of pictorial literacy on the part of those who were destined to handle them, although not necessarily so). Personal talismans contained a somewhat different cluster of iconic elements, most often associated with gender-specific roles and agricultural fertility. All were related to the overarching religious ideology, yet each was tailored to fit a particular niche.

Workshop technology sheds light on spatial organization, investment of labor, and, especially critical to the present inquiry, the ordering of Moche visual vocabulary in ceramic production. The development of multiple-part molds, and the attendant technical sophistication in multiple-part joinery, was largely programmatically driven. In other words, three-dimensional forms might have been sculpted from clay, without the use of molds, hand built one by one. But they were not. At Cerro Mayal, the emphasis was not on creating singularly beautiful or expressive works of ceramic art (even though many such artworks exist) but on creating large numbers of relatively specific forms with meaningful symbolism. Basic forms, such as jars and bottles, which might well have been more efficiently mold made (if absolute numbers were the goal), were mostly hand built, whereas the symbolically loaded imagery embellishing them, relating to religious ideology and temple ritual, was systemically programmed and reified by means of iconographically fixed molds.

This suggests that these specialists possessed, and to some extent controlled, detailed esoteric knowledge. The degree to which others in Moche society may also have had access to specialized esoteric knowledge is unclear. It is quite likely that oral explication and storytelling accompanied the portable artworks far into the hinterlands, and some individuals may have been more pictorially literate than others, allowing them to read the visual images with greater depth of understanding.

The development of an ideologically based social hierarchy generated a definite need for a means by which political and religious messages could be widely communicated. The degree to which basic press molding techniques were used to create multiple-part compositions reflects a technological adaptation to external pressures and limitations. Complex mold technology arose in response to particular demands for certain kinds of imagery and vessel forms. Molds were a means by which pictorial signs could be correctly replicated, even though in many cases employing them caused extra labor. The use of molds formed a key element in how iconographic clarity became increasingly standardized and spread. The large-scale production of specific imagery on ritual-use ceramics through mold technology at workshops like Cerro Mayal provided a means by which consistency of imagery occurred and a mechanism by which pictorial references came to be used independently from specific vessel forms.

PART II

Interpretation of Moche Iconographic Configurations (= Extraction)

CHAPTER 4

Issues of Iconographic Analysis

By the eighth century, Moche elite arts had assumed many aspects of a regularized system of signs and symbols. It was a pictorial tradition with religious ideology as its organizing matrix, even though, as with most products of visual culture, it also communicated a range of other messages and social imperatives. Visual imagery occupied a key position in the juncture between society's larger remembrance of myth history and the commemoration of particular religious observances conducted at temples and other sacred sites. Specific technologies, such as muralism and ceramic mold use, were evidently developed and refined over time in response to particular social needs and expectations. Significant patronage resources were devoted to the construction of enormous monuments, artworks, and manufacture of ritual-use ceramics, as well as other specialized paraphernalia, like metal ornaments and elaborate costume elements. The level of political and economic resources invested attests to the intensity of social commitment shared throughout Moche society.

Previous chapters explore various social contexts, focusing on strands of evidence related to the cultural milieu, monumental architecture, and production of ritual-use ceramics. Combined, they suggest how communication technology was cultivated and how it served the agendas of elites to propagate and maintain the artistic traditions. The contextual evidence grounds the imagery within a meaningful framework, exposing the kinds of social motivations that would support the development of a complex visual notation system.

The chapters that follow inquire about how best to understand Moche images from the standpoint of internal ordering, attempting to locate the intersection between orality and visual notation and investigating its connections to language. To what degree were notational structures or linguistic correlates present? How best to categorize them? These analytic exercises are the extractive processes the Houston refers to as "hermeneutic."[1] To address these issues, the focus of inquiry turns to the internal structures and semiotic arrangements evident in the pictorial system itself.

Is It Discursive?

Visually discursive forms must have recognizable differentiated signs and symbols, and they must have syntax. Yet meaningful signs are not always linguistically charged; nor are all systems of syntax modeled on spoken language. Discourse occurs when humans exchange ideas. It is extratextual and phenomenological, representing the larger sum of communicative parts, often encompassing speech, gesture, and the use of common systems of visual signs, assembled as a result of human agency.[2] Discursive visual forms are thus intended to contribute to a larger communicative purpose. Studies of word and image tend to echo the Saussurian dialectic, generally placing writing and figural imagery in opposition; visual signs more closely related to words have been posited as having a higher degree of *discursiveness*, and those that are more imagistic have been regarded as more *figural*.[3] The degree to which a visual system conforms to a linguistic sequence, its level of pictorial verisimilitude, and the manner of its schematization combine to determine its position within the larger domain of images.

As a conventionalized corpus, Moche imagery lies somewhere between glottographic writing and expressionistic picturing—well placed within the realm of semasiography and notation, an area of visual structuring laid out according to conventionalized rules of visual interaction, rather than by rules of linguistic sequence or pictorial veracity. Such designations, and the location of Moche visual arts within them, warrant additional clarification in what follows. To assert that the Moche pictorial system constituted an arrangement of regularized signs is to invite an investigation of structures of ideation and linguistic paralleling, which, presumably, underlay the iconography's complex levels of visual metaphor and metonymic syntax.

Glottographic and Semasiographic Signs

The graphic scripts most familiar today are those that reflect human speech, the glottographic forms. Such systems distill and codify sounds into a manageable set of symbols, no small feat considering that spoken human languages are composed of many thousands of meaningful units (morphemes), which are themselves composed of lesser numbers of separately distinct sounds (phones). The discrepancy between the large numbers of morphemes that most languages feature and the more limited number of distinct sounds that human vocal chords are capable of uttering has led, in part, to a distinction among linguists of script forms that record speech according to phonetic values (phonographic) from those that do so according to meaning (logographic). Many script traditions include elements of both.

Phonographic writing systems record phonological units (phonemes) and are characterized by limited numbers of (mostly) arbitrary or abstract signs that represent the specific sounds integral to particular language groups. Phonetic systems are generally classified as segmental, whose scripts denote individual phonemes in single-unit signs (such as Roman, Arabic, and Cyrillic alphabets); syllabic, which inscribe whole syllables and use additional graphs for multisyllable words (as with Linear B cuneiform); or featural, whose graphs represent compound aggregations of phonetic features (such as Pitman's shorthand or Korean hangul).[4] Alphabets usually have between twenty and thirty-five characters, and syllabaries may have as many as forty to ninety signs.[5] In terms of visual ordering, these notational systems usually contain a relatively high level of syntactic correspondence to the grammars of the languages they represent, although no written form ever entirely reproduces language.

Logographic writing is based on morphemic units of meaning.[6] A morpheme can be either a whole word or any part of a word that has particular meaning, such as tense markers or case markers. Chinese script is among the most often cited examples of logographic writing. Sequences of Chinese logographs contain a separate graph for each word or morpheme. Chinese is an "isolating" language, in that it strings separate words and morphemes together; therefore, if one wants to change meaning, one selects another word sequence rather than modifying the words themselves. This characteristic makes the exclusive use of logographic writing viable, even though Chinese (like all languages) has thousands of morphemes and hence, thousands of graphs.

Much has been made of the *ideographic* nature of Chinese script. Modern Chinese writing is composed almost entirely of arbitrary symbols whose meanings are understood by convention; however, early Chinese graphs apparently had a strong representational relationship to the things they represented. The degree to which a symbol actually looks like the thing it represents is its level of *motivation*. Some logographic scripts are highly motivated, whereas others are almost entirely arbitrary, and not all logographs picture that which they represent. A logograph representing the concept of "tree" may resemble a tree or not. The perception of a close degree of motivation in early Chinese script led to the notion that Chinese logographs are ideographic; that is, they represent ideas directly, examples of one-to-one pictorial correspondences intended to conjure mental images of nonphonetic, experiential cognition based on shared cultural concepts. This representational quality creates a degree of polysemy, in the sense that motivated characters signify meaning in more than one way. Yet, as signs for specific units of a particular spoken language, Chinese logographs are ultimately glottographically informed.

Motivated symbols are also sometimes referred to as *pictographic*, a term that works well to describe individual signs but which becomes problematic when used to describe entire graphic systems. Often associated with widely disparate Amerindian artistic traditions, the designation can be confusing

FIGURE 4.1. Illustration of the rebus "I saw Aunt Rose."

because its specific connection to language is poorly defined. The ambiguity allows it to be applicable to any number of artistic traditions, whose motivated symbols may or may not be logographic and whose inner workings may differ radically from one culture to another. Similarly, the concept of *rebus* is useful to understand specific signs or clusters of images, but it is not ultimately a term that would apply to an entire graphic system.

Rebus devices use pictures whose pronunciations are homonymic to the vocalization of the message desired, as in Figure 4.1. It is a picturing technique that has been described as a type of "visual pun" or "puzzle writing," merging logographs, images, and phonetics—a visual rhetorical device commonly used by hieroglyphic or other pictorially based sign systems to indicate words whose semantic meanings are too difficult to otherwise express. Rebus devices are essentially tied to specific languages, and some languages lend themselves to rebus constructions more easily than others. Rebus is a logographic technique that occurs often in New World visual systems in conjunction with pictures and script.

Graphic scripts that do not directly reflect speech are characterized as nonphonetic or *semasiographic*.[7] They are as controversial as they are intriguing, with many linguists insisting that these forms are not "true" writing, specifically because they do not reflect speech. The general absence of scholarship in certain areas of picture theory may well be underlain by long-held ideas about alphabetic (or cultural) superiority. Best exemplified in a coda elaborated in 1974 by Ignacio Gelb, an "evolution" of writing places pictures at the primitive end of development and alphabetic writing at the apex.[8] Yet it would be a mistake to summarily lump (and dismiss) nonlinguistically tied signs as too idiosyncratic or illogical to merit investigation.

Semasiographic systems can be genuinely ideographic in that they represent ideas directly. They function on the same cognitive level as spoken languages, within the structures of their own systems, but are not representations of specific linguistic construction. These notational forms can be understood outside of language once one understands the concepts that drive and order them. They constitute systems conceptually comparable to grammar, though not necessarily similarly ordered. To be given voice, semasiographic constructions require mediation on the part of an informed viewer.

Semasiographic systems have been described as either "conventional," in that meaning is indicated by the interrelationship of symbols that are arbitrarily codified (such as with mathematical, musical, or dance notations), or "iconic," where meaning is indicated through the use of symbols that are more directly motivated (e.g., those symbols having strong relationships between images and referents). Almost all semasiographic forms will include some arbitrarily conventionalized elements, and, as Elizabeth Boone notes, the distinction between conventional and iconic systems is blurred.[9]

Mathematical symbols are an excellent example of a conventionalized semasiographic system. Equations express quantities and spatial relationships that can be understood by anyone familiar with the system, regardless of their native language. Numerals, letters, and specialized signs (operatives) stand for numbers, things, and actions, respectively—functions that could be thought of as analogous to spoken language. Yet mathematical notation also includes a spatial aspect, whereby meaning is conveyed through the relative position and size of the symbols. For example, 2^a means something quite different from a^2 or $a/2$ or $2/a$. All use variants of the same symbols, but the differences in arrangement convey meanings in a way that is not directly paralleled in spoken language.[10]

International road signs are familiar instances of an "iconic" semasiographic system. They feature images describing road conditions, events, activities, rules, and commands. When translated into speech, the system is composed primarily of descriptive noun phrases, having a high degree of correlation between image and referent, combined with several arbitrary conventions used to convey specific instructions to the viewer on how to respond, such as a circle with a diagonal slash to mean prohibition or a yellow triangle to signal caution and so forth. The context within which the message operates is strictly limited and understood as a given; the viewer is in motion, moving forward, driving on the road. The system was devised to avoid the use of specific language; the system depends, instead, on a pictorial vocabulary or shared tradition of pictorial understanding common to all drivers, regardless of one's native language. Its icons correlate to verbal expressions in a relatively direct manner, partially because, in this particular system, messages are conveyed in the form of simple autonomous phrases, rather than as sequences of ligatured ideas. There are virtually no structures from one road sign to another that one might construe as analogous to sentences. The system is limited in that it expresses almost no complex information about spatial or temporal relationships outside of the viewer's immediate experience.

Like mathematical notation, these iconic road signs include an element of spatial interaction that requires secondary elaboration. The viewer is presumed to be engaged in a particular activity (driving a moving vehicle) translatable to a sequential narrative whose parameters are generally known to the creator of the visual sign. The physical demands of driving—making appropriate stops, avoiding potholes, negotiating dangerous curves—are signaled to the viewer in a way that presupposes a spatial relationship among sign, driver, and road. The visual system expresses its message within the parameters of its unique schema, yet it requires mediation to find expression in verbal or other communicatory modes.[11]

Syntax and Semiotics

Internal ordering, or syntax, is a critical factor in how a system is used in actual practice (and in how it is subsequently categorized). Syntax governed by linguistic patterning is, for many scholars, among the most defining features of writing. For example, in *Mesoamerican Writing Systems*, Joyce Marcus distinguishes early writing from complex iconography by its format, commenting that "even when we are unable to read or interpret certain examples of writing, we are able to infer that a certain text is writing by its organization.... [W]riting has a linear format, either in *rows* (as in the case of Mesopotamia) or *columns* (as in the case of China and the Maya region). This linear format implies the order of reading."[12] Nonetheless, Marcus, like many other scholars of ancient American script, raises the question of mixed writing systems. The various syntactic ordering mechanisms governing nonlinguistically tied semasiographic and mixed notational forms are less readily apparent and, because they are so contextually dependent, vary significantly from one system to another. Marcus notes that some Mesoamerican writing systems, like Mixtec, which uses hieroglyphic labels to clarify specific details of pictorial scenes, should be thought of as mixed forms because they dispense with a rigidly columnar format, adopting styles that can be considered as "labeling" or "caption" scripts.[13] In the Americas, such systems seem to have been the norm rather than the exception.

Charles Peirce began the discussion of semiotic relationships with his theory of signs, the fundamental elements of which have become familiar in the last century. His triadic division of signs into icons, indexes, and symbols addresses the dynamic relationships among object, sign, and viewer.[14] Yet, because Peirce characterized ideographs and hieroglyphs as icons of a "nonlogical" kind, associating them with the evolutionary development of "primitive" writing, his analysis generally skirted discussion of how nonglottographic sign systems may work.[15] The presumption of an antipodal model of visual communication, couched in the evolutionistic vocabulary of the times and generally accepted as universal, caused mixed, hieroglyphic, and semasiographic notational systems to be placed into a single amorphous category, where they languished for some time, unloved by scholars and primarily defined by what they are not.

As later researchers began to explore the implications of semiotic theory related to pictorial communication, intellectuals such as Susanne Langer took up the issue. Langer's primary writings tend to divide the world of symbols along the lines of the presence or absence of linear ordering; for her, the great divide was between "saying" and "showing." Spoken language and models of spoken language guided her fundamental assumptions about the formation of cognition and ideation. In Langer's estimation, discursive forms are "linear," marked by individual signifying units, syntax, and the possibility of translation.[16] This allowed her to contrast discursive forms with what she calls "presentational" forms, which, for her in the 1940s, included abstract modern painting. She asserts that presentational forms are not composed of context-free signifying units; their sense is inseparable from their embodiment. Presentational images or compositions, she asserts, were meant to be perceived as whole *gestalten*. She writes that "a work of art is a single symbol, not a system of significant elements which may be variously compounded."[17] Their forms are stylistically conditioned; their sense is inseparable from their embodiment in an articulated form. They are not divisible into elements of grammar. Purely presentational artworks are free of the processes of double articulation; in essence, they have no systematic ordering prior to visual delivery.

Yet, just as Peirce discovered, hieroglyphs, picture writing, and other nonlinguistically tied communicative forms constitute problematic areas within the oppositional schema Langer proposes, for they include aspects of both, plus a range of other variables. For these, she coined the term *presentational symbols*, noting that they derive their meaning through the viewer's understanding of the whole, and thus are symbols (in the Peircian sense) rather than linguistic signs, and that they employ a presentational mechanism (in the sense of being whole units involved in a simultaneous, integral presentation, even though there may be groups of such symbols placed in proximity to one another).[18] Although a somewhat ill-fitting designation, it opens the way for further articulation of the ambiguous territory between the two extremes.

In attempting to define a middle ground along a perceived word–image continuum, Charles Owen's work on the internal functioning of diagramming systems attempts to explain exactly how a system can be both discursive and presentational simultaneously.[19] Owen proposes to categorize various notational and diagramming systems according to their degree of linear syntax, asserting that linear sequential symbol systems are more directly analogous to grammatical structures than those with less linear sequence.[20] Owen notes that because sequential systems (such as phonetic writing) are encoded linearly, they must be transmitted, received, and decoded in a strictly defined order. Conversely, presentational systems are usually not linear/sequential in their method of communication and therefore may be decoded from more than one starting point.[21] Systems that occur somewhere in the middle of this continuum—and there are many (for example, symbolic diagramming, music notation, transit system notational forms, dance notation, complex process diagramming, and sequence experience notation)—have greater flexibility in the order and manner in which they may be successfully decoded. These notational forms are characterized as having *configurations* of symbols, rather than strings of symbols.

Although enlightening, none of the proposed models fits without caveat. James Elkins addresses the quandary in a consideration of text–image relationships, with a proposition that the root cause might actually stem from a flawed premise, the very foundational model that insists on a dialectic opposition and an evolutionistic continuum between picture and script. Instead, he argues for the adoption of a tripart classification of visual images. In *The Domain of Images*, Elkins asserts that the word–image dichotomy is demonstrably untrue, stressing that all images are both "read" and "seen," in the sense that they simultaneously mix words, letters, marks, and iconic signs. We cannot read a book without simultaneously seeing its color, substance, and visual format; we cannot appreciate the meaning of a picture without reference to a range of syntactic, linguistic, and formalist constructions. In short, Elkins asserts that there is no such thing as a purely visual picture, or a page of writing uncontaminated by nonverbal elements, or a chart that conveys data alone with no other visual elements.[22]

Within the world of graphic constructions, maps, diagrams, emblems, and schemata, rightfully, are neither writing nor pictures. Rather, they constitute a third node of visual communication, which Elkins calls *notation*, a term referring to images that convey meaning according to rules other than the formats associated with pictures or linguistically informed writing systems.[23] Notations, he asserts, employ syntactically disjunct characters possessing levels of semantic unambiguousness. Yet their primary ordering structures, whence meaning is derived, revolve around formalized spatial arrangements, rather than the dictates of linguistic patterning. Their organizational structures depend on the relationships created by visual ordering devices, such as grids, axes, or other formalized spatial conventions. Rather than a dichotomous semasiography, the world of mixed symbol systems is better imagined as having three interlocking parts (Figure 4.2).[24]

Disallowing a model of dichotomous opposition, Elkins identifies and situates mixed notations in a triangulation, based on how they combine pictorial representation with syntactic ordering in relation to each one's degree of linguistic similitude. His triadic Venn diagram tentatively proposes a way to consider all the many varieties of mixed graphic forms, bringing home the point that mixed images are quite common throughout our visual experience. His proposal places semasiographs, emblems, and schemata in the regions most nearly sharing all three areas of overlap.[25] The tripart relationship is liberating in several regards. Graphic forms that are not "writing" need not necessarily assume additional "pictorial" qualities under pressure of analysis. In providing notation a legitimate residence, the mixed script forms and pictographies so prevalent in ancient American societies are released from paradigmatic structures that, in some regards, bind them to Eurocentric biases. In accepting mixed pictorial forms as neither pictures nor writing, it becomes possible to address these graphic systems for what they are, rather than for what they are not.

In operational terms, what do the different visual systems do differently? Are there reasons why one might serve a community better than another? If writing systems do not "evolve" from simple to complex, as was once thought, are there other factors playing into their development?[26] Some have noted that semasiographic systems seem to work best, and occur most often, within strictly limited areas of reference, even though, in theory, it need not necessarily be the case.[27] According to W. C. Brice, "The more restricted the context the better [semasiographic systems] function"; therefore, we should expect that the most successful semasiographic systems will function within limited or restricted contexts.[28] Moche art's strong emphasis on ideologically loaded symbolism tied to ideological practice constitutes one such area of limited reference.

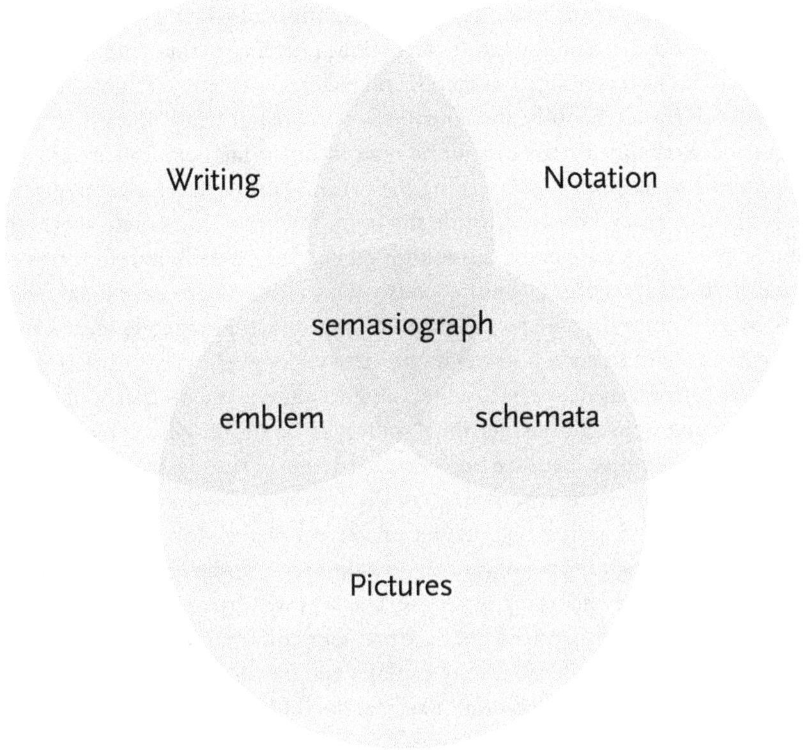

FIGURE 4.2. Domain of images as an interlocking triad: pictures, writing, and notation (based on Elkins 1999:86).

Owen and Langer both recognized that a broad range of visual systems exists, functioning somewhere between strictly linear and purely presentational. Langer's "picture languages," with their "presentational symbolism," are precisely the "mixed" writing systems that ancient Americanists identify and seek to clarify. Houston notes that the standard evolutionary model of how writing evolves is flawed in its insistence that one form replaces another, when in fact, the systems are most often "bundled" with each other.[29] He points primarily to Maya script but might just as well include Teotihuacano, Olmec, Mixtec, and others. What he terms bundled scripts are strongly analogous to what Janet Berlo once described as "embedded texts."[30] Coining the phrase in her discussion of Mesoamerican graphic systems, Berlo recognized the existence of combined logographic and ideographic symbols, noting that specific symbols corresponding to precise linguistic meanings were sometimes embedded within single iconic figures or iconic clusters having less linguistically precise but still conventionally understood meanings. Together, they functioned to convey meaning simultaneously, rather than as separate ways of telling the same material. Such embedded signs appear, very often, as part of complex pictorial compositions.

While Berlo's observation refers to the manner in which particular signs are to be decoded, it also constitutes an oblique reference to the syntactic ordering of iconic clusters of signs, symbols, and pictorial elements. If signs are to be understood simultaneously, then obviously they are not "read" in a proscribed sequence. Embedded texts cannot be read in linear fashion. The eye travels around the overall image, discerning the various parts and registering meanings as they are encountered, while the brain forms an immediate synthesis of all elements. In Langer's terminology, embedded texts are hybrid forms of presentational symbolism, simultaneously discursive and presentational.

Martin notes that the pictorialism of the iconographic mode means that the entry level of its code is low and open to a wider readership. Readers need not have high levels of specialized training to understand at least some level of the iconography. The reader must, however, be thoroughly versed in the larger cultural milieu, because the (re)construction of the message requires an element of collaboration on the part of the viewer. In contrast, because glottographic scripts feature a high degree of conventionalized coding, its readers must possess a high degree of literacy to gain access to the content. Provided the reader has the necessary expertise, the text will become readable upon decoding, and the reader need not have previous cultural knowledge to reconstruct the message. Semasiography exploits and blends these, by turns inviting literal reading and collaborative re-creation of text through memory and extrapolation on the part of the viewer.[31]

Locating Grammar and Internal Order

To place Moche iconography within larger taxonomies of writing, pictures, and notations, it remains to separate out elements of visual grammar and internal ordering. How best to identify a corpus of differentiated signs? Where to locate specific aspects of syntactic patterning? Clearly, Moche iconography does not systematically reproduce language. If it did, then we might expect to see an alphabet of Muchic language phonemes or a visual system reflecting the language's other grammatical features (a syllabary, for example). Instead, we find a tradition whose visual ordering is both conventionalized and richly iconographic but which does not bear the kind of linear patterning described by Marcus. It is neither strictly linguistically ordered nor purely presentational in format. The iconography is composed, instead, of individual pictorial units and clusters of units, which, in some cases, may have had limited linguistic correlates and which appear to have been arranged according to nonsequential, configurational syntactic structures.

Formal Analyses Building from Previous Studies

A rich body of scholarship lays the foundation for investigations of Moche art as a cohesive iconographic corpus. Initial interpretations celebrated Moche's remarkable realism. The imagery was thought by scholars, such as Gerdt Kutscher, Rafael Larco Hoyle, and Arturo Jiménez Borja, to portray all aspects of daily life, including flora, fauna, and social portraiture.[32] Numerous studies were devoted to identifying specific imagery at its most basic level, identifying plants, animals, and so forth.[33] It was eventually remarked, however, that certain fundamental aspects of human life were absent from the pictorial record, such things as children playing, adults farming, and the preparation of food—a discrepancy that cast doubt on a straightforward scenes-of-daily-life interpretation. Perhaps the single most important shift in iconographic interpretation came when it was observed that Moche artwork repeatedly depicts a limited number of specific themes with recognizable characters that appear in various forms and renditions. The recognition of specific characters, and the discovery of variations in the iconographic attributes associated with each, provides a cornerstone for the present discussion.

Scholars like Donnan, Benson, Castillo, Hocquenghem, Bourget, and many others have articulated some of the major themes found in Moche art.[34] Such themes are basically pictorial versions of well-known narrative episodes. To date, roughly sixteen to twenty recognizable themes have been identified, although these are far from discrete and many have significantly overlapping aspects. As with all narrative structures, themes are characterized as having the key components of action, identity of participants, locality, and temporality.[35] In addition to the Sacrifice Scene, the Warrior Narrative, and the Ribbon Dance mentioned previously, others include the Dance of the Dead, the Deer Hunt, and the Burial Theme.[36] Each scene is composed of an array of primary and secondary characters engaged in particular activities. Many of the principal characters are found in a number of different scenes. Donnan suggests that a "complete" version of a theme would have all members, both principal and secondary, present.[37] The more complete the scene, the more apparent is a pictorial narrative structure.

Only rarely, however, are *all* possible members present. Luis Jaime Castillo points out that in reality it is almost impossible to say when a motif is complete, because Moche pictorial scenes almost always include some amount of variation.[38] Castillo's observation raises the likelihood that no scene is ever 100 percent complete, given the fluidity of the iconographic symbol system. It is perhaps more productive to think of thematic content in terms of having greater and lesser degrees of narrative elaboration, rather than in terms of "completeness." Most scenes are shown in abbreviated form, omitting the least essential elements. Any given artwork may present a complex scene, a simplified scene, or just one specific element of a scene, but all are essentially referential to the larger narrative and are, therefore, interrelated. The modular nature of the iconographic corpus is a key element in how semantic units are differentiated and ultimately in how the pictorial sequence is ordered.

Moche's basic artistic canons follow consistent patterns, a factor that significantly contributes to thematic cohesion.[39] In general, the relative size of figures conforms to realistic scale, with some important exceptions. Landscape elements, such as mountains, houses, and large trees, may be reduced in size. Scale may also indicate an individual's status in relation to other figures within the same register. Conventionalized use of costume elements denotes status. Body parts, such as heads, hands, and sexual organs, are sometimes enlarged for emphasis. Depth of field is indicated by scale and aerial positioning, while perspective is generally shown through the combined use of profile and frontal views; rarely are three-quarter or oblique views used. Objects that in profile would appear unrecognizably thin or flat are usually depicted frontally.[40] Action or stasis is indicated through specific, conventionalized positioning of the torso, arms, and legs; the entire body need not necessarily conform to a naturalistic posture for these indicators to function. Moche artistic conventions are highly consistent over time, making the recognition of thematic contexts and specific icons possible.

Present Inquiries

Modern comprehension of archaeological finds, like those at Sipán, San José de Moro, Cao Viejo, and Moche, would be greatly diminished without the insights allowed by previous work on Moche pictorial conventions. It bears reiteration that the occupants of the royal tombs at Sipán and San José de Moro, by virtue of their costume and accoutrements, demonstrate that Moche iconography depicts high-status elites in specific social roles.[41] Excavations at various Moche sites confirm that many of the activities depicted in art occurred in real architectural space, and the remains of multiple prisoner sacrifices at Huaca de La Luna further demonstrate that images of blood sacrifice do describe real events. Whether art imitated life or life imitated art, Moche iconography correlated strongly to the real world, even though it was often cloaked in religious references and symbolism. The correlation between images and artifacts makes it clear that a larger cultural narrative involving living people, places, and events was the principal mechanism informing the imagery.

There are several areas where Moche's visual grammar and syntax might be made apparent. For example, if the Moche people were indeed unified by a cohesive ideological thread (an oral text), then the technologies developed by endogamous communities of artists, whose specialty was the construction of ideologically meaningful products, would be the likely locus for the development of script communities.[42] A common narrative informed the artistic production of artwork, in monumental contexts as well as in smaller portable arts. A study of technological processes sheds light, in what follows, on how artists approached the task of creating meaningful iconography. Ceramic mold technology provides unexpected insights into how artists themselves thought about visual phrases or semantic units.

Linguistic analyses allow for the proposition of basic structural patterns of communication; parallels among structure, syntax, vocabulary, and the artistic corpus provide grounds for analogy and, ultimately, an indication that a limited number of possible logographic signs may have been embedded within the overall visual structure. Visual anomalies, such as human–animal hybrids, transformational images, and compounds of objects bearing little logical relationship, are often telltale signals of logographs, rebuses, or other complex signs in various script traditions. Moche's artistic tendency toward composite constructions resembles language in several intriguing regards and may signal some degree of linguistic correspondence.

And finally, Moche pictorial systems incorporate a high degree of narrative structure, often incorporating visual storytelling techniques, such as sequence, perspective, and the use of registers, to accomplish a narrative purpose. Despite its strong representational canons, however, Moche imagery is not solely made up of pictorial representation. A significant portion of the artwork incorporates value-laden icons, and many such icons are themselves composed of elements with iconic meaning. Groups of nested, ligatured ideographs provide a conceptual ground. A formal analysis of specific constituent elements outlines the nature of the relationship between pictorial vocabularies and syntactic, or internal, ordering.

CHAPTER 5

Mold Technology and the Formation of Semantic Units

The ceramic technologies and methods of manufacture documented at Cerro Mayal support the idea that Moche artists conceptualized iconic elements as differentiated units of meaning. Mold construction techniques effectively facilitated the parsing of meaning into a system of signs capable of communicating coherent concepts and visual phrases. Such phrases are integral to discursive forms. Iconographic elements could be separated to mix and match, depending on the desired result, and they could be used as pictorial modifiers in ways suggestive of language structures.

A series of inscriptions on the exteriors of ceramic molds from various workshops, described in what follows, offer tangible evidence that the ceramists themselves understood the notational character of particular iconic markings. It was a technology that seems to have been widespread among a particular class of artisans, with a significant geographic distribution and a lengthy duration of use. The inscriptions go far toward the assertion that Moche artists deliberately attached meaning to images at the level of abstract signs. This basic outline of spatial and temporal parameters, although sparse, establishes a cultural space where a specialized script community seems to have developed. Within those contexts, mold technology emerges as a key factor in how particular elements of ideological narrative became distilled and were made durable in plastic media.

A Typology of Inscriptions

Of the 368 molds or mold fragments closely analyzed from the Cerro Mayal sample, sixty-nine had exterior inscriptions—a figure equal to roughly 19 percent of the molds. The markings were deliberately made. Many refer to common Moche pictorial themes, insinuating that the meaning and function of the inscriptions and the iconographic content of the ceramic products were directly linked to a broader symbol system.

Three basic types of markings are evident: those that roughly reflect the mold's interior imagery, such as eyes, nose, mouth, or feet, which served as pictorial alignments assisting the potter in positioning imagery on the finished product; those with hash marks incised perpendicular to the edges of the mold, which were used as register marks to align multiple-part mold pieces, front side to back side or right to left; and still others that are small, sketchy pictorial drawings having no visible resemblance to the imagery on the mold's interior and not appearing to serve any purpose overtly related to the manufacture process. Instead, the iconic inscriptions of this third group bear reference to larger concepts. Among this last category of molds, a conceptual leap is presented by the discrepancy between the molds' interior and exterior imagery, one that suggests that those who were iconographically savvy thought of the symbol system abstractly, as signs, and that a Moche iconic "shorthand" was used to communicate specific information in an abstract notational form.

Pictorial Alignments

Inscriptions that reflect the mold's interior bear a simple one-to-one correspondence between image and meaning. Eyes, nose, mouth, or other features were often crudely sketched upon the mold's exterior surface, positioned to echo the mold's interior. A functionalist explanation proposes that such markings were probably useful in assisting the ceramist to position imagery on the ceramic object; he or she would be able to use the exterior markings as guides. Furthermore, the inscriptions may have helped the artists to quickly differentiate one mold from another without being forced to scrutinize each mold's interior prior to selecting it for use.

Pictorial alignment markings are often among the simplest of inscriptions, although their simplicity does not necessarily indicate the quality of the finished product. A mold whose only inscriptions are a simple circle and line positioned in direct correspondence to the human image depicted on the mold's interior, as, for example, in Figure 5.1a, presents a contrast to the finesse of the image created by the mold. In this case, the mold, which was probably used to make figurines, was delicately detailed and well executed. A second example, Figure 5.1b, features equally simple inscriptions, although the subject of the imagery is not human. The telltale circle around the eye and the suggestion of a round beak identify the image as an owl. Though the beak is only vaguely insinuated on the mold's exterior, the eye circle allows a positive identification of the mold's subject.

FIGURE 5.1.
Pictorial alignment inscriptions on figurine and appliqué molds with facial details indicated on the exterior.

Although technically simple, pictorial alignment inscriptions sometimes make reference to complex concepts. One mold, for example, produces a human figure whose tilted head bears a grimacing expression with a wide "banded mouth" (Figure 5.1c). By late Moche times, the banded mouth, a stylistic conceit where the lips are depicted as a continuous band encircling the mouth, was an artistic convention with a longevity of almost a thousand years in coastal art.[1] It appeared most often as part of the identifying characteristics of fanged deity figures and other supernatural creatures and was rarely associated with ordinary people. We may not know the precise identity of this mold's character, but the visual shorthand of the banded mouth motif nonetheless signals that it was somehow related to an idea cluster associated with the supernatural fanged deity. That it appears as a key identifier on the mold exterior suggests that, in the mind of the artist, the banded mouth was among the image's most salient features.

Likewise, the inscriptions on the exterior of the large Wrinkle-Face Whistler mold (Figure 5.2) are keyed to the position of the character's features and the specific identity of the subject depicted by the mold interior. In this case, the wrinkles surrounding the pursed lips are the principal diagnostic indicator of the character's identity. As it would scarcely be necessary for the potter to draw so many wrinkles simply to position the character's eyes and mouth on the vessel, the specificity of the inscription suggests that the character's identity was also being communicated.

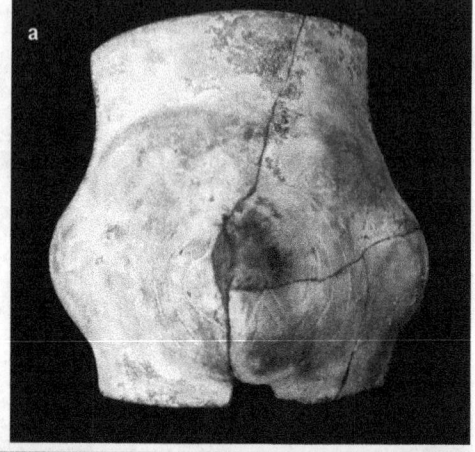

FIGURE 5.2.
Pictorial alignment inscriptions on Wrinkle-Face Whistler mold: **(a)** exterior detail; **(b)** interior of mold and impression.

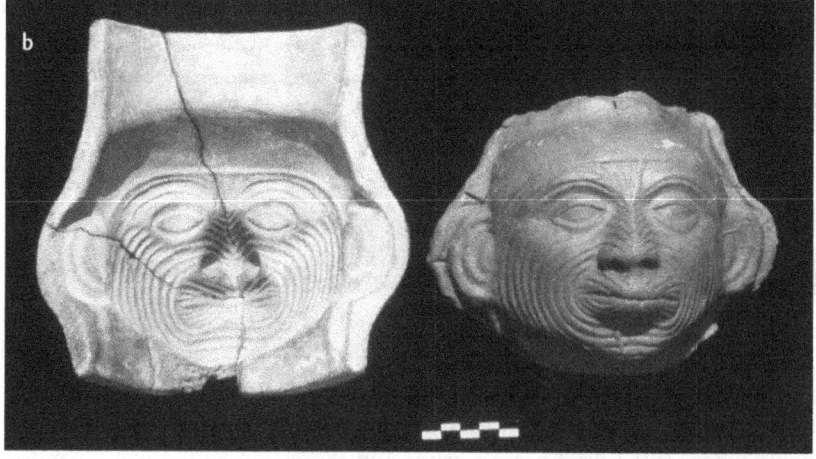

Specific references to particular characters' narrative roles are signaled in various ways. The animal depicted in the jar neck mold shown in Figure 5.3a, probably a lizard, wears a specific type of headdress and cylindrical earplugs and is shown with a banded, fanged mouth—all diagnostic traits of this character, despite variations in scale and media. The artist includes references to the specific mouth type as well as to the headdress on the mold exterior inscriptions. Some examples feature exterior inscriptions clearly intended to signal something about the character, traits that may not actually be shown in the finished product, as in the appliqué mold shown in Figure 5.3b. In this case, the mold, which creates a very realistic fox head, is inscribed in the area of the animal's eye with two concentric circles, each terminating in a stylized bird head motif. Although its meaning is unclear, the presence of the added graphic elements signals that the artist considered some abstract element of the image's larger associations to be significant.

What those associations might have been is a topic open to speculation. Perhaps the bird heads are ideographic references to messengers or emissaries,

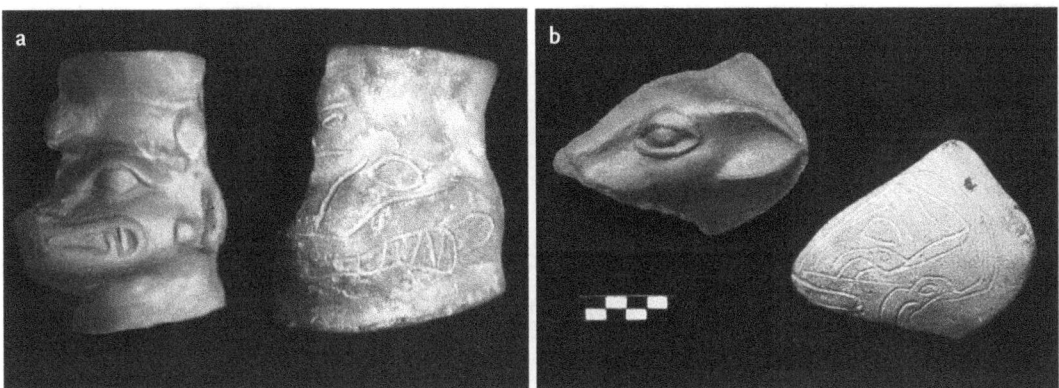

FIGURE 5.3. Pictorial alignment inscriptions: **(a)** Fanged Lizard mold and impression; **(b)** Snarling Fox mold and impression.

a meaning that may have combined with the natural persona of the fox to signal a modification in a standardized metaphoric construction.[2] Perhaps the bird heads should be read as artistic devices related to the kind of visual periphrasis, described as "kennings" by John Rowe, common to the Chavín tradition of terminating lines with zoomorphic heads.[3] Alternatively, the connection might have been linguistic. If homophonic correspondences existed, the two images, when juxtaposed, may have constituted a rebus device. Although the evidence is inconclusive, each interpretation is based on the assumption that the artist understood the inscription motifs in ways consistent with the use of script notation.

Register Marks
Other mold inscriptions feature straight-line incisions leading off their edges to serve as register marks. These nonpictorial features helped the artist align two-part or multiple-part molds. They are found alone or in combination with other kinds of incisions, and their technical purpose seems self-evident. Register marks continue to be used by modern potters to align multiple-part mold pieces, front side to back side or right to left. Molds such as the large frog and the portrait head, shown in Figure 5.4, were clearly used in pairs, as numerous finished vessels in museum collections will attest. Each mold depicts a symmetrically divided subject; the edges of the molds themselves show that the images were split along obvious lines of symmetry. The exterior of the large frog mold, Figure 5.4a, was inscribed with marks indicating the position of the frog's main elements (eye, legs, mouth). Secondary iconographic elements (beans, corn, *aji* peppers) were not included, suggesting that they were not integral to the essential identification of the subject matter. The line indicating the location of the frog's mouth runs off the leading edge of the mold. The opposing counterpart mold (now missing) was probably inscribed with the

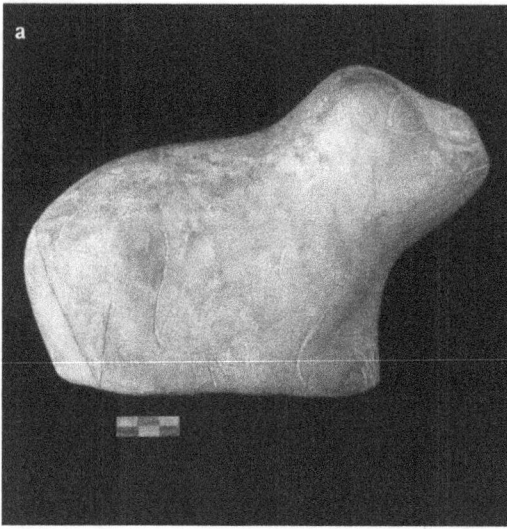 

FIGURE 5.4. Edge register marks: **(a)** large frog mold; **(b)** portrait face mold.

continuation and termination of the mouth line. Such a line served as a register mark aiding in mold alignment.

A similar register mark is visible on the human face mold in Figure 5.4b. The mold terminates in the front along the face's axis of vertical symmetry (between the eyes and down the nose ridge) and along the left side of the head just behind the ear. If the finished piece was a full portrait head, the points of division evident in the mold suggest that it was made using at least three (or perhaps four) separate molds (two for the face and one or two for the back side of the head). The exterior of the mold has a crude circle corresponding to the interior location of the eye and a horizontal line running across the bridge of the nose. The horizontal incision shows no point of termination and surely continued to the right-side counterpart, forming a point of alignment for the two mold halves.

Iconic Inscriptions

Pictorial alignment marks and register marks are seen as directly related to the ceramic production process, even though they may also refer to specific attributes of particular characters being depicted. A third type of marking found on Cerro Mayal's molds is more abstractly notational. This type of inscription generally consists of small diagrammatic images whose pictorial content bears little or no direct resemblance to the imagery on the mold's interior. Nor does this latter category of markings seem related to any technical feature of the manufacture process. Instead, they replicate, in abbreviated form, motifs conceptually linked to the larger iconographic repertoire and other abstract concepts.

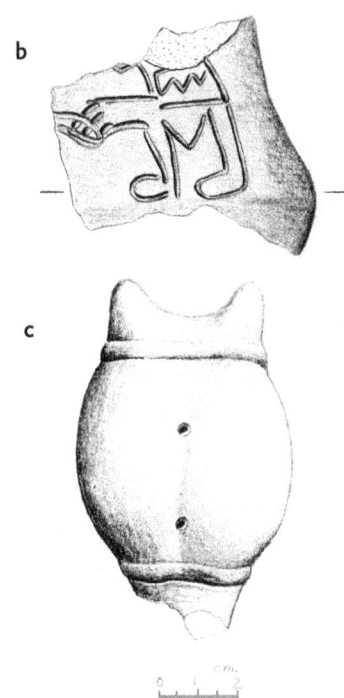

FIGURE 5.5. (a) Rattle mold with rattle player inscription; (b) detail drawing of rattle player inscription; (c) double-chamber rattle (CM190-12).

A case in point, the mold in Figure 5.5a produced a double-chambered rattle, similar to that shown alongside in Figure 5.5c. The mold interior is smooth; a rattle produced in this mold would have clean lines with no impressed relief designs or images. The exterior inscription, however, is quite unexpected; it does not depict a rattle. Instead, it depicts someone *playing* a rattle (Figure 5.5b).

Although the mold is fragmentary and the inscribed figure's head is missing, certain details are evident. The figure's feet are shown in profile, the figure's right arm extends perpendicular to the body, and the hand grasps a slender object that appears to be a handle (probably a rattle handle). As is typical of Moche artistic canons governing profile figures, the subject's upper body is depicted frontally, even though it is intended to read as a profile. The triangle between the legs indicates the droop of a loincloth, a male garment, while a horizontal line at the waist corresponds to the upper limit of the loincloth and the lower edge of the customary shirt tunic. Just below where the head would be, the figure's chest displays a zigzag motif characteristic of high-status individuals who wore fancy headdresses secured by zigzag-decorated chin straps, much like that worn by the musician in Figure 5.6a. We can infer that the figure depicted is a musician. Yet Moche musicians are not always shown wearing this costume, as illustrated in Plate 9 and Figure 3.11e; nor are rattle players consistently depicted as male or female. Therefore, it is not correct to assume that

FIGURE 5.6. Rattle players: **(a)** rattle player effigy vessel (894.100072, Collection of the Field Museum, Chicago); **(b)** large hollow figurine with rattle; **(c)** rattle player figurines and molds, Cerro Mayal.

the inscription refers to the relationship between the rattle produced and the social identity of the person who would use it.[4] The conceptual link is, instead, between the object and its future use, meaning that the inscription signals a specific action or event.

In linguistic terms, such a visual assembly might be construed as a verb clause, rather than a noun phrase. Whereas the subject of linguistic ordering will be considered at greater length in the following chapter, at this juncture it is worth noting that Fernando de la Carrera, a colonial author and scholar of language, observed that the indigenous Muchic language had what was essentially a derivative relationship between verbs and nouns, where verbs were created from nouns. He wrote, for example, that the verb phrase "I dream" was created by use of an appended noun phrase that translates literally as "I am a dream."[5] In the present discussion, a linguistically tied pictorial notation

FIGURE 5.7. (a) Birth mold with rattle inscription and mold impression, Cerro Mayal; (b) "Birth Bowl" (from *The Mochica*, by Elizabeth Benson, © 1972, Praeger Publishers; reproduced with the permission of Greenwood Publishing Group, Inc., Westport, CT).

could function in a similar manner; the verb phrase "I rattle" might have been constructed of the noun phrase "I am a rattle" (e.g., an interpretive conflation of object and function). This suggests that the inscription depicting someone who rattles could be read in the sense of a naming convention, or logographic sign, identifying the object that the mold created, a rattle.

Such linguistic ordering seems to signal a methodology by which to proceed, even though many inscriptions seem inscrutably far from interpretation at present. One enigmatic example (Figure 5.7a–b) is a peculiarly shaped mold producing an image situated on the interior of a concave vessel. A relatively rare theme in Moche art, it depicts a female contorted into a posture of giving birth, with the newborn's upside-down, crowning head visible at bottom. A similar bowl, Figure 5.7c, shows a woman in an attitude of parturition, suggesting how the finished vessel might have appeared. The mold's exterior inscription is entirely different from the interior theme. Instead of any pictorial reference to the interior image, the inscription shows a double-chambered rattle with a long umbilicus-like tail or tassel cord attached, identical to those being held by the rattle players in Figure 5.6.

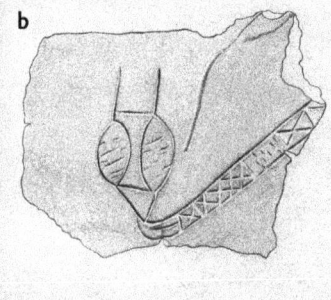

FIGURE 5.8.
(a) Mold with rattle inscription, exterior view and interior impression; **(b)** drawing of exterior inscription; **(c)** photo and drawing of rattle inscription from birth mold (C1-3576).

More significant is the fact that the rattle inscription on the "Birth Bowl" mold is not an isolated sign. A second mold fragment (Figure 5.8) from Cerro Mayal carries almost identical exterior markings. Because of its fragmentary condition, the interior imagery produced by the second mold is only recognizable to the point of determining that the mold clearly does not produce a rattle; the form produced is cylindrical, with a single extension emerging from one corner, devoid of any markings or impressions.

How should these inscriptions be interpreted? Is there a connection between a woman giving birth and a double-chambered rattle? Explanations are speculative. It may be that the double-chambered rattle was conceptually linked to the act of giving birth. Perhaps the rattle form, with its long umbilicus tail, was a metaphor for the uterus itself. The double-chambered rattle may have been conceptually linked to fertility rituals, perhaps to shamanism, or it may have been linked to the musical iconographic complex in some other conceptual fashion. In the case of the Birth Bowl, the inscription seems to be a visually "nominal" clause, while the interior subject of the bowl is active. Close reading of linguistic sources does not uncover any vocabulary for words such as *birth, fertility, rattle, to give birth, to play music,* or *to make sound* or any such related concept.[6] Thus, it is impossible to know if perhaps a homophonic (rebus) or other linguistic connection existed.

With so many variables, the question remains open to further study, yet, regardless of how one interprets the image, it seems clear that this type of inscription is not connected in any literal sense to the physical shape of the

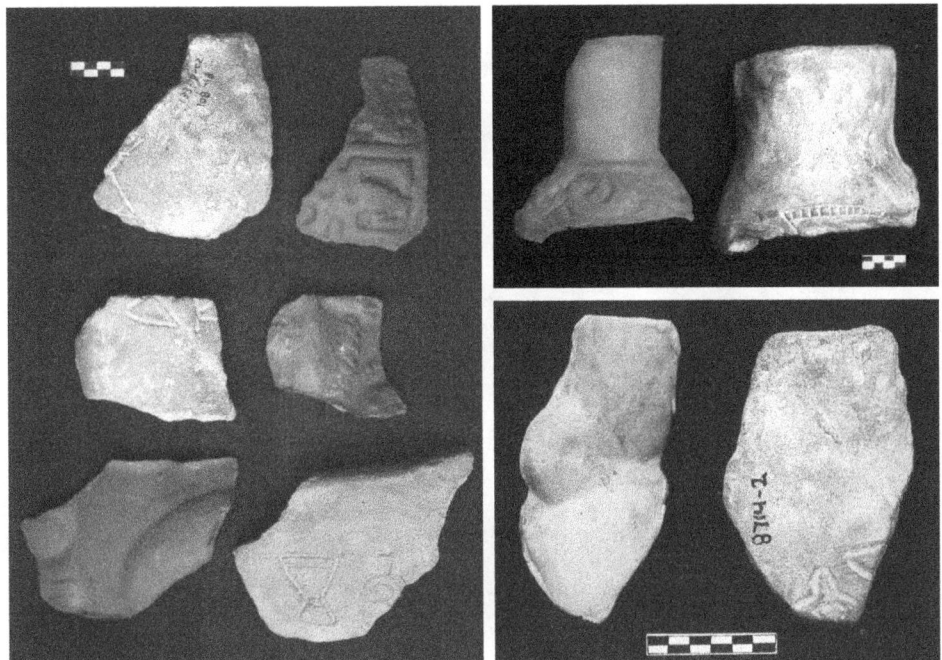

FIGURE 5.9. Molds with "ritual vessel assemblage" inscriptions.

object produced by the mold. There is no one-to-one direct correspondence. Here, the imagery has been consciously, deliberately used to denote an abstract cultural reference. Reduplication of the rattle sign in multiple units constitutes an example of a recognizable visual "vocabulary" unit that functioned as part of a larger grammar composed of consistently repeated signs.

Other examples of consistently repeated signs are present on other mold exteriors. Inscriptions of what might be termed a "ritual vessel assemblage" motif are found on a group of molds mostly related to bottle production (Figure 5.9). Typical ritual or funerary assemblages often include stirrup-spout bottles, hourglass-shaped *floreros*, and tall globular jars (see chapter 2, Figures 2.11–2.12). No two molds produced the same interior imagery, yet all have the same motifs inscribed on their exterior. Recognizable as ceramic forms by their distinctive silhouettes, the inscriptions show stirrup-spout bottles and hourglass-shaped flaring vases drawn in minimal detail and lined up in a row.

The quick, abbreviated lines of the inscriptions are analogous to those seen in painted imagery, as, for example, in Figure 5.10, illustrating well-established visual precedents for depicting this type of ritual vessel in a minimalist manner. Often associated with death scenes and offering rituals, stirrup-spout bottles, floreros, and offering plates were emblematic.[7] They functioned as icons in their own right, referencing funerary rites, offertory practices, and human actions associated with performing such activities. Again, the mold inscriptions do not carry a literal correspondence to that which the mold produces

FIGURE 5.10. Bottles with painted "vessel assemblages": **(a)** seated man surrounded by (left to right) a stirrup-spout bottle, stacked gourd bowls, thread spindles, and a flaring vase (ML006439, Museo Larco, Lima); **(b)** human and skeleton, with painted vessels, stirrup-spout bottle motifs, copper rectangles, crescent headdress, more copper rectangles, and stirrup spouts (from *The Mochica*, by Elizabeth Benson, © 1972, Praeger Publishers; reproduced with the permission of Greenwood Publishing Group, Inc., Westport, CT).

FIGURE 5.11. Face molds with exterior geometric "textile pattern" inscriptions.

but, instead, make reference to the overarching ideological narrative informing the entire visual system. Specifically, the "ritual vessel assemblage" motif constitutes an ideographic sign cluster, one that was conceptually keyed to a sequence of actions but denoted in the form of nominative referents.

One final cohort of mold inscriptions has no obvious pictographic references at all. Typically connected with face stamp molds (Figure 5.11), these are completely geometric, composed of zigzags, triangles, and abbreviated step frets. Their motifs are strongly reminiscent of textile patterns, particularly patterns seen on warriors' tunics and belts. In various parts of the Andes, and most likely on the North Coast as well, particular textile motifs seem to have functioned as emblems of a person's rank, ethnicity, or place of origin.[8] It is possible that the significance of the inscribed geometric icons derived from textile patterns, whose meanings, in turn, were based on associations with specific persons or offices.

Sharing Mold Technology

Mold inscriptions are seen in workshop contexts other than Cerro Mayal, a finding with significant implications regarding the distribution of a particular technology and notational iconography. Similar markings were made on ceramic molds from at least two other known ceramic workshops, Huaca de La Luna in the Moche Valley and Huaca Sialupe in the Jequetepeque Valley.[9] The distribution of particular mold-handling techniques was likely much more widespread, yet because of limited data—very few ceramic workshops have been excavated—the overall temporal and spatial parameters of the technology are not well defined at present.

Nonetheless, the initial findings on this point bear mentioning because they demonstrate conclusively that mold inscription techniques were transmitted to valleys north and south of the Chicama. The tradition existed for at least two to three centuries in the Chicama and Moche valleys and persisted into the transitional centuries of the Middle Horizon in the Jequetepeque Valley. The Huaca de La Luna workshop was approximately contemporaneous with Cerro Mayal, active mostly during Moche Phase IV, and Huaca Sialupe dates to the Middle Sican period, two to three centuries later.[10] Cerro Mayal's notational forms were not an isolated phenomenon; to the contrary, the technology seems to have been widespread among a particular class of artisans with a significant geographic distribution and throughout a lengthy duration of time.

The ceramic workshop at Huaca de La Luna produced ceramics that were generally very similar to those produced at Cerro Mayal, including the same general form categories, such as jars, bottles, floreros, and figurines, as well as many of the same motifs, animals, warriors, fanged deities, and the like. The production technique employed at the Huaca de La Luna closely paralleled that at Cerro Mayal in terms of using combinations of hand-building and mold-making techniques. Significantly, the ceramic workshop at the Huaca de

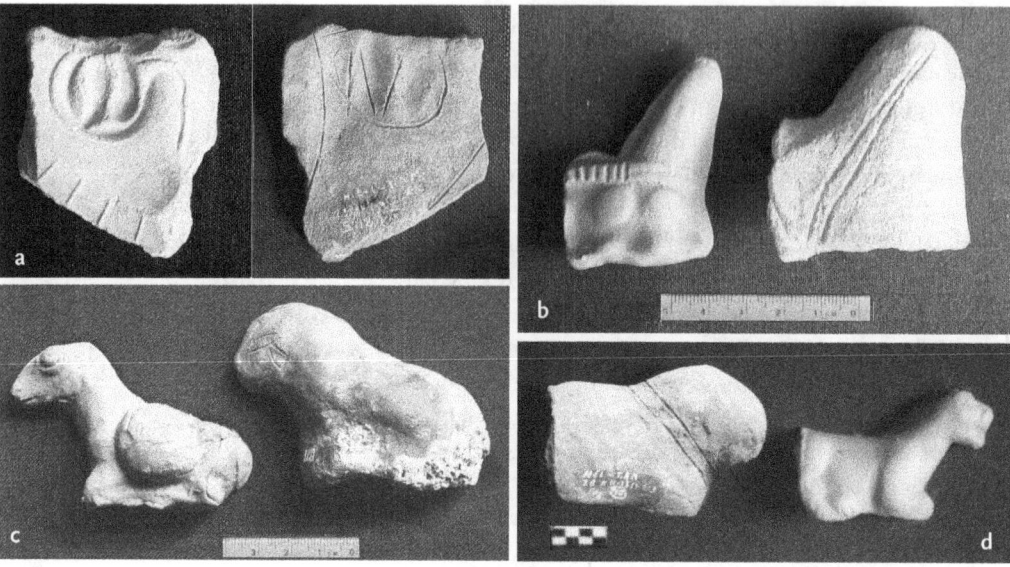

FIGURE 5.12. Huaca de La Luna mold inscriptions: **(a–c)** mold fragments with exterior alignment marks (*chirimoya* rattle, llama, fanged mouth); **(d)** mold with register marks (sea lion).

La Luna produced molds whose inscriptions can be roughly divided into the same three categories as those of Cerro Mayal: pictorial alignments, register marks, and abstract signs.

Examples of pictorial alignment and register mark inscriptions from the Huaca de La Luna workshop are similar in most respects to those of Cerro Mayal. For example, the Huaca de La Luna face mold in Figure 5.12a has exterior inscriptions that echo the interior mouth and fangs of what was probably a Fanged Owl. The exterior markings in Figure 5.12b–c, likewise, echo interior imagery. Parallel register marks on a two-piece mold depicting a sea lion (Figure 5.12d) extend around the exterior of the mold from one edge to another, providing an effective aid for the alignment of the two halves. And, as with similar two-piece molds at Cerro Mayal, inspection of the Huaca de La Luna mold suggests that the incisions were made while both halves were in place.

Moreover, as is the case at Cerro Mayal, Huaca de La Luna's mold inscriptions include those that are abstract. For example, in Figure 5.13a–b, a mold producing the image of a person attired in high-status regalia, including shield, libret, club or staff, and large stepped-crescent headdress, has simply an abbreviated crescent headdress inscribed on the mold exterior. Whoever the subject of the depiction may have been, it is clear that in the mind of the artist he was reducible to this one sign, a royal crescent.

In a second example, a mold that produces a bird head (Figure 5.13c–d) was inscribed with an image of a *porra* (war club) on the exterior surface. Any connection between a bird and a war club is not readily apparent. Moche war

FIGURE 5.13. Huaca de La Luna molds with inscribed signs: (a–b) crescent headdress sign; (c–d) porra sign.

clubs are strong icons in their own right, often functioning as metonymic references to warriors, yet in this case, the mold was one piece of a two-part appliqué, suggesting that the war club icon was a visual reference to a larger compositional concept.[11] Such an appliqué would have been integral to the construction of the elaborate bird-headed headdresses worn by high-status individuals depicted in large-scale portrait vessels (Plate 10). If used as an abbreviated indicator of a larger concept, the war club icon functioned as a fully developed abstract sign, far removed from any directly motivated connections.

Huaca de La Luna ceramists shared more than technological concepts with their Chicama Valley counterparts; in at least one example, signs common to both workshops are present. Inscriptions depicting "ritual vessel assemblage" signs found at Cerro Mayal (Figure 5.9) were also found at the Huaca de La Luna (Figure 5.14). Again, abstract references are suggested by the discrepancy between inscription and ceramic product; in Figure 5.14, the mold is inscribed with a florero sign, but it did not produce a florero vessel.

FIGURE 5.14.
Huaca de La Luna molds with inscriptions: **(a–b)** "ritual vessel" motifs; **(c)** bean with X marks; **(d)** warrior figurine mold with porra inscription.

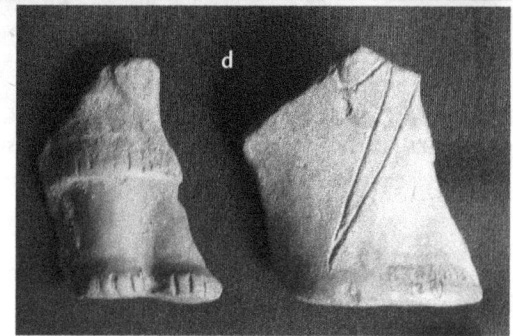

A well-documented workshop at Huaca Sialupe, in the Jequetepeque Valley, provides good evidence that similar mold technologies persisted well into later times, even though vessel styles changed significantly.[12] Middle Sican ceramic vessels tend to be fully mold formed, with much less incidence of variable components. Full body molds, used for making bottles, most often include stirrup spouts already formed as part of the vessel body. The technique represents a change from Moche, where spout handles were always handmade and added after the molding process. Likewise, complex joinery techniques continued to be used, with multiple-part appliqué molds used for multiple-part joinery, but with far less frequency. It is hard to know if the shift came as a result of technology or if technology simply followed the popular demand.

FIGURE 5.15. Huaca Sialupe molds with iconic tassel inscriptions: **(a–b)** small face neck fragments with "tassel" motifs (SIA_0022/0023); **(c)** vessel mold fragment with iconic "tassel" inscription and plain interior (SIA_0077).

The artists of Huaca Sialupe continued to employ similar kinds of inscription techniques, in spite of significant changes in iconography. A strong proliferation of a motif known as the Lord of Sicán is seen, in combination with what appears to be a diminution of iconographic variability. Nonetheless, the same three basic categories of mold inscriptions are seen, including those indicating pictorial alignments and those used as register marks for mold alignment during manufacture. Although precise figures were not available for study, visual inspection suggests that of these two types of inscriptions there was a lesser incidence of one-to-one (pictorial alignment) inscriptions and a proportionally higher incidence of register marks. Additionally, the register marks appear to have more variations, a fact that would most likely be an outgrowth of the technical complexities of using full body molds. As at the Cerro Mayal and Huaca de La Luna workshops, a number of molds had inscriptions that did not correlate with the imagery produced by the mold. A "tassel" symbol appeared on several examples (Figure 5.15). Other molds had various geometric inscriptions, including chevrons and checked patterns (Figure 5.16).

It is possible that, because artistic emphasis shifted to full body mold construction techniques, there was significantly less impetus to think of molds as programmatic variables. It is quite likely that the composition of the artist community itself accounts for changes across time and distance. Additionally,

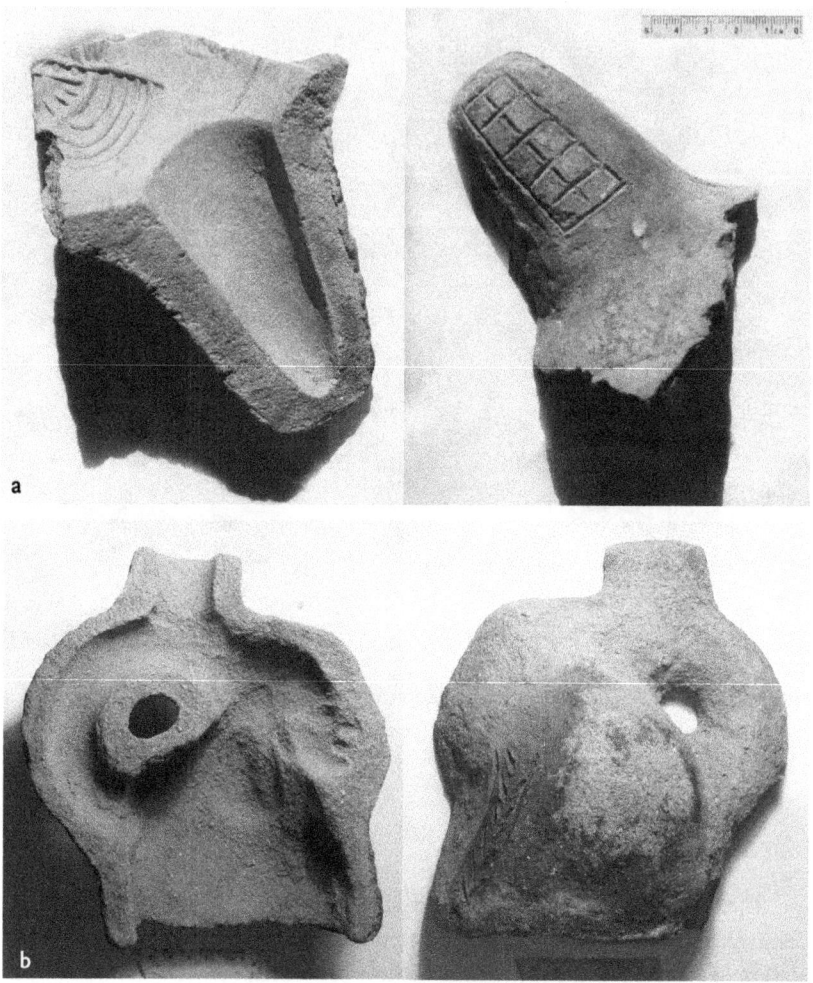

FIGURE 5.16.
Huaca Sialupe molds with iconic checked and chevron inscriptions: **(a)** pointed spout (or tripod leg) mold with checked motif inscription (SIA_0019/0021); **(b)** full body stirrup-spout mold with sitting figure and "chevron" inscriptions on the exterior (SIA_0055/0056).

it is far beyond the scope of this investigation to speculate about the meaning of Sican imagery at Huaca Sialupe. It is valid to note, however, that the technological tradition of using mold inscriptions continued in at least one workshop despite centuries of time and distance. In particular it bears reiteration that at least some percentage of the signs in use at Huaca Sialupe were abstract, idiographic signs, very likely linguistically tied to particular words, concepts, or individuals known to local ceramic specialists.[13]

Mold Inscriptions and Textual Communities

Many mold inscriptions were not connected in any direct sense to the imagery of the objects produced by the molds. Instead, their meanings derived from complex distillations of well-understood associations. Abstract motifs are not limited to isolated examples, and, in several cases, nearly identical inscriptions appear on more than one mold. The time depth and spatial distribution of this pattern, even in its presently limited form, give testament to an intentional notational value implicit in the reproduction of groups of repetitive icons.

If mold inscriptions functioned within workshops to signal specific information (technological or other), then we can assume that most of the ceramists understood the significance of the markings. Skilled workers tend to develop and learn to read specialized signs that are intrinsic to their jobs; they develop a type of occupational literacy.[14] Occupational literacy is generally a direct outgrowth of technical processes; it comes about in response to need. It may be common only to a single community or used by other communities engaged in similar activities. Whether linguistically motivated or conceptually tied to culturally resonant moments, in certain technological contexts ceramic mold inscriptions functioned as ideographic or logographic notations legible among a particular group of artists.

Ceramic mold inscriptions are distinct from the kinds of inscriptions found, for example, on adobe bricks. The differences signal very distinct technologies in action. Adobe brick makers' marks seem to have been used as unique signatures for groups of people who are thought to have contributed brick lots to the huaca construction project. As such the marks themselves would be idiosyncratic and unique, presumably produced by disparate people having various degrees of education and status. If the bricks were, in fact, the Moche equivalent of taxable goods, we might expect to find some method of accounting. The apparent lack of such a system is one of the more perplexing aspects of Moche studies. A method of counting was proposed by Larco, in the form of beans with various configurations of stripes and spots, a schema that may have had some, as yet poorly understood, correlation to the brick markings. Yet there seems almost no point of correlation between brick markings and the imagistic signs and visual icons populating Moche monumental and liturgical arts. Curiously, such arts seem to be almost entirely devoid of numerical signs, with the exception of some images depicting the aforementioned beans, leading to the suggestion that systems for recording numerical information and imagery related to religious observance were kept separate, perhaps overseen by distinct groups of specialists.

Technological reasons helped to fuel Moche ceramists' development of iconic notations. Returning to Stephen Houston's observations about how graphic systems arise, the technological need was accompanied by cultural predisposition.[15] By right of status and the nature of the subject material, fineware ceramic artists were informed members of what might be termed a textual community. Textual communities are those that share some form of dominant "text" as a foundation for a common cultural matrix.[16] Such communities learn, read, and interpret texts together; the shared commonality allows for the creation of joint identities. Because *text*, broadly defined, can refer to any coherent arrangement of signs, texts can take forms other than strictly alphabetic.[17] In cases where they integrate with speech, for example, oral "texts" become stylized performative voicings or recitations. The texts become a locus of common ground shared by all. In his discussion of textual communities in medieval Europe, Brian Stock writes, "One of the clearest signs that a group had passed the threshold of literacy was the lack of necessity for the organizing text to be spelt out, interpreted, or reiterated. The members all knew what it was. As a consequence, interaction ... could take place as a superstructure of an agreed meaning."[18]

Stock's observation readily relates to what is understood about Moche social practice. All evidence points to Moche religious and cultural foundations as oral texts, transmitted in the form of encompassing narratives and ritual enactments. These would have been the fundamental matrices for Moche sociopolitical, religious, and visual structures. Specialized workshops, like Cerro Mayal and others, would have provided ideal environments for artists, as members of a larger textual community, to develop into "script communities." The persistence of a technology involving abstract inscriptions and featuring a relatively constrained iconographic vocabulary over a period of centuries argues in favor of the existence of mechanisms for the consistent transmission of skills. And indeed, the workshop appears to have operated under the patronage of Mocollope. For a script to survive, it must have some system of apprenticeship whereby all members share in the constant construction of the script form.[19] Such an arrangement appears to have been in force at specialized workshops like Cerro Mayal, where the archaeological record suggests a close attachment between specialized ritual-use fineware and social hierarchy.

Here, mold technologies are important because they provide material evidence that Moche artists contrived and manipulated signs whose meanings were known and deliberately replicated. Mold technology played a defining role in the maintenance and transmission of a shared ideological text. Discussion of the deliberate production of glyph-like signs leads, however, into controversial territory, for the development of notation and writing in the Americas is a contested subject. This technology does not fit with generally accepted expectations about how writing "evolves." As late as 1974 scholars such as I. J. Gelb were still arguing in favor of the eighteenth-century notion that ancient scripts began with primitive picturing and gradually evolved into more abstract symbols, ultimately leading to alphabets. It was a pronouncement that placed New World graphic systems at a disadvantage and masked the alternative communication technologies that existed. The paradigm has never enjoyed an easy fit in the Americas, precisely because indigenous iconographies, hieroglyphs, and mixed notational forms generally developed along somewhat different trajectories.

The evolutionary model, what some call the Pictographic Theory, is increasingly under attack, and the strongest challenge has come, somewhat ironically, from ancient Near East studies. Denise Schmandt-Besserat has noted that the maxim is not consistent with the archaeological data related to cuneiform development. She proposes instead that the antecedents of phonetic writing, at least in the ancient Near East, were actually counting devices.[20] In her research, Schmandt-Besserat puts forward the use of tokens (small bits of modeled clay) as having been developed in response to the needs of an expanding economy and to the rise of ever-more complex social structures. Tokens originally represented the concrete counting of physical objects. They later evolved into complex tokens with inscriptions, punctates, and subcategories. More than a simple one-to-one object correspondence, tokens represented an entirely new level of abstraction. The conceptual leap was to endow each token shape with a specific meaning. Thus the token shapes became abstract signs.

Corresponding to the increase in bureaucracy, methods of storing Near Eastern tokens in clay "envelopes" and archives were devised. Tokens enclosed inside envelopes were represented by impressed markings on the exterior of the envelopes. Scribes soon realized that actual tokens were not necessary, replacing the hollow envelopes with solid tablets bearing only the relevant markings. These markings became a system of their own (Archaic cuneiform), which developed to include not only impressed markings but also a range of legible signs traced with a pointed stylus. Schmandt-Besserat makes an important observation in noting that the substitution of signs for tokens was a first step toward writing. She likens the systematized inscriptions to "picture signs" or "pictographs" because they represented pictures of the tokens used as counters in the accounting system.

A key point for the present discussion is the realization that, in the Near East, alphabetic writing resulted from bureaucratic demands and from the invention of abstract counting. Scribes invented ever more efficient accounting methods; in the process they invented signs for cardinal numbers that were not linked to concrete counting, as they had been previously. As a by-product, the scribes were left with pictographs that could represent objects independently from numerical accounting. In other words, writing came as an offshoot of a technical development unrelated to narrative speech and unrelated to narrative picturing.

Schmandt-Besserat's tracing of the development of alphabetic writing is relevant to the present study in several regards. First, in challenging the dominant paradigm (the Pictographic Theory), she allows room for an exploration of other mechanisms by which written forms might arise. In particular, by pointing out that alphabetic script probably came about as a by-product of a social function other than the direct impulse toward recounting narrative, she opens the way for the suggestion that the attachment of meaning to iconic forms, as seen in Moche, could possibly have come as a technological by-product of occupational specialists. Second, in pinpointing the moment that the conceptual leap from a one-to-one imagistic correspondence to a "pictographic" (or "logographic") system occurred in the Near East (e.g., scribes making pictographic notations of tokens), she identifies an important distinction that finds parallels in the case of Moche mold technologies.

These archaeological materials make it clear that the Moche artists who created elite imagery thought of the various themes and related concepts in terms of set visual phrases. Icons representing specific conceptual compounds constituted abstract signs. Signs, once abbreviated and placed into circulation among a comparatively closed group, communicated particular information autodidactically, largely because the community shared an overarching narrative text. The shared textual matrix allowed members to communicate from the convenience of a superstructure of agreed meaning. The presence of the inscriptions with strongly glyphic characteristics in the technological context of ceramic production makes it clear that Moche artists themselves thought of the iconic repertoire in terms of meaningful signs.

In many regards, the technological development heralds a nascent script form in use among a particular group of occupational specialists, the beginnings of a script community sharing a common vocabulary of well-established signs. The signs carried relatively specific denotative meanings, which, in turn, established a conceptual base on which connotative meanings could build. It may be that certain repetitive signs were linguistically informed, that they constituted logographs, as, for example, with the mold inscriptions whose interior products and exterior markings appear to be mediated by linguistic structure.

The molds' intrinsic form and use naturally created semantic boundaries and discreet iconographic packages. Because the artists lived and worked within endogamous communities, informed by shared ideologies that circulated as long-lived oral texts, the artists shared a base of knowledge from which ever-more abstract communications were possible. Their membership in what might be termed a textual community allowed the development of a script community. In it, an underlying oral text, understood and reiterated by all, was played out often, allowing for a form of glyphic signing to be used among them. Among this group of specialists, it came as an outgrowth of technology, shared cultural text, and shared language.

That the artists differentiated semantic units during artistic production is clear. The mold inscriptions were abbreviated signs, inscribed, most likely in response to technological demands and within the context of specialized manufacture taking place among a relatively closed group of people. In other words, like the cuneiform tablets, a specific group of signs came as an offshoot or by-product of a different technology that was already in full swing and had been so for a very long time. The mold inscriptions demonstrate not only that these craftspeople thought about the variable visual vocabulary of which their product was composed (as articulated in an earlier chapter) but that, by later Moche times, the pictorial units were standardized to the point that they thought of them as discreet units, which were, in fact, motivated signs. It is but a small step to imagine that the use of specific signs and semantic units in common use at ceramic workshops, as given substance by these mold inscriptions, may also have found application elsewhere.

CHAPTER 6

Muchic and the Linguistic Analogy

Discursive forms have recognizable units from which their grammars are composed, and when language elements are encoded into a society's visual culture, evidence of it should be apparent. In semasiographic, emblematic, or mixed pictographies, telltale indicators may include the presence of conventionalized signs directly incorporated into visual imagery or visual phrases echoing language structures. Conscious and consistent reduplication of signs is a prerequisite for recognition and reading; therefore the presence of repetitive phrases is also an indicator. One might reasonably expect to find visual phrases reflecting the use of rhetorical phrases, metaphors, or other kinds of formulaic, ritualized speech. Additionally, numeric systems tend to adapt readily into visual or tactile forms. For example, the "bean writing" described by Larco Hoyle may refer to tactile counting devices, somewhat similar to the small stones manipulated by *khipu* users.[1]

Building from the idea that the Moche artists who created elite imagery thought of themes and concepts in terms of set visual phrases, an investigation of linguistic evidence, seeking traces of logographic signs, is an approach that offers promise. Although Moche visual vocabulary does not appear to include alphabetic signs, it does include graphic elements that suggest the possibility of linguistic connection. The mold technology and inscription practices described in the preceding chapters highlight the fact that Moche modes of production lent themselves very well to something like grammatical parsing and demonstrate that artists thought of icons and narrative actions in terms equivalent to discreet semantic units. It would not, therefore, be surprising to find logographs or rebus devices embedded into the pictorial structures, something that semiotic analysis seems to predict.

The indigenous Muchic language, *Yunga*, as the Spaniards called it, was still spoken in the sixteenth century. Some of its grammar was recorded at that time, and small bits survive from various subsequent investigations. Although languages change and evolve over time, as a remnant, colonial Muchic (Yunga) indicates certain things about basic patterns of semantic order, patterns of parallelism, and syntax. Its vocabulary is relevant, as well as its numerical constructs. An examination of the basic structures of the Muchic language and its semiotic relationships to Moche pictorial language and an exploration of parallels between Moche art and analogous Mesoamerican notation systems form the subjects of the present chapter.

Introduction to Muchic

The primary sources of linguistic information for the North Coast of Peru date to the early conquest period, written by Spanish priests. The native language that they encountered, while probably not identical to that spoken by the Moche, was most likely directly related to it and similar enough in form to be useful in constructing a working model of linguistic semiotic patterns. In the sixteenth century, Yunga was spoken throughout much of the Peruvian coastal area (particularly the northern regions) and constituted one of the four largest language families in the Andes, in company with Quechua, Aymara, and Puquina.[2] The most comprehensive source for the language and the basis for the present study is a grammar by Fernando de la Carrera, *Arte de La Lengua Yunga*, originally published in 1644. Carrera, who was born in Trujillo, Peru, and eventually became the vicar of San Martin de Reque (near present-day Chiclayo), was a native or near-native speaker of Yunga.[3] His book translates a Catholic *confesionario* (confessionary) into Yunga and attempts to instruct the reader on learning to speak the language. Subsequent scholars have sought to analyze the internal structure and grammatical rules by which the language functioned, as well as to place the language within the larger classification schema of Central and South American language groups; their efforts are summarized below.[4]

Nomenclature

Linguistic scholarship on Muchic lacks consensus, to the degree that even the correct nomenclature of the language is a cause of considerable confusion and controversy, as is the classification of the language within the larger schema of indigenous South American languages. Although Carrera called it "Yunga," later linguists articulate a number of reasons why the name is not necessarily the best choice for the language Carrera's grammar described. Carrera wrote that his grammar described the indigenous language of the Bishopric of Trujillo, stating that in the seventeenth century some forty thousand speakers of Yungas dialects lived in the Corregimientos of Trujillo, Zaña, Piura, and

Cajamarca.⁵ Rademes Altieri points out that in Carrera's time people living in the Corregimientos of Chachapoyas, Luya (Chillao), and Palas (Cajamarquilla) would also have been considered Yunga speakers, even though these areas are disparate and diverse.⁶ It seems clear from the eighteenth-century chart of Bishop Martinez Compañon, which gives comparative word lists from seven different Yunga languages found in the Bishopric of Trujillo in 1785, that "Yunga" referred to more than just one language and included a number of dialects.⁷ Therefore, the term *Yunga* ("Yünka" or "Yunca" according to some spellings) best describes a larger language family with local dialects.⁸ That is the sense in which it is used here while, for reasons described below, the language described by Carrera is referred to as Muchic.

According to Antonio de la Calancha (in 1638), the Yunga language spoken in the Moche Valley was called Quignam. Unfortunately, almost no record of it survives today.⁹ He writes that Quignam was spoken from Pacasmayo (the southern tip of Jequetepeque Valley) as far south as Lima, further naming related North Coast dialects as Mochica and Sec.¹⁰ In contrast, Carrera (in 1644) specifies that the Muchic dialect of Yunga that he describes in his book was spoken in "todo el valle Chicama," specifically including the Chicama Valley towns of Paijan, Magdalena de Cao, and Chocope.¹¹ By this reckoning, Muchic was spoken in the Lambayeque, Jequetepeque, and Chicama areas, with its southern range overlapping Quignam somewhere in the Chicama or Moche Valley; Quignam was spoken in the Trujillo area and south, and Sec was spoken farther north, near Piura and Sechura.¹² This point is relevant to the present inquiry, because Chocope is the contemporary town adjacent to the ruins at Mocollope and Cerro Mayal, and Magdalena de Cao is adjacent to Huaca Cao Viejo. Carrera's specifications suggest that, in all probability, even in antiquity, long before the colonial epoch, some or all of the Chicama Valley population spoke Muchic or close variants of it.¹³

Further name designations cloud the issue. Uhle referred to the indigenous language of Trujillo and the North Coast as "Chimu," after the later culture group dominant in the region at the time of the Spanish conquest. Middendorf called the language described by Carrera the "Language of Eten," "Mochica," or a German variant, "Muchik." In recent years the name "Muchic" has gained favor among scholars, perhaps in part because of John Rowe's use of the term in a widely circulated article, "The Kingdom of Chimor."¹⁴

After Carrera's grammar, the second important source on the Muchic language, *Das Muchik öder die Chimu Sprache*, was written in 1892 by E. W. Middendorf, a German scholar who studied the language near the small town of Etén. Middendorf's account is relatively complete and complements Carrera's work in many ways, providing additional vocabulary and further instruction on the pronunciation of words. Other word lists have been compiled by Adolf Bastian, Federico Villareal, Enrique Brüning, Walter Lehmann, Rafael Larco Hoyle, Jorge Zevallos Quiñones, and, finally Paul Kosok, who reported that by 1951 there remained only a few people in Etén who spoke or remembered even three or four words of Muchic.¹⁵

In a 1968 dissertation titled "Mayan Affinities with Yunga of Peru," Louisa Stark addresses the grammar and syntax of the language in comparison with the Mayan language Ch'ol. She suggests that the total number of Yunga words available from all sources is approximately 1,742, or 806 words when corrected for duplications.[16] Her study is intriguing in its suggestion that a linguistic affinity between coastal Peruvian and Ecuadorian languages and Central American Maya languages is stronger than affinities with Andean Quechua languages. Alfredo Torero attempted further studies, and more recently, extensive linguistic analysis has been conducted by Rodolfo Cerrón-Palomino; his book *La Lengua de Naimlap* presents a comprehensive overview.[17]

Basic Characteristics of Muchic:
Sounds, Grammar, and Syntax

Carrera's documentation of the different sounds of the Yunga/Muchic language is often problematic, writing as he did in seventeenth-century Peru in colonial Spanish and Latin. Because it is now extinct, it is difficult for the modern scholar to gain a sense of how Muchic might actually have sounded. Like most other aspects of Muchic linguistic studies, the issue of phonetics lacks consensus, yet this element is fundamental. A correlation of Carrera's orthography with other sources (Appendix B), suggests that Muchic had the following six vowel sounds: /a/, /e/, /i/, /o/, /u/, /æ/.[18] The vowels *a*, *i*, *o*, and *u* could be either short or long. Additionally, Muchic had twenty-one consonants, as shown in Table 6.1.

The vowel (V) and consonant (C) syllable structures of Muchic words are V, CV, VC, or CVC.[19] There are no word initial or final consonant clusters, but sequences of two consonants may occur medially, and medial vowel clusters of as many as three may occur.[20] Cerrón-Palomino notes that the language's internal morphological structure is complex; vowels are often altered in inflection or according to rules of syncopation, contraction, harmony, or apocopation, while consonants remain relatively stable.[21]

Certain linguistic patterns serve as signature characteristics for this language and may well be useful to construct analogues of visual vocabulary. Such patterns include the fact that Muchic was morphologically agglutinative, using mostly suffixes, with occasional prefixes and infixes, to modify root words. The person and number of verbs are commonly indicated by suffixes, as are each verb's tense and aspect.[22] The concept of possession is expressed in the form of a genitive suffix added to the possessor noun, with an additional suffix added to the object(s) of possession.[23] Almost every type of clause in this language had some indication of possession; the rules governing the genitive case are complicated. Carrera states that each noun has two nominative forms, as well as three different genitive forms.[24] The genitive would be used to construct passive sentences, prepositional phrases, and adjectival phrases using pronouns. The language also included the concept of inalienable possession; for example, words for body parts are phrased in the genitive case.[25] Like Quechua, Muchic had complex kinship terminology that changed relative to

Table 6.1. Muchic Consonant Sounds.

Carrera:																					
d	f	c, qu	l	ll	xll	m	n	ñ	ng	p	r	rr	s, ss	cɥ	ch	t	Ç, z	tzh	y, j	x
Phonetic correlate:																					
d	f	k	l	lʸ	ł	m	n	nʸ	ŋ	p	ř	ř̃	ŝ, ŝ:	čʰ	č	t	s	ts	y	š

the speakers' relationship to the referent.[26] Nouns often have suffixes indicating the nominative's location (such as in, on top of, or under).[27] However, Muchic does not indicate gender; thus, adjectives do not change to indicate gender, nor do adjectives change to indicate number (e.g., adjectives do not have concordance with nouns and verbs).[28] Plurality was usually indicated by adding a suffix to the subject noun.[29] Muchic does have occasional examples of reduplication, albeit not very common.[30] In general, the use of the third person plural pronoun ("they") was carefully avoided, preference being given to the use of an adjective such as "those."[31] Sentence structure in Muchic followed a fairly regular pattern of subject + verb + direct object + locative.[32]

Concerning a Linguistic Analogy

Most people intuitively know that speaking is not the same as showing. Anyone can observe that these seem to function in two completely different modes of operation. The assertion marks a fundamental dichotomy lying at the root of most modern studies of script and pictorial image. In the "word–image" debate, script is regarded as the representation of spoken sound and pictures, as representations of visual experience. The perception of a clear distinction between these modes of communication, however, has created a binary opposition within academia that casts semasiographic or mixed notational forms in the awkward position of having no clear means of analysis.

How best to discover the connection between conventionalized icons and script-like elements and language structures? What was the nature of the relationship between oral and visual forms, and to what extent did the Muchic language inform Moche imagery? Were elements of spoken language directly incorporated into Moche imagery as standardized signs? Are parallels between the semiotic arrangement of the visual system and Muchic's linguistic structures evident? Semiotic analyses and investigations of other ancient American script forms identify areas where generative, homologous, and interpretive functions are found, providing cues about where one might expect to encounter script-like information.

A Semiotic Model (Benveniste)

In 1969, Emile Benveniste proposed a semiotic model by which disparate discursive forms might be compared. He asserts that the common characteristics of semiological systems are their signifying property (meaning) and their composition into units of meaning (signs).[33] Accordingly, he writes that semiological systems are characterized by (1) their mode of operation (the perceptory sense to which the system is directed, such as seeing or hearing); (2) the domain of the system's validity, that is, the area of human activity in which the system imposes itself (such as dance, religious practice, traffic management, and so forth); (3) the nature and number of the system's signs, which are generally determined by the functional dictates of the preceding two areas; and (4) the system's type of operation, referring to the internal relationship among the signs that confers their distinguishing function on them.

It proves to be a useful model, in that it allows for general identification of constituent parts of any given semiotic system. According to this schema, the first two characteristics (the mode of operation and the domain of validity) provide the external empirical conditions for the system. The third and fourth (the nature of the signs and their type of operation) indicate the system's internal semiotic conditions. The first two, because they are externally conditioned, can allow for a certain amount of variation, whereas the second pair, because they represent a system's internal semiotic conditions, cannot sustain structural variation without either falling apart or transforming into a different system.

Levels of interchangeability are determined by the locus and nature of difference between systems. Systems whose external aspects differ may ultimately be convertible, but systems whose internally conditioned elements differ substantially cannot translate directly. In most cases, semiotic systems whose third and fourth aspects are fundamentally at odds will find little or no grounds for direct transference of meaning. By way of illustration, Benveniste points out that the alphabet, Braille, Morse code, and the deaf-mute alphabet are all interchangeable. Their signs are all based on the premise of one sound to one letter, and their type of operation is a sequential transmission/reception of individual signs. Even though their modes of operation are quite different, their internal characteristics function in a like manner.

When Benveniste's criteria are applied as a comparison of Muchic language with Moche visual imagery, several important points of correspondence and divergence appear (see Table 6.2). A Moche iconographic system would have a *visual* mode of operation, that is, permanent marks or images were created in plastic media and addressed to viewers via the sense of sight. The system's domain of validity was in the realm of *ideology* and religious practice, and the physicality and presence of the artworks carried social and political subtexts. The nature and number of signs were in the form of hundreds of *icons* having specifically identifiable attributes, signs related to a particular conceptual base. And its type of operation was essentially a *configurational syntax* composed of icons or groups of presentational statements having a limited degree of linear sequence. The Muchic language, in turn, had an *oral/aural* mode of operation. Its

Table 6.2. Comparison of Moche Linguistic and Pictorial Domains		
Semiotic Categories	**Moche Imagery**	**Muchic Language**
(1) Mode of Operation	Visual/manipulation of plastic media: sequential and/or presentational	Oral/aural: paradigmatic and syntagmatic
(2) Domain of Validity	Specialized; religious belief and practice, with political subtext	Most aspects of social interaction, including religious practice
(3) Nature and Number of Signs	Hundreds of icons having specifically identifiable attributes; signs related to a particular conceptual base	Spoken phonemes, combining into thousands of morphemes
(4) Type of Operation	Groups of visual statements with limited internal syntax; occasional pictorial narrative episodes	Sound segments arranged into linear sequences ordered by well-defined syntax

Source: Based on Benveniste 1985.

domain of validity was much larger, encompassing most aspects of *social interaction* and human activity. The nature and number of its signs were in the form of twenty-eight spoken *phonemes* and an unknown number of morphemes. Its type of operation featured a complex system of *grammatical syntax* that combined and arranged the sound segments into defined sequences.

The comparison is illustrative in several regards. It points to certain incontrovertible differences between the two communicatory modes. Speech and vision appeal to two fundamentally separate sensory faculties; they are manifested and processed in distinct cognitive domains. They are not redundant—one cannot exactly replicate the functions of the other. In identifying their differences, however, points of common ground are revealed, areas where the possibility of translatability exists and becomes evident. Consider, for example, the relationships between Moche's semiotic systems based on each of Benveniste's four conditions:

1. Visual and spoken modes utilize different physical senses for their primary *modes of operation*, yet each also entails a constructive and interpretive aspect, as they deal in paradigmatic and syntagmatic ways with meaningful signs. The correspondence signals a relationship of homology, where an equivalence is perceived but not explicitly stated.

2. Within the systems' *domains of validity*, the spoken language was used in all areas of social interaction, whereas the use of the specialized visual language was considerably constrained. Very little correspondence is found between these domains. They are characterized by an explicative relationship, at most, where language interpreted or complemented pictorial subject matter. The imagery may have triggered memories of

particular narratives and religious activities or perhaps communicated indirect messages related to status, oral history, or the performance of religious duty, yet within this domain, visual imagery operated primarily at a performative level.

3. In terms of the *nature and number of signs*, linguistic signs outnumber visual signs dramatically. Yet a homologous relationship between meaningful icons and morphemes is apparent. Some amount of conceptual parallel exists, in the sense that both systems were built around a basic cohort of phonemes or thematically tied visual signs that could be combined and disassembled to create an incalculable number of viable combinations. Furthermore, in both systems, there seem to have been certain combinations that were not acceptable or that did not combine to create coherent meanings. Within this condition, some signs may be directly translatable to language as logographs or rebus devices; however, because not all Moche images are recognizable signs independent from the contexts in which they appear, not all will translate.

4. The *types of operations* seen in the two systems differ considerably, yet there are some areas of overlap. The spoken language arranged sound segments into linear sequences ordered by a complex system of grammatical syntax. The visual system, although it did employ narrative sequencing on occasion, was generally presentational in its mode of operation, ordered by a hybrid nonlinear, configurational syntax. Thus, the relationship is only partially homologous. Portions of Moche narrative imagery could be seen as having a derivative relationship to language, and it is in narrative structures that modal convertibility is most evident.

Linguistic Homology (Kubler, Teotihuacán, Taube)

The homologous relationships between visual and oral languages suggest the possibility of structural echoing of certain formal characteristics of spoken language. Such analogues would include the presence of nominative subjects and depictions of actions (analogous to verbs) and the possibility of linear visual structures approximately conforming to patterns of spoken sequences. Muchic language structures of agglutination and word order are promising areas of inquiry. Likewise, linguistic patterns of verb suffixing or genitive markings, which suggest how subjects and objects relate to each other, may ultimately be correlative with specific artistic conventions, offering insight as to how signs should be read in relation to each other.

George Kubler's work at Teotihuacán represents one of the earliest attempts at this type of formal structural analysis of an indigenous American culture's iconographic system. In "The Iconography and Art of Teotihuacan," Kubler states that Teotihuacano "painters and sculptors were seeking forms of logographic clarity.... [They were] interested in combining and compounding associative meanings in a quest for viable forms of writing."[34] Although he did not single out any elements that were logographic per se, Kubler challenged the assumption of the time that the city's murals, present in various temples and elite buildings, represented actual biological species and utilitarian objects. Instead, he analyzed the murals' constituent parts in terms of grammatical functions, as verbs, adjectives, and nouns. He concludes that because the images contain a high proportion of "nominal" and "adjectival" forms and a relatively low number of "verbal statements," the images should be likened to a litany rather than to a narrative. A litany is described as a recital of the names and qualities of the deity being worshipped, together with the favors being requested from it—"grammatically poor but high in metaphors and titles."[35]

Karl Taube has gone on to suggest that it should be possible to decipher Teotihuacán's glyphic labels through making contextual inferences based on certain kinds of graphic conventions and visual coefficients. We should expect that specific visual compositions will signal, as framing devices, the presence of logographic configurations of signs.[36] He notes that numerical coefficients function in the iconographic system to identify the graphic nature of (usually) calendrical signs and that consistently reduplicated hieroglyphic signs seem to signal place-names.[37] He pushes the research further by proposing additional points of intersection and visual contexts where one might encounter script-like information. Taube mentions that individuals tend to have glyphic labeling, most likely serving as naming devices, and that framing devices, such as speech scrolls, highlight the fact that certain images operate at the level of signs. His work at Teotihuacán reminds us that, for hybrid notational systems, specific canons and artistic conventions will be the consistent framing devices onto which signs are grafted.

Christopher Donnan has proposed a similar homology for Moche imagery, stating that "in many ways, [the Moche] system is similar to the symbolic system of a language," suggesting that objects, people, and things depicted in Moche art might be thought of as "artistic nouns."[38] These, he proposes, were modified using a set of symbolic elements to serve as "artistic adjectives" to impart additional information to the viewer. Actions (verbs) could, likewise, be modified with "artistic adverbs" to suggest information such as direction or speed.

Moche imagery differs from Teotihuacano in the sense that, if the latter is like a litany of metaphors and titles, the Moche is more obviously referent to ritual actions and activities (more like verbs)—activities that ultimately revolved around the maintenance of a socioreligious power base. The artwork features iconographic phrases that are consistently referential to culturally systemic narratives.[39] Even in those artworks having no narrative sequential structure, whose characters are like "set pieces," "icons," or "noun phrases," an image's primary significance is most often derived from its relationship to specific actions and ritual activities. Such "noun phrases" function because their "verb predicate" is understood, even though omitted. In short, rather than passive recitation of titular phrases, Moche iconography is characterized by frequent visual reference to actions and narrative sequences.

Equivalence of Signs:
Moche Logographs, Mixtec Analogues

If phonetic correspondences are present in Moche iconography, then they should, in theory, appear at certain junctures and not at others. For example, we can anticipate that Moche language will not be represented in a purely logographic form. Logographs adapt most easily to single morpheme language structures; Muchic's agglutinative structure, with its variable inflections in root words, nominatives, and genitives, would make the use of a solely logographic system unwieldy. Logographs, if present, would more likely occur as part of a larger notational scheme.

Indeed, Moche imagery does regularly incorporate a number of highly conventionalized, glyph-like motifs juxtaposed into pictorial space, especially in later phases. Based on studies of fineline paintings, Donnan and McClelland identify specific examples of pictorial modifiers. Calling attention to what they identify as "locators," they note that such signs indicate particular kinds of places within the coastal world, such as desert, ocean, ceremonial precincts, and scrub forest (Figure 6.1).[40] Absent direct linguistic evidence, locators are understood ideographically. Once they are recognized, however, it remains to investigate the possibility that such signs may have had direct correlations to specific Muchic words or phrases, thereby functioning as logographs.

The Mixtec pictorial writing system of Mexico (A.D. 1200–1600) provides an excellent framework by which to consider the question of Moche logographic signs.[41] Although the temporal separation of the two cultures would seem to preclude any suggestion of direct interchange, several Moche pictorial conventions bear uncanny similarity to graphic signs later developed by the Mixtec, a circumstance that invites direct comparison.[42]

No longer in use, Mixtec writing was documented in southern Mexico at the time of the Spanish conquest and later studied in depth by Mary Elizabeth Smith.[43] Sometimes described as a "pictographic" system, Mixtec notation is an example of a hybrid writing form. Mixtec writing was essentially composed of pictorial narratives with glyphic elements, including logographs indicating specific words, pictographic homonyms linked to linguistic sounds, and directly ideographic symbols that were nonlinguistically tied semasiographic forms. Painted parchment codices, read in a "meander" pattern, largely expound on the genealogical histories of local rulers, important actions completed by those rulers, and descriptions of lands held by particular polities.

Mixtec notation employed highly conventionalized icons to make general information known to the viewer but did not use "genre" figures. In other words, no figures other than those having specific identities integral to the overall message were included; nothing was included as visual "filler." Events were recorded, but the actual vicissitudes of the stories were not depicted.[44] Streamlining was an important element in how the visual syntax of the pictorial system functioned.

FIGURE 6.1. Rollout drawing of animated helmet and prisoner bottle with examples of geographic indicators (drawing by Donna McClelland).

Smith has observed that some Mixtec iconographic configurations had no linguistic connections; they were pictorial conventions only. Specific examples are the conventionalized symbols for "road/warpath," "conquest," "death/sacrifice," and "speech." This type of sign is purely ideographic. Others were "unmotivated" logograms, that is, abstract codified signs that did have direct linguistic counterparts but whose meanings did not correspond to their formal appearance. Because they were also generally "ideographic," they could also be understood without reference to language. For the Mixtec, these mostly referred to calendrical names and numbers. Still others, called "place signs," were logograms whose specific pictorial elements were the equivalent of one or more words in the Mixtec language. These signs were usually highly "motivated," and many times included additional rebus components. Typically, place signs were composed of a geographic element (a substantive) and a modifying element (a qualifier).[45]

Smith has identified several of the main pictorial conventions (or glyphs) that served as geographic substantives (Figure 6.2). The glyph for "town" is a horizontal rectangle having a "geometric frieze" pattern. The "hill" glyph is described as a bell-shaped form with a border, having small protruding bumps. A "temple platform" is indicated by a horizontal base that has a "rondel frieze" pattern and a stairway at one end. A "valley/plain" is shown as a horizontal rectangle whose interior is divided into bladelike units that represent feathers. The place sign for "river" is trough shaped with a blue middle and a wavelike top. Modifying elements might include almost any type of qualifying reference: color, size, Deity, numerals, calendrical signs, animals, plants, objects, weapons, and so forth. Though less well understood because they were in many cases linguistically tied, modifiers are recognized by their position within the composition. For example, in Figure 6.3 the "hill" glyph has a "head" on top of it, and the "temple platform" glyph has a distinctive flower attached. Even though Smith does not supply translations for them, it is clear that these markers specify and name something particular about the hill and the temple platform.

The pictorial conventions identified by Smith comprise particular images that appear with regularity in certain kinds of contexts or as part of repetitive

 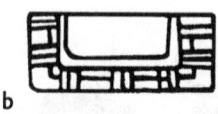 

FIGURE 6.2. Mixtec place glyphs, Codex Muro: **(a)** town; **(b)** river; **(c)** hill (after Smith 1973b).

FIGURE 6.3. Mixtec place glyphs with modifiers, Codex Muro: **(a)** hill; **(b)** temple; **(c)** town (after Smith 1973b).

themes, in many ways very similar to the kinds of framing devices Taube reports at Teotihuacán. Smith recognizes the symbols as conventionalized to the point of being signs, hypothesizing that some of the signs could be correlated with Mixtec words to make logographs. Finally, she notes that the graphs were sometimes combined with other conventionalized images to create compound signs. Her methodology is instructive.

Moche iconography includes analogous artistic conventions, stylized images that, over time, came to signify particular things. Stepped pyramid images are a case in point. Often depicted in Moche artwork, they were ubiquitous architectural forms that represented the locus of political and religious power on the North Coast for centuries.[46] Images of them are relatively consistent; in sculptural form the vessel body conceptually parallels or explicitly depicts a platform mound with a building on top. In painted form, the platform is depicted as a sequence of horizontal rectangles topped by architecture. As background for narrative scenes, they can be read as "locators."[47] In its most abbreviated form, the stepped pyramid came to be symbolized by a step-fret icon.[48] In one example (Figure 6.4), a sculpted, three-dimensional pyramid is shown painted with a repetitive stepped motif reminiscent of textile patterns common to men's tunics. What is most likely a temple sits atop the pyramid, itself fitted with a stepped-crescent headdress. As this headdress type is consistently associated with the religious and political power of warrior lords, it serves here, along with the wall motifs, to convey information about the building to which it is attached.[49]

Headdresses are consistent indicators of rank and social role in Moche art. They often function as stand-alone symbols for the roles or persons with whom they were associated (an aspect of representation discussed at greater length in

FIGURE 6.4.
Stirrup-spout bottle with stepped pyramid temple (photo courtesy of Ethnologisches Museum Staatliche Museen zu Berlin, VA17632).

the chapter that follows).⁵⁰ Therefore, both the stepped-crescent headdress and the stepped pyramid were independently meaningful. Both can be found separately in other visual contexts, but when seen in combinations like this one, they meld together to become a compound icon interpretable in terms of noun substantive and adjectival modifier.

Several interpretations are possible. The "stepped pyramid" symbol may have functioned as a geographic substantive with the "step-fret crescent headdress" functioning as a qualifier or modifier signaling specific information about the building or its owner. It perhaps refers to a specific place, modified by an emblem associated with a particular ruler or polity, thus functioning as a place-name. If so, the vessel may refer to a specific location with a proper name, such as "Pyramid of the Lord of [X Territory]." Alternatively, the qualifying element perhaps functioned as an adverbial phrase, metonymically referring to a specific activity engaged in by the person(s) associated with the qualifier, leading to a more obscure kind of place-name reference, for example, "pyramid where rulership occurs." A third interpretation is one in which the qualifying element functions in a straightforward adjectival sense to describe the substantive, in this case possibly a possessive adjective (e.g., "the warrior's pyramid").

A comparison between the Moche fineline drawing with a seated leader (Figure 6.5a) and a detail from a page in the Mixtec Codex Muro (Figure 6.5b) illustrates interesting correspondences in the manner of depicting elite architecture, suggestive of additional areas where Moche logographs might be

FIGURE 6.5. (a) Moche Lord from the "Presentation of Plates"; (b) detail of seated Mixtec Lord after the Codex Muro (Smith 1973b).

discovered. In these two images, the most immediately obvious similarity is the spatial positioning of the imagery. Both feature an important figure, probably a ruler or other elite person, sitting inside an architectural structure depicted in cutaway profile, an artistic device creating what looks like a T-shaped building.[51] The buildings are atop stepped platforms, an architectural form related to the political and religious practices of both cultures. The two principal seated figures are identified through their costume elements and by the accouterments that surround them. The Mixtec figure is specifically identified through the addition of an attached glyph in the pictorial space above his head; the Moche had no such naming conventions that we know of.[52] The buildings have ornamental forms across their ridge crests; the Mixtec's are L-shaped, while the Moche's are in the form of T-shaped mace heads; in fact, the remains of such decorative mace heads have occasionally been recovered from Moche monumental contexts (Figure 2.10).[53] In both examples, the presence of distinctive roof combs serves to identify a specific function or type of building and may well refer to something particular about the individuals seated there.

The Mixtec manuscript includes both pictographic and logographic elements. To date, however, no examples of directly logographic elements have been identified within the Moche symbol system.[54] Nonetheless, Moche iconic references, such as the stepped pyramid, may be more linguistically tied than previously supposed. For the Mixtec, we know that the signs for "town" and "hill" are linked to geographic locations because they consistently correlate with Spanish glosses of specific Mixtec words; town, hill, and altar translate to *ñuu*, *yucu*, and *chiyo*, respectively.[55] Like Mixtec signs, Moche iconography includes an enormous array of possible adjectival qualifiers; however, several iconographic elements that may have been geographic locatives appear with consistency: the stepped pyramid is one of them.

Jorge Zevallos-Quiñones and others have long noted that toponyms are among the most conservative of linguistic forms. If logographic elements did exist in Moche art, the stylized *huaca* icon could well be one of them.[56] The word *macɥæc*, as mentioned in Carrera, is most often interpreted to mean huaca, idol, or place where idols are worshipped. Yet the words for worship, place of worship, and object of worship all stem from the same root word, *mæcha*, with their exact meanings communicated by means of appended modifiers. Several examples of usage in Carrera allow us to understand that the term was interpreted by the Spanish with a great deal of cultural slippage and misunderstanding, in much the same way as the Quechua term huaca, "sacrality," was both place and thing.[57] Furthermore, in describing mæcha in Hispanicized form, Calancha makes explicit that "the word *mochadero* is the common name with which the Indians name their places of worship."[58] When one considers that the Spanish suffix *+dero* can be added to either person or place, it may be that the word *macɥæc* is the Yunga equivalent of the Quechua word huaca.[59]

Thus, if *macɥæc* was used in a general sense to mean sacred place of worship, or huaca, the conventionalized stepped pyramid icon may well have had the word *macɥæc* as a linguistic counterpart. As a symbol with a motivated linguistic counterpart, the stepped pyramid icon would therefore constitute a logograph. Otherwise, as a standardized sign not linguistically tied, the huaca icon functioned as an emblem.

Some languages lend themselves more easily to logographic script than others. Languages where each morpheme is only one syllable long and syllables are clearly delineated and easy to identify provide a comparatively easy transposition of spoken language to logographic form.[60] One would not expect to find a purely logographic type of writing, with one graph for each word, in use for languages that inflect their root words; for example, English inflections of the word *eat* (eat, ate, eaten, eats, eating, etc.) would each require a separate graph. The use of logographs to represent such languages would lead to an overwhelming number of graphs, making the script unusable.[61] Similarly, some languages readily lend themselves to rebus writing, while others do not. Spanish, for example, is particularly difficult to translate into rebus because of its conventions for indicating number and gender.

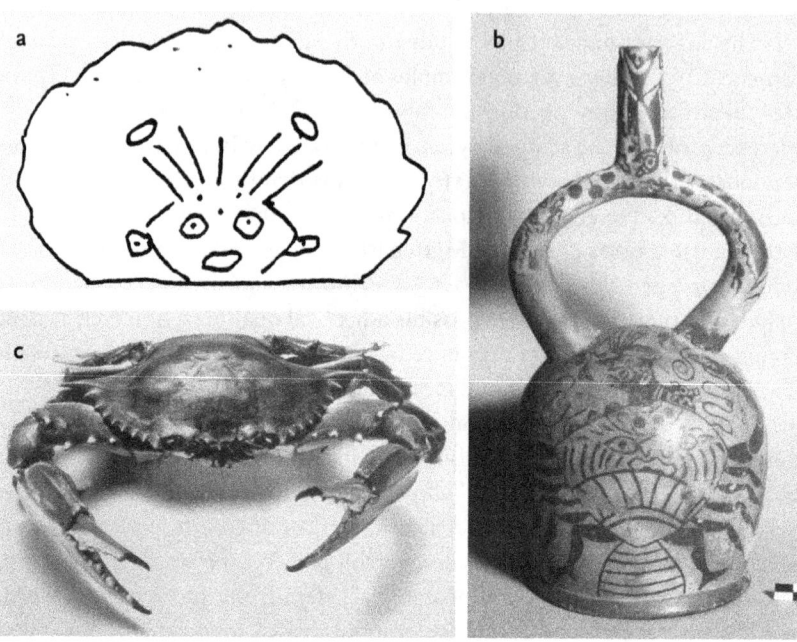

FIGURE 6.6. Xian crab: **(a)** sketch of *cangrejo* (by Walter Lehmann, after Schumacher de Peña 1991); **(b)** stirrup-spout bottle with crab (894-100106, Collection of the Field Museum, Chicago); **(c)** photo of a live Grapsidae crab.

Available evidence does not point to rebus as a primary organizational concept for the Moche pictorial system. If Muchic employed rebus as its principal notational vehicle, we would expect to see two obvious components. First, conventionalized pictorial elements agglutinated to each other in seemingly arbitrary fashion would be present. Moche pictorial style does display this characteristic to some degree, allowing for the possibility that rebus was employed, but not to the exclusion of all else. Second, we might expect complex rebus constructions to roughly follow the language's grammatical structure: subject + verb + direct object + locative (adverb). If exclusive, sequences of rebus signs would be configured according to spoken patterns, rather than in conjunction with other kinds of pictorial structures.

All indications suggest the possibility that the Moche system did incorporate rebus devices in some capacity. At least one example of homonymic correlation has been noted. Walter Lehmann states that the word *xian* (*xiăŋ*) meant both "sun" and "crab," that their names were pronounced identically.[62] Lehmann's elderly informant explained that they were the same because "the crab has a crown same as the king of the sun."[63] And indeed, there is a species of crab on the North Coast whose shell has a marking that appears to have a face with a rayed corona surrounding it. Lehmann includes a rough sketch of it (Figure 6.6a), an image that correlates closely to what is seen in Moche art (Figure 6.6b). Benson identifies the crab species as likely a member of the

Grapsidae family (Figure 6.6c).[64] Lehmann suggests that the coincidence of language and image explicates various representations in the artwork—that the "crab-god," who is often shown fighting various other persons, appears to have been conceptually linked to the "sun-god."

Lehmann's observation represents at least one reasonable possibility of rebus construction in the Moche iconographic corpus. Additional connections may come to light with further linguistic work. It has been noted that Moche's fantastic supernatural creatures seem to be composites of parts.[65] If present, we should expect rebus devices to be most evident in the juxtapositions of seemingly unrelated conventionalized images, such as those seen in compound icons.

Commentary

Although Muchic is an extinct language, what remains of its vocabulary forms an important source for searching out logographic or rebus correspondences, as well as information about any grammatical predilections that might underlie Moche's visual semantic units. Although much remains unstudied, semiotic models hint at the junctures where linguistic correspondences might be found, as well as areas where such constructions are unlikely to occur. The iconography appears highly conventionalized and pictorially ordered in ways very suggestive of visual syntax, although direct connections remain elusive. Its component parts appear codified and in many cases seem to function as pictorial subjects, verbs, direct objects, and locatives. The internal structures governing the placement of the elements within pictorial space, however, are not reliably sequential in their construction. This suggests that although underlain by a culturally shared metanarrative, and sometimes overtly thematic, the pictorial order was not strictly tied to language or linguistic patterning, even though this did occasionally occur.

Linguistic analogies cannot address the segments of the visual language that are semasiographic or ideographic, what Benveniste might have referred to as conventionalized iconic signs. Nor can they approach aspects of communication that were delivered through nonvisual means, such as performance of ritual, social interactions, or elements that achieved codification through rules that differ from those of linguistic ordering. Nonetheless, some correspondences may be embedded. Moche art lies squarely in the interstices among writing, notation, and pictorial representation. As such, a model of hybrid mixed notational forms predicts that some linguistic correspondences will exist. It remains to investigate Moche imagery's schematic and emblematic qualities.

CHAPTER 7

Hybrid Presentational Syntax in Moche Iconography

In its early phases, Moche visual arts depended heavily on emblematic configurations of images. Later, Moche art increasingly included narrative pictorial structures that integrated into earlier traditions of iconic compounding—an enduring characteristic of the overall visual corpus. Regardless of narrative content, the iconography is neither entirely pictorial nor made of abstract signs alone.

While the preceding chapters identify specific images as semantic units, the task of the present chapter is to hypothesize the ways in which the discreet signs and pictorial elements fit together syntactically to deliver particular information into permanent forms. Compound icons, functioning as signs set into representational scenes, suggest the possible loci where syntactic structures become discernable. These embedded signs derive meaning from Moche's artistic canons, specifically from the practice of using key themes, reiterated with lesser or greater amounts of detail or "completeness," composed of recognizable characters or suites of activities, and reproduced with differing degrees of elaboration.[1] Allusions to myths and happenings refer to the same cast of characters, whether in solitary emblematic form or in complex iconographic sequences; both formats were keyed to core ideological constructs, creating a basic organizational framework for the visual code.

The rules by which Moche artistic programs operated, therefore, seem founded on at least two main principles. First, the imagery utilized generally accepted groups of signs and symbols—clusters of elements, which were combined, disassembled, and recombined to provide variations of meaning. Second, strong conventions governed the manner in which objects were represented, the spatial arrangement of objects within the picture plane, and the depiction of serial actions. Narrative examples used sequencing, perspective, and registers to convey messages (although not necessarily in every composition). Additionally, the images incorporate a multivalent aspect that goes well beyond simple narrative. The iconographic content of many artworks functioned in a vertically compressed, or metonymic, manner, involving clusters of compound icons whose constituent elements were themselves symbols and which, in some cases, may have included linguistic or logographic elements.

As compound clusters of signs, these operated under their own system of logic, in a manner that deserves to be considered at length. Moche iconographic syntax was organized along a horizontal axis of sequential passages (as in complex narrative scenes), as well as a vertical axis of iconic linkages (as nested symbolic indexes). The conceptual ligatures indicated by horizontal and vertical syntaxes, as well as the nature of the semantic units in use, suggest that the iconography worked in a configurational manner, in what Langer might have described as a hybrid presentational syntax.[2] What follows is an exploration of how certain aspects of visual syntax are apparent in the art.

Themeology and the Narrative Construct

The correlation between image and artifact makes it clear that a larger cultural narrative involving real people, places, and events was the principal mechanism informing the imagery.[3] Lavish investment of resources on monuments like Huaca de La Luna, Huaca Cao Viejo, and others testifies to the importance of the ideological matrix at society's highest levels. Key connections between pictorial images and burgeoning numbers of artifacts discovered in the spectacular tombs and temples in recent years have been made, as scholars realized that Moche imagery could be categorized according to distinct themes. Themeology became an interpretive medium, an effective methodological approach for making images understandable as narratives, even when significant parts of the pictures were otherwise unintelligible. The approach allows for an ever-expanding field of research, one based on the premise that each scene, in its most complex form, will be composed of a full array of primary and secondary characters but that any given artwork need not necessarily include all possible variants. An individual artwork may present an entire scene, a partial scene, or just one specific element of a scene.[4] The more complete the scene, the more apparent is a pictorial narrative structure.

A goal of researchers has been the reconstruction of Moche ideology through the reconstruction of narrative sequences. Identifying specific themes and their various constituent elements has proven useful—not every vessel depicts every component of every theme, but taken as a group the overall parameters of stories become apparent.[5] The narratives are particularly evident in scenes where an elaborate cast of characters is shown, because often such compositions will also include registers, conventions of scale or perspective, and characters actively engaged with each other. In ceramics, complex scenes appear most often in fineline paint or low-relief press wares. In contrast, vessels embellished with a single motif or icon are often interpreted at face value, as are emblematic applications of images in architecture and other media.

Archaeological evidence supports the idea that Moche iconography correlated strongly to the real world, even though veiled in a language of religious ideology. The relative naturalism of Moche forms masks the fact that Moche art contains a high degree of convention and abstraction. Unexplained visual anomalies, such as human–animal hybrids and strangely placed visual elements, show clear deliberation on the part of the artists to use imagery as signal units. The art additionally includes iconic elements that are in no way realistic and that cannot be seen as part of a verbal narrative sequence yet are somehow tied to a larger contextual statement.

Conventions and Icons

Horizontal Axis

Moche visual narrative sequences tend to be thematic, and the sequential narrative format became an increasingly important vehicle for the communication of social and political values, as evidenced by the fineline painting tradition that grew in frequency and complexity toward later Moche phases.[6] What appear to be political references are especially pronounced in Phase IV.

To interpret a Moche narrative image, begin with the assumption that all elements serve an expository function—there are no figures that are simply decorative and no elements whose strict purpose is to depict "realism." Neither are there any generalized, nonspecific, or generic background characters.[7] All characters are present because they convey information, have identifying modifiers, or are themselves modifying elements.

Roland Barthes observes that narratives share certain structural commonalities, analysis that proves useful here.[8] Four main components, he notes, function within a hierarchy of importance, as follows. The primary elements or characters in a narrative, the parts without which it cannot function, he calls the nuclei. Secondary elements that function to support the nuclei and move the narrative forward, he labels catalysts (or "catalysers"). A narrative will also have indexical semantic units, which Barthes refers to as indexes and informants. He notes that indexes have implicit signifieds and always involve an element of decipherment, which distinguishes them from informants, which communicate elements of data explicitly, imparting immediate signification.

In his analysis of Moche narrative structures, Simon Martin employs Barthes's terminology to identify the major characters of the Sacrifice Scene (Figure 2.1). He identifies the primary nucleus of the scene as being the moment when the Warrior Priest (whom he calls the Rayed Deity) receives a goblet from the Owl Warrior.[9] The exchange is clearly the dominant narrative moment in the composition. Other participants are characterized as catalyst characters (they include the Priestess, the praying Priest, and several smaller warriors). Their status-identifying elements, such as the Spotted Dog, particular headdress, fancy sedan chair, and spatulate scepter, serve as indexes and informants.[10] These convey direct information about the participants, as well as indexical references to factors outside the picture and to preceding or succeeding plot points. In the lower register, a cluster of images shows a not-quite-human priest drawing the prisoners' blood; this constitutes a second nucleus, drawing attention to an artistic trend in later Moche visual art toward incorporating multiple narrative moments. A key observation here is that in recognizing the primary and secondary nuclei, secondary catalyst characters, indexes, and informants, it becomes possible to recognize them when they appear as singular units elsewhere, away from larger narrative scenes, and to understand in what capacity they may function as semantic units.

Barthes's structural analysis in practical application also recognizes the mechanics of how meaning transfers between characters central to narrative function and indexical references. Narrative sequences, when keyed to oral telling, naturally include linear progression, a horizontal movement (or recounting of events) from a beginning point to a finish. In Barthes's vocabulary, these narrative elements are "distributional," because the elements occur sequentially, chained to each other through the order of their occurrence. The relationships between these semantic units and their correlates are basically syntagmatic; the units function on the same operational level.[11] Pictures whose visual representations seek to illustrate spoken stories in a serial manner provide clear examples of this. Barthes contrasts these horizontal, lateral connections with vertical, indexical relationships. These he calls "integrational," observing that their meaning is grasped from one level to the next.[12] In other words, not all syntactical units function on the same modal level; they can function on different levels, with the significatory power of some units deriving from frames of reference understood through other shared frameworks or social convention but not necessarily through the images shown. Furthermore, although the relationship between any given unit and its correlate may be as Barthes proposes (with nuclei and catalysts as distributional and indexes and informants as integrational), he also points out that such units may sometimes combine more than one aspect simultaneously.

Barthes's description of narrative structures provides a framework by which to speak about parts of stories. Within those passages, the constituent parts correspond in many ways to grammatical elements. The brief pictorial narrative passage in Figure 7.1 provides an example of how a horizontal, or syntagmatic, visual phrase might read. The interaction between two human figures (A, B, and C) forms the nucleus of a scene. The gesture that unites them (B) is the key iconographic element that allows the viewer to understand their primary relationship. Internal pointers suggest a directionality of action analogous to speech. The story might go something like, "The soldier defeats an adversary in the desert." We read the direction and movement of the scene based on several cues: the characters are arranged in a roughly horizontal

FIGURE 7.1. Drawing of a Warrior Confrontation: **(a)** subject; **(b)** verb; **(c)** direct object; **(d)** locative element (drawing by Donna McClelland).

sequence, as are the gestures and focal direction of the subject images; likewise, the general shape of the vessel surface and the mechanical action required in its rotation suggest a framework of time. In grammatical terms, the order of the visual phrase echoes Mochica's general structural pattern (as outlined in the previous chapter):

The soldier	/ combats (defeats)	/ an adversary	/ in the desert.
subject +	verb +	direct object +	locative
A	B	C	D

Although outwardly sequential, each clause is nonetheless subject to significant internal elaboration through the addition of modifying elements (informants and indexes). The communication of those elaborations was governed by convention. The first soldier (A) is identified by his costume elements and specific headdress, with particular markings indicating status, clan, or other affiliation; these elements are indexical and/or informational. Combat (B) is indicated by specific conventions for fighting and victory; these include raised war clubs, figures positioned face to face, attitudes of confrontation or being stricken down, and knees bent as if in motion. In Moche art, conventions will indicate who loses, such as the winner grasping the loser by the hair or the loser's weapons and emblems of rank being captured; the loser is sometimes shown as a naked captive with a rope around his neck. The adversary soldier (C), as with the soldier above (A), has identifying costume elements, a specific headdress type, and particular markings indicating status, clan, or other affiliation. In this example, an unknown graphic element floats in the picture plane just above the figure's forehead. Spatial locatives and geographic "locator" elements (D) include conventionalized elements like rolling hills, pointed hills, sandy ground, and pyramids; specific types of plants indicate particular microclimatic environments, for example, reeds and cactus; catfish would indicate swamp, desert, riverine areas, and so forth.[13]

Vertical Axis

It has long been observed that Moche iconography incorporates certain kinds of pictorial abbreviations. In attempting to trace the implied patterns of expansion or compression apparent in these, an impressive web of interstices emerges, demonstrating significant, and surely not coincidental, vertical depth of indexical meaning. A warrior, for example, may be shown engaged in a narrative scene, as in Figure 7.1 and in Plate 11, or may be shown alone, provided only with the insignia of his rank (Figure 7.2). When solo, he represents his office and the things related to his office metonymically. By extension, when the very same emblems (helmets, war clubs, and such) appear alone, they represent themselves, as objects, while simultaneously referring to the warrior as an individual, to his offices and activities (Plate 11).[14] Their true significance is in their value as references to the important activities of the state, of warfare, prisoner capture, and sacrifice, meaning that would not be lost on someone who was completely familiar with the overarching social narrative informing them (Plate 12). In reducing the warrior to the symbols of his rank alone, his specific person has been condensed into an ever-more abstract iconic signifier in a way that can be likened to vertical telescoping. When figures of speech or visual phrases carry more significance than the sum of their parts, they have the potential to stand alone as meaningful units. They are both emblematic and nominative, serving as indexes that, in most cases, are themselves metonyms for larger themes.

The vertical compression of imagery, it seems, could occur in virtually any part of a visual phrase, be it noun, verb, adverb, or adjective phrase. Just as nominative characters could be reduced to distilled signs, actions were also shown in condensed versions. Such signs may have presented more difficulty, however, because concepts surrounding verbs and adverbs do not "telescope" or compress so neatly as do nouns; the previous "warrior/helmet" example moves from one noun substantive to another, and both have concrete physical forms that can be depicted. A symbol's value becomes more arbitrary in transactions involving verbs and other less concrete phrases, giving rise to signs that are less directly motivated and more glyphic. As a consequence, visual contractions involving verbs and adverbial phrases will employ more abstract kinds of symbols than do noun phrases.

As an example, note that in some renditions of the Warrior Narrative, where the warriors are reduced to their accoutrements alone, they are made animate

FIGURE 7.2.
Seated Moche lord wearing step-crescent headdress (photo courtesy of Christopher B. Donnan).

through the addition of arms and legs. Such elements serve as nominal modifiers, leading to images such as an animated helmet in the act of taking a prisoner (Figure 6.1) and two animated weapon bundles that confront each other (Plate 13). In both, the image clusters stand in place of full depictions of warriors; in fact, they are warrior indexes. For whatever reason, the artist did not feel the need to take up pictorial space with a full figure. Clearly the action phrases were the primary messages of substantive value in the overall telling of these events.

In some cases, what appear to be symbols or indexes may actually be linguistically tied signs. Whether logographs or pictographs, the Muchic language does suggest how artists may have conceived verb phrases. The language is notable for its relative lack of verbs.[15] Verbs were often created by taking nouns and appending them with particles that signaled tense, number, and so on. Fernando de la Carrera gives the following example: *fœp* is the word for "dream" (noun); with the addition of the verb particle *+eiñ*, the word becomes a verb, *fœpeiñ*, which strictly translated means "I am a dream" but which in spoken language is understood as a verb phrase meaning "I dream."[16]

Given Muchic linguistic structure we might expect compressed or abbreviated verb phrases to appear somewhat like noun phrases but also to include some evidence of an "action marker." Consider, as an example of how a verb phrase might compress, a Moche fineline bottle whose design shows a richly arrayed

FIGURE 7.3. The "Presentation of Plates," rollout drawing of fineline bottle (drawing by Donna McClelland).

lord seated inside a structure atop a stepped pyramid (Figure 7.3). The lord appears to gesture toward the funerary vessels immediately surrounding him. A standing figure faces him, and they appear engaged in an interaction, presumably involving the presentation of the many rows of paired gourd bowls behind him. The bowls are noteworthy because they illustrate a previous point: there are no insignificant figures in Moche art—no nondescript servants are shown carrying these bowls; only the bowls themselves merit inclusion in the illustration. They are shown as having feet, literally walking themselves toward the pyramid.

On top of another stepped pyramid, shown on the opposite side of the same vessel, several less elaborately dressed figures, perhaps priests, sit facing the lord. One figure is dressed almost identically to the seated lord, lacking only the feline headdress. It is unclear whether this figure represents the same lord at a different moment in the narrative sequence or a different person altogether. All appear to be chanting or singing. On their right are rows of tall-necked jars with convex lids. (Incidentally, these are the same types of jars and lids commonly produced at Cerro Mayal [Figure 3.3].) Like the paired offering plates, the jars are also notably anthropomorphized through the addition of feet and ropes around their "necks," conceptually equating them to prisoners. Just as sacrificial prisoners are paraded to the pyramid to have their blood let, so these "captured" vessels walk themselves to the pyramid to pour out their liquid contents into shallow offering bowls, an offering that comes as the focal point of a complex ritual cycle.[17] The addition of feet serves as an artistic convention indicating movement (an "action marker"). Thus, these nominatives are modified to be understood as active; paralleling Muchic language, nouns become understood as verbs through the addition of modifying suffixes.

In understanding that such modifications are possible, renditions of similar plates or jars, when shown as stand-alone icons, take on enhanced meaning; their indexical value becomes more clear. A sculpted vessel depicting two gourd bowls filled with peanuts and chilies (Figure 7.4) is almost certainly an indexical reference to the same activity of making offerings, like that shown in the fineline bottle with stacked plates (Figure 7.3).[18] The sculpted version, however, shows no

FIGURE 7.4.
Stirrup-spout bottle with gourd plates (45.001184, Collection of the Field Museum, Chicago).

particular evidence of any "action markers." Instead, the depiction stands as a metonymic reference to the activity of making offerings; in linguistic terms, it functions as a noun. The activity of making offerings—the act of making these particular offerings—may well have been associated with specific rituals, which themselves were triggered by certain events (if, for example, peanuts were only offered at certain times of year, or *aji* peppers only in certain circumstances), but it is a meaning that required constructive effort on the part of the viewer. Its meaning depended on a cultural nexus that was provided by the social context in which the object was used and by the person using it.

The passive communication of single icons, however, does little to explain the syntactic structures present in more complex scenes. Verb phrases are key in these because they allow emblematic and abbreviated icons to become episodic phrases more actively tied to larger social narratives. The development of action-based visual cues in later Moche iconography seems to signal an important development toward pictographic notation. It is in this area that semasiographic conventions come into play.

Syntax and Semasiography

A basic tenet of the present study holds that Moche art is informed at its deepest levels by a broadly based societal narrative related to ideology and ritual practice. The performance of that narrative probably included oral components, like the public recitation, acting out, or telling of myths and legends, and may itself have been the subject of recollection—orality in any form always includes an aspect of sequential ordering, most minimally as single sentences and more extensively as epic tales. Barthes's model applies most readily to images that include multiple components arranged in configurations recognizable as sequential narratives. In Moche art, that translates to a relatively small, but important, portion of the entire visual corpus.

By far, however, the majority of the art employs iconic or emblematic configurations of signs. These images feature visual phrases, or clusters of signs, which are understood by various conventionalized means (logographic, rebus, indexical abbreviation, etc.), placed within the pictorial space with very little precondition on the viewer in terms of how the image must be decoded. They tend to include internal pointers that guide the viewer from one sign or sign cluster to the next.

In a previous example (Figure 7.1), the image glossed as "The soldier defeats an adversary in the desert" follows a visual pattern readily familiar because of its left-to-right sequence and the directionality of its visual signs. There is little reason to assume, however, that Moche visual syntax will always be so; its signs and symbols might also be arrayed from right to left or vertically. In the case of a visual tradition where no widespread literary habits existed, the semantic units might be arranged, as in this example, in a pattern of subject, verb, object, locative. The order perhaps reflects a cultural preference determined by speech, but that speech preference might just as easily have been graphically arranged from right to left. In a second example (Figure 7.5), the main protagonist, a warrior, captures another warrior, signaled by the grasped forelock, flying nose ring, and loss of headdress. Informants arranged around the perimeter (locators and symbols equivalent to adverbs and adjectives) modify the action, and an image of a weapon bundle serves as an index for the larger significance of the act, a pattern that would read as locative, object, verb, subject in linguistic parlance. Yet, in a culture where no widespread literary habits existed, again, such categorizations find little substance, save for our own purposes of decipherment. The various modifiers (symbols and locators, informants and indexes) tend to hang in space, loosely arranged around the perimeters of the primary action in variable order. The pattern of viewing is dictated by the mechanics of the vessel format in relation to the viewer's eye and hand, but within the image cluster, the active element of the interaction, what corresponds to the verb, is the pivot on which the meaning of the scene rests.

The construction of this type of visual phrase lies at the foundation of what increasingly appears to have been semasiographic visual notation. Moche's short visual statements, best categorized as configurational or presentational, corresponded to variable units of meaning capable of enlarging or amplifying

FIGURE 7.5. Drawing of a Prisoner Capture (drawing by Donna McClelland).

the narratives on which they were based. The ability of a pictorial code to do so is an important distinction between an iconography and a semasiography. Returning to Martin's observations, semasiography is differentiated from iconography by its ability to create and record new narratives; that is to say, it has discrete parts that can be combined, disassembled, and recombined to create new meanings.[19] The degree of facility with which a system can do so is linked to the kind and number of internally conventionalized elements it employs. Martin and others have noted that although semasiography lacks the flexibility and expressive depth to be a comprehensive communication system, it nonetheless functions well within certain kinds of contextually limited applications.[20] An important benefit of semasiography is its ability to excel in circumstances where an interpretive community plays an active role in supplying contextual data and constructing meaning within a broader cultural frame—just the sort of interpretive community formed by an oral society whose primary communication technology found its meaning in the reiteration and enactment of key myths and religious rituals.

Here, once again, comparisons to other indigenous American semasiographies are instructive. In Mixtec graphic notation, the figures are standardized: When used as narrative nuclei, their significances are indicated by a limited range of body postures, hand gestures, and the manipulation of significant objects; these include images of victors grasping the hair of their captives or facing figures displaying particular gestures. Remarking on their resemblance to Late Moche narrative depictions, Martin posits that the main difference between the two lies in the semantic role of the Mixtec image clusters, suggesting that the Mixtec figures are distinguished because they "begin to function like independent verbs in a statement" and noting too that the same analogy arises in Kubler's work on Teotihuacán semasiographic texts.[21]

FIGURE 7.6. The Revolt of the Objects, rollout drawing of fineline bottle (drawing by Donna McClelland).

Although Mixtec often concerns itself (in contrast to Moche) with lengthy genealogical recitations and calendrical signs, particular elements within Mixtec semasiography parallel what is evident in Moche, for example, the use of specific conventions of body posture, costume elements standardized to the point of becoming independent signs, and particular hand gestures and other visually leading devices intended to guide the "reading" of the figures. Perhaps most intriguing is the idea that some clusters of figures in semasiographies will begin to function as independent verb statements, because it is precisely these kinds of configurations that generate syntactic movement within Moche visual imagery, pushing it further toward a notational system.

Hybrid Presentational Syntax

When single emblems, abbreviated icons, or embedded signs are clustered within pictorial narrative structures, what follows is truly a mixed pictorial system. Approaching the constituent elements as configurations of sign clusters is perhaps useful, especially in cases where imagery is densely figured. The conventions of placement and spatial movement are populated by characters, which are themselves composed of indexically informed signs nested together and embedded within conventionalized storytelling formats. As an example, scenes like the Revolt of the Objects, which initially seem chaotic, tend to resolve into order when individual groupings are addressed as series of visual phrases (Figure 7.6). Clearly loaded with numerous compound icons and conventionalized elements, the scene has sparked various interpretations, none of which necessarily runs directly counter to the present assessment.

The scene provides ground for the analysis of presentational syntax in a complex narrative construction, precisely because of its intricacy. The story is told through a series of vignettes, each with a primary subject and one (or more) direct objects, linked by an action marker. These create the same sort of verb clauses mentioned by Martin in his analysis of Mixtec semasiographic

FIGURE 7.7.
The Revolt of the Objects, details of narrative clusters from rollout drawing of painted bottle: **(a)** Feline Warrior with captive belt(?); **(b)** Fox Warrior with captive nose ring and Priestess; **(c)** animated back flap with captive warrior; **(d)** Rayed Warrior Priest; **(e)** Feline Warrior with captive helmet, pectoral, and earflares; **(f)** Priestess gesturing to staves and weaving implements who bring captives, one of whom is part human, part deer; **(g)** Owl Warrior approached by animated sling and war club with captives (after drawing by Donna McClelland).

notation. The scene depicts a frantic battle, where clothing, weapons, and other objects are shown as animate beings struggling against human and anthropomorphic warriors. Painted in fineline technique onto a globular stirrup-spout bottle, several distinct cohorts are spread among three main visual foci. Three major characters, recognizable from the Warrior Narrative and Sacrifice Scene, command the dramatic action of these three areas, the Rayed Warrior Priest, the Priestess, and the Owl Warrior (Figure 7.7d, f–g).

Atop and alongside the stylized pyramid, the Owl Warrior (Figure 7.7g) and the Priestess (Figure 7.7f) meet with animated weaving implements, clothing, and weapons who forcibly drag captive human prisoners forward. The directionality of pose gives momentum to the sequences; meanwhile, the very specific hand gestures exchanged between the two leaders and the victorious animated object warriors seem to signal possession. These hand gestures are particularly conventionalized, as are other indicators of combat and capture. A series of combatant pairs, located through the vessel midsection, divide the lower region from the upper. In the upper areas, the battle appears to turn in favor of the Rayed Warrior Priest and his allied anthropomorphic warriors. Here, the animallike warriors take the animated objects as captives, while the fully arrayed Warrior Priest engages in an exchange with a seated figure, whose hand gestures, again, are highly conventionalized. The fact that the Priestess is shown twice lends credence to the idea that the activities occur over a period of time, depicting more than one episode or moment.

What is actually going on in this image is a matter of lively debate. The Revolt of the Objects has been interpreted as a depiction of an important mythological moment set in ancestral time.[22] Its name and some interpretations derive from events recorded in the colonial period *Huarochiri Manuscript*, where, according to the narrative, there was once a time when the Sun died and during the ensuing darkness, inanimate objects rose up against humans.[23] The stones banged against each other, mortars and grinding stones began to eat men, and domestic llamas began to herd humans. The story has been likened to a similar tale recounted in the *Popol Vuh*, a Maya creation story from Mesoamerica.[24] Some scholars take issue with these interpretations, pointing to the absence of particular characters (mortars, metates, pots, pans, llamas) and the abundance of militaristic elements (which are not strongly featured in the oral source versions), proposing alternative interpretations.[25]

More recently, the scene has been linked to a series of fineline depictions, which place the event within a longer narrative sequence and seem to indicate that the battle of the animated objects preceded a boat journey taken by a high-status female (apparently the Priestess).[26] Called the "Waved Spiral Narrative," the sequence concludes with a ritual presentation of a goblet, presumably containing the blood of the prisoners. Confusion arises, however, because this is not the same scene of blood sacrifice as shown in the more familiar Warrior Narrative and Presentation Scene. In those narratives, warfare and prisoner capture immediately preceded the procession of nude captives to the temple, where they were sacrificed. The divergent imagery has led to controversy about the meaning of the scene and to speculation that possibly more than one sacrifice narrative existed for the Moche.

This perplexing scene, while problematic, is nonetheless of service in a search for variable semantic units and syntactic structures. It is remarkable for the number and variety of visual devices it employs. Visible in it are pictorial conventions that serve to carry the story forward and oft-repeated visual phrases combined within a contiguous picture plane. Its conventions include arms and legs that animate; headdress and raiment that indicate status; grasped forelock and inverted war club to show defeat; architectural structure, flora, and fauna to show location; and eminent rays to indicate power. Each one of a specific cast of characters participates as a primary subject of an action clause, and in at least one instance, the role of a character is shown as variable.

FIGURE 7.8. Confrontation of Bean Warriors and Deer Warriors (drawing by Donna McClelland).

If the Revolt of the Objects depicts a culturally familiar myth about inanimate objects that arose through supernatural means, then the various pictorial elements, the nose rings, war clubs, spindles, and other animated objects, function horizontally, as secondary characters to the primary narrative. The animation of these objects, represented by the addition of arms and legs, functions as a semasiographic convention. If, instead, they represent visual abbreviations of particular persons, whose actual physical likenesses are omitted, then the image perhaps signals a different battle narrative. Under this proposal, the animated objects both identify and make indexical reference to particular rank, origin, or affiliation based on information signaled by the various elements of costume and accoutrement.

Either way, multiple action clauses, numerous small nuclei focusing on the act of taking prisoners (presumably for purposes of sacrifice), are key to the syntactic momentum of the depiction. They push it forward by means of very specific conventions. Various internal pointers and gestures make clear the nature of the interaction and the direction of movement. The image clusters function as small visual phrases, imparting meaning in a semiautonomous manner. They float in a pictorial space, ungrounded by realistic conventions of landscape. Instead, the internal syntax of the semantic units (the image clusters) guides the viewer's gaze toward the primary focal points (on one side of the bottle, the Rayed Warrior Priest, and on the other, the anthropomorphic Owl Warrior who stands atop the pyramid).

In this composition, the syntactic structure of the visual system allowed for variable configurations of semantic units, emphasizing that any given phrase might combine different kinds of signs. For example, the captive (part human, part deer), led by the animated weapon in Figure 7.7f, is nude and is led by a rope, but his status is additionally clarified through an indexical reference to the Deer Hunt, a deeply elaborate narrative sequence in its own right (Plate 14). In it, the elite hunt for deer functions as a metaphoric reference to the quest for sacrificial captives.[27] The theme holds a definite undercurrent related to political legitimation, and it is not unusual to see visual indexes making reference to this (Figure 7.8). Viewers familiar with the metaphor would immediately recognize the reference, even as brief as it is in the Revolt of the Objects rendition.

Enumerating each visual phrase helps to identify what elements function as internal modifiers (informants and indexes) and which signal syntactic conventions. Not all animated objects presented elsewhere in Moche art necessarily belong to this particular narrative. Nor are all anthropomorphic creatures necessarily supernatural beings. As one of the more complex Moche images, the scene employs an impressive selection of semantic and syntactic conventions, as well as iconography thoroughly mixed with clusters of abbreviations, indexes, and other kinds of signs, seemingly compounded one atop another. The scene, although highly complex and intent on narrative depiction, does not escape the strongly emblematic conventions typical of Moche art. Its multitude of small characters forms a series of clusters, each comprising its own subject–verb–object sign configuration. The meaning of the overall event is, thus, constructed of various action phrases, which the viewer strings together by means of spatial conventions, gestures, and compositional elements, constructed in a way that exemplifies Moche's unique combination of hybrid presentational syntax, indexing and abbreviation, and pictorial narrative structure.

Commentary

Moche pictorial art utilized compound icons embedded with various modifiers (symbols, locators, informants, and indexes). Internal order for most visual imagery appears to have resulted from conventionalized components, derived from horizontal and vertical associations and from what were possibly linguistically motivated signs (logographs). When shown as individual icons, images derived meaning through indexical relationships with larger narrative themes. In compositions having multiple characters, visual syntax tended toward dynamism, with visual sequences ordered as single or multiple clusters of signs configured around active elements of interaction.

The presence of action markers in the visual corpus, either as internal pointers or as outright semantic units, goes far toward indicating syntactic structures. Configurations of abbreviations and icons were embedded within emblematic and sequential compositions. Such structures are most evident in the more elaborate narrative compositions but are also identifiable in shorter visual phrases. The internal syntactic arrangements of emblematic configurations generally differ from those of overtly narrative structures, but in Moche visual culture the two formats are fundamentally linked, overlapping to such a high degree that the respective modes of operation cannot be separated—a distinctive characteristic of Moche visual communication.

Within the image clusters, active gestures, the visual equivalent of verbs, were the focal points on which meaning and syntactic motion rested. Visual phrases containing these active elements provided direction for what increasingly appears to have been semasiographic visual notation. Moche's short visual statements corresponded to variable units of meaning capable of enlarging or amplifying the narratives on which they were based. The ability of a pictorial code to do so is an important distinction between an iconography and a semasiography.

Moche visual vocabulary was capable of creating and recording new narratives by means of combining and disassembling variable iconographic units.

Semasiographic notational forms, which depend on the cultural fluency of the viewer, find their syntax in spatial patterning, more so than do fully phonetic forms, which rely on the specialized training of the reader. This factor may have had some bearing on the retention of emblematic iconography, even when other factors increasingly favored more linear compositions for the conveyance of complex narratives. That a single icon could retain its significance, even when far removed from any obviously narrative context, reaffirms the idea of a widespread ideological underpinning for the artistic corpus. Taken in this light, it is not surprising that Moche themes never seem quite complete; artists could add any number of indexical referents and iconic informants. The individual components of various narrative phrases were vertically telescoped to progressive levels of abbreviation, each retaining resonance within the overall construct. Composed of clusters of variable pictures and signs, the visual vocabulary represents an open-ended semasiography, for which total "completeness" would not ever have been possible.

The analogy to spoken language falls short, however, when it comes to the expectation that visual syntax will directly echo speech patterns into the realm of indexes and informants, even though the chains of associations evident in progressive levels of abbreviation and telescoping indicate the conceptual basis on which symbolic allusions and indexical signs may have been based. The linguistic structure of Muchic suggests that it is reasonable to predict that certain kinds of markers would be needed to convey narratives in visual form, especially if the content was an already abbreviated phrase. Specifically, Muchic's linguistic predilection for noun substantives made active through suffixing suggests that visual phrases will also find a similar disposition in the form of visual clusters of objects with action markers. This was perhaps an organizational structure habitual to Moche artists as Muchic speakers. Direct syntactic ligatures present in speech disappear, however, when indexes transcend from one reference framework to another. Often several indexes refer to the same signified, and the order of their occurrence in the discourse is not linguistically tied—that is, not reflective of sentence structures—nor is that order always pertinent. Although complex narrative scenes sometimes incorporate sequential storytelling devices, within shorter visual phrases, the syntactic order tends to be variable and clustered around indicators of primary actions.

Thus, Moche's mixed visual system was neither strictly linguistically informed nor purely pictorial. Rightly categorized as visual notation, it included elements of both but conveyed meaning according to rules other than those associated with either. Moche pictorial syntax operated in a simultaneously horizontal and vertically layered manner, involving clusters of compound icons whose characters were themselves composed of well-understood signs. In a nonlettered society such as the Moche, where visualization was integrally linked to oral and performative transmission, graphic imagery was a key element in the success of the communication strategy.

CHAPTER 8

Concluding Comments

This study represents a multidisciplinary approach to understanding Moche art and visual culture. Adopting a strategy of external and internal analyses, the preceding chapters integrate studies of Moche culture and monumental arts, the production of pottery, and discussion of discursive forms to address the larger cultural influences shaping Moche visual communication. Investigations of mold inscriptions, Muchic linguistics, and presentational syntax in Moche iconography continue the analysis, with the goal of identifying instances of pictorial codification. The existence of such a graphic system is the premise on which the study operates and the thesis by which these disparate investigations are united.

Moche Visual Culture

The logic of Moche iconography is seen here as underlain by cohesive social groups, artists, occupational specialists, or other elites whose common bonds and perceptions amounted to what constituted textual communities.[1] All evidence points to a moment in which we can assume a degree of cultural consistency, united by an overarching ideology and social narrative. This is reflected in the traits of material remains found throughout Moche territory, despite time and distance. Shared beliefs were surely transferred through performance and retelling of oral narratives in communal observations of ritual events and through the broadcast and reiteration of those events in various visual forms. In such a milieu, mutual knowledge of narratives, what some call oral texts, resulted in a collective cultural base, understood to varying degrees by all members of society. The cultural matrix, held together through a superstructure of agreed meaning, was generated and reinforced by social events and socioeconomic structures. Specific art, artifacts, and ritualized objects were key elements in the mechanics of how social memory was constructed; monumental and portable arts occupied complementary niches in the overall fabric of communication exchange.

Monumental iconography, especially in its relationship to portable arts, demonstrates an undeniable cultural predisposition to pictorial communication. Elite Moche monuments were the central foci of important political and religious activities on which the iconography of smaller, more widely distributed art forms were based. Monumental proclamations of ideology and political legitimation, seen on oversized multilevel pyramids, spoke to the society in ways that were apparently top downward, as emblematic images aimed to subject classes below. Patronized by elites, such constructions communicated down the social hierarchy, as well as across horizontal social levels between elites who were, perhaps, competing with each other in various inter- and intravalley exchanges.

Ceramics used for liturgical practices were encoded with signs of ideology and references to ritual and were distributed far and wide. They functioned as vehicles for communication of narrative, even though the successful transmission of information required mediation. When distanced from temple contexts, iconography metonymically keyed to the larger religious body depended on a mnemonic function and level of visual literacy not necessarily evenly held by all members of all communities. In translating the imagery from monumental to portable contexts, therefore, elements of narrative continuity provided by architectural structures and the liturgical sequences associated with them must necessarily have been replaced by human agents, whose ideological knowledge was required to fill the void.

Small-scale arts helped to reinforce social integration through pictorially referring to overarching beliefs and through the performative responses dictated by their actual physical forms. Ritualized arts encoded messages about ideologically bound social narratives while simultaneously serving as mnemonic prompts for those who enacted that ideology. Some images were more explicit than others. Their mnemonic value was bound up in each vessel's basic formal structures and ordered sequences of picturing or notational imagery and was keyed to ritual practices effected by individual practitioners.

The specialization of crafts, ceramic arts in particular, resulted in the clustering of artisans into what were most likely endogamous groups. It is a scenario strongly supported by various strands of ethnographic and archaeological evidence. Such an arrangement would, in turn, allow the development of script communities—what could, in effect, become a mechanism for the consistent transmission and interpretation of meaningful signs related to an overarching social narrative text—left in place for a sustained period of time.

Ceramic production technology relied heavily on the modularization of recurrent themes and elements, as shown in the workshop examples presented here. Advances in mold technology were most likely driven by a desire to convey imagery accurately. Mold use served the purpose of faster production, but more importantly, it allowed for the control of key iconographic features and specific esoteric knowledge. Patronage of small-scale ceramic arts would simultaneously serve various political and religious functions, including the demands brought by feasting and social reciprocity, while generally publicizing and reinforcing temple events and the elites responsible for those events.

Mold technology, elaborated here through an analysis of workshop data, points up two interrelated aspects of how visual information was constructed. First, artists thought of visual phrases as set iconic packages, capable of being distilled into discreet elements that could then be configured in various ways (e.g., mix-and-match use of multiple mold-made elements). Second, they were conscious of doing so, made evident by the use of notational inscriptions on mold exteriors. Such markings were deliberately set for the purpose of transferring information autodidactically. The fact that many inscriptions bear little or no relationship to the subject matter of the mold is further indication that workshop artists were well schooled in a mutually understood system of visual notational signs.

That artists were members of a pictorially literate script community also speaks to some degree of elevated social status. Highly specialized workshops apparently enjoyed patronage in the form of provisioning, and master artists were possessors of special esoteric knowledge in the form of visual signs keyed to larger ideological narratives. The same level of esoteric knowledge is evident in the construction of mural and frieze iconography at the major monuments. Portable and monumental arts share remarkable consistency in terms of how compound images are configured, and the inclusion of sacrificial elements into the friezes suggests that at least some artists were active participants in the construction of social narrative at the public level.

A high degree of standardization and abbreviation attests to the idea that Moche imagery was more than just generally symbolic. As a cohesive iconography, it constitutes an important example of a mixed notational form, whose presentational syntax included embedded elements with conventionalized meanings. Spoken language must have informed the graphic system to some degree. This is implied in the tendency toward nominative clusters and verbal abbreviations (as a syntactic structure), as well as some suggestion of intermittent use of rebus devices (creation of semantic units). The relationship between Moche verbal and visual domains was undoubtedly mediative, as language functioned to interpret and translate larger societal actions enacted elsewhere. Simultaneously, the relationship seems to have included many generative elements, in the sense that narrative language, words, or phrases directly led to the generation of specific pictorial units and repetitive visual phrases. It seems probable that a number of logographs existed, embedded as signs within larger pictorial structures, although scant linguistic evidence renders this point inconclusive.

Images were to be read, however, in sequences that were not necessarily linear. Within a vessel format, after the vessel's basic vertical orientation was established, a composition could be viewed in any order, a few visual phrases at a time. The viewer's starting point was rarely an issue because the entire message was composed of compressed iconic phrases, each expressing a selected aspect of a larger narrative. The visual compositions were discursively organized along two main conceptual axes: *horizontal/sequential* (as in narrative structures) and *vertical/iconic* (as in nested symbolic indexes). The range of complex relationships characterizing Moche iconography can be likened to literary tropes in some ways. Vertical telescoping, for example, constitutes a form of visual synecdoche; the connections between full and ever-more distilled elaborations of characters and their accouterments are easy to see. The indexes make specific references without the presence of the entire figure. Because of the heavy dependence on stereotyped expression and mnemonic visualization as a means of remembering, the use of periphrasic tropes is relatively common in oral cultures.[2] Their employment in Moche art is evident in the form of vertical indexes and abbreviations. The system's visual syntax can thus be characterized as a type of "presentational symbolism" or embedded text, that is to say, as a semasiography (or pictography) made of emblematic visual phrases, often compounded and layered with variable modifying elements, arranged as clustered configurations and loosely ligatured sequences.

The narrative structures within these image clusters rely on aggregates of icons arranged as action phrases. Iconic statements become action phrases when given animating modifiers. Each small nucleus has an internal logic and semantic units, which may include configurational arrangement of icons, indexes, or other kinds of signs, some perhaps phonetically keyed. The larger, more elaborate scenes take on narrative meaning when nuclei are considered as points in a story—the exact sequence of the story is determined, however, by the person doing the interpretation. As is characteristic of semasiography, the specific telling of any given story is determined by the reader (the human agent). Semasiographic notation depends on a high level of social embeddedness, in this case oral transmission and performance of ritual. Later versions and artistic trends in Moche visual arts (fineline painting from San José de Moro as a particular case in point) have the most determined use of conventionalized pictorial devices designed to signal the direction of the correct narrative sequence. This supports the idea that artists (and informed patrons) were increasingly concerned with recounting lengthy and elaborate renditions of key religious rituals and ideological narratives and that the repertory of visual images had reached a level of development and internal organization that could support a growing complexity of visual discourse.

The differentiation between images found in ceramic imagery and in monumental arts points out an important divergence in how visual imagery was intended to function. It is quite clear that both artistic genres utilized the same iconography and were underlain by mutually shared cultural beliefs. It is also evident that specialists, fully conversant with the full range of pictorial conventions, and certainly known to each other, directed the iconographies of both. Yet the majority of monumental images are boldly emblematic. Examples of narratively structured murals and friezes are rare by comparison (the Complex Themes at Huaca de La Luna and Cao Viejo, the Sacrifice Scene at Pañamarca, and the Revolt of the Objects at Huaca de La Luna being four primary examples). The oversized images of the Decapitator, the Prisoner Procession, the arachnids, and others have little or no internally signaled syntactic relationship with each other. Instead, their "reading" was determined by the relationship of the viewer to the architecture and by the sequence of ritual performance conducted there. In monumental arts, the chain of events, punctuated by the architectural configuration, shaped the narrative. The contextual experience of the viewers and participants supplied the cultural nexus into which the visual signs were embedded. The situation differed significantly from that of portable arts, whose meaning was derived from their function as liturgical objects and whose legitimacy was invoked through the retelling of the narratives that they signaled.

The thematic approach allows us to understand that Moche visual images are based on long-standing cultural narratives. It works best when narrative remains constant over time; with fixed themes, all iconography, from simple to complex, will necessarily be related to the (re)presentation of fundamentally unchanging stories related to gods, myths, legends, and morality tales, put forward in symbolic iconography. Later Moche art, however, began to move away from single-icon representation, seemingly in search of more self-contained narrative with more abstract systems of signs. In the face of change over time, therefore, the approach must serve as a valuable starting point but cannot serve as a final answer to decryption.

The social pressures driving the evolution seem likely to be associated with politics and patronage. The Moche pictorial system functioned within a limited context to communicate shared ideology. It was created by specialists who were proficient in assembling the internal structure of the visual phrases through vertical indexing not necessarily in linear order. If Moche elite were concerned about political legitimation through public display of sacrifice and liturgy, as it seems that they were, then the addition of a widely disbursed pictorial system noticing their deeds would surely be endorsed by them and worthy of patronage. Whereas artists may not have been overtly manipulating imagery to suit particular agendas, it bears notice that certain kinds of images, characters, and themes, such as portrait vessels, the Rayed Warrior Priest, and the Warrior Narrative, appear with greater frequency in later periods.[3] These later additions appear to reflect subtle changes to prevalent, well-established narratives.

An important element separating visual notation from pictorial representation is the ability for the constituent semantic units to be disassembled and reconfigured in different ways, to create variable meanings. Changeable meaning is a key element for creating new discourse. Thus, a dynamically changing visual corpus not only will repeat narrative but has the potential to compose or incorporate new narrative elements. If Moche themes were purely representational, then they would concern themselves with repetition only. And indeed, there is a significant level of repetition in the iconographic vocabulary. The evidence suggests, however, that by at least mid to later Moche (Moche Phase IV), artists had begun to manipulate familiar visual phrases in various ways, to achieve greater elaboration of indexical references and narrative content. Judging by archaeological evidence from later monuments and workshop production, it was an artistic trend that held sway for several centuries.

It is unknown why the Moche pictorial tradition did not continue its development. It seems clear that during the transitional Middle Horizon, between the Moche and Chimu periods, sometime after A.D. 800, a radical transformation of some kind occurred in coastal society, one that precluded the continuation of this type of communication technology. It has been suggested that political collapse occurred, possibly linked to environmental stress, devastating El Niño events, or conquest. It is beyond the scope of this study to draw any conclusions. The visual record is, however, in agreement with the archaeological, in the sense that strong change did occur. Monumental architecture and urban configurations reflect a significantly altered emphasis during the Moche to Chimu transition. Monumental murals and friezes became less overtly pictorial, with Chimu friezes increasingly repetitive, geometric, and abstract. The monuments themselves increasingly included administrative configurations, such as *audiencias* and storage chambers.

Changes in iconographic content seem to signal accompanying changes in ideology. Whereas certain kinds of imagery survived the transition into Chimu times, other kinds of imagery did not. Very few of the familiar cast of Moche characters continued into the Chimu period.[4] In general, those iconographic features that were retained reflect some of the oldest and most broadly accepted of Andean beliefs and customs. These include the feline/blood sacrifice metaphor, the ritual use of *chicha* and *Spondylus*, the institution of ancestor worship (with its conception of an afterlife and reciprocal interchange between the dead and the living), the institution of social stratification (which allowed elites to enjoy status-dictated burial sites and ride in litters), and the association of hunchbacks, owls, and religious specialists as mediators to the spirit world.

The technology of ceramic manufacture became less fluid. Specifically, there was an abandonment of fineline painting, complex narrative, and portrait images in ceramics. Ritual vessels were increasingly formed entirely in large molds with significantly less appliqué work, reducing the possibility of creating variable compositions. The change in technology perhaps represents an alteration in the patronage arrangement between ceramists and the elite. A disruption in patronage would surely alter the mechanism for transferring information from one generation of artists to another, thus compromising specialized textual communities.

Moche visual notation seems to have served a purpose so specialized that it did not find application apart from its role in religious practice, in the sense that it was not used, for example, to make mathematical calculations or apparently to record genealogical descent, financial transactions, or calendrical dates. What slim evidence on these points survives points to the idea of record keeping as performed by separate mechanisms, for example, bean counting, marked adobes, and later on, *khipus*. It seems likely, therefore, that a significant change in the political and religious structure of the society had a direct impact on this visual system, so directly keyed to the performance of a very specific liturgical remembrance.

Future Directions

Although it ultimately did not survive, Moche visual culture did flourish for at least eight hundred years on the North Coast of Peru. In those centuries, the iconography enjoyed great consistency, even in the face of changes that occurred over time. This remarkable visual tradition developed to the point of semasiographic notation, one of very few ancient American examples to do so. As such, various lines of research are suggested by the results detailed here.

Chief among them, the relationship between portable and monumental arts deserves further inquiry, to pursue the hypothesis that Moche visual imagery was fundamentally linked to ritual events staged at monumental pyramids located throughout the Moche region. As the primary social matrices on which Moche visual culture rested, the monuments' familiar icons were dedicated to the veneration of blood sacrifice rituals, directly glorifying the participants and self-reflexively making reference to events that took place there. And yet discrepancies between the iconography of monumentalized pageantry and what is suggested in complex narratives point to a disjuncture where differences in iconographic content may perhaps be profitably exploited.

Also, particularly stubborn questions remain regarding the use of specialized liturgical ceramics. Answers to unresolved questions about them may well reside in the contextual data provided by archaeological fieldwork, which gives rise to an ever-increasing body of information in need of synthesis. Because strategies of communication are multisystemic, all manner of production technology, household and workshop economy, and allied elite arts played a role in how the iconography functioned, the agendas that it served, and the meanings it evoked.

The evidence in favor of a fledgling notational form in use among a certain segment of Moche society calls for further study. Preliminary results are tentative, especially for the most complex and value-laden scenes; however, configurational analysis of presentational syntax seems to signal a methodological approach that is alternative to what has gone before. Moche iconography routinely employs iconic elements whose syntactic correlates may or may not be included within the immediate visual space; these are the indexes and informants to which semiotics refers. Additional formal analysis of indexical and informational elements present in iconic clusters, interpreted as phrases, may bring additional insight into the workings of Moche's compound references. In isolating them, a body of recognizable notational conventions will accrue over time.

It seems likely, as well, that some visual anomalies are not, in fact, indexes but, rather, logographic elements. These could be linguistically motivated, as suggested by the homonymic correspondence of *crab/sun/xiăŋ* in Muchic language, or conceptually motivated, conventionalized signs, as proposed with the *huaca/macyæc* correspondence (both examples described previously). The rudimentary investigation of Muchic language presented here signals a starting point for further investigations in the linguistic arena.

The conventionalized elements of Moche visual art invite comparison to other ancient American semasiographic traditions and to revised understandings of literacy. The present study advances a theory of proto-literacy seeking to make a contribution to what is known with regard to the rise of literacy and visual communication in early societies. Admitting Moche art to an increasing circle of ancient American mixed notational forms, such as those from the Mixtec and Teotihuacán, will suggest new models for comparison and the means of identifying mechanisms of conventionalization.

In studies of ancient indigenous American graphic notations, the distinction between glottographic and semasiographic notation is blurred, making clear the need of a fresh classificatory schema. New World written forms seem to mix elements of both visual systems in ways that do not easily fit the models as they have been articulated. Shifting paradigms in studies of writing and notation offer an interpretive framework in which to situate visual forms that, like the Moche system, convey meaning in neither purely linguistic nor purely pictorial ways. Visual arts whose purpose is to graphically communicate specific messages reside in an area that shares, to greater or lesser degrees, elements of both but also systematically achieves distinctive purposes, through structures and modes of operation tailored to unique demands.

Considering Moche visual art under an umbrella of semasiography challenges the paradigm of how visual culture arose in ancient America and allows a better vantage point from which to study this and other similar discursive forms that were simultaneously pictorial and notational. Moche's tendency toward iconic imagery is well known, yet the tactic presented here represents a new approach to a difficult problem. Through addressing the visual corpus in terms of notation, suggesting areas where signs and syntax are apparent, Moche takes its place among larger inquiries related to pictography and notation in the ancient Americas.

APPENDIX A

ANALYSIS AND CROSS-TABULATION OF CERAMIC FORM AND IMAGE
FREQUENCIES (CERRO MAYAL, 1992 FIELD SEASON)

Appendix A. Incidence of Iconographic types and Ceramic Form types, Cerro Mayal workshop.

Image Group	Image Desc	basin	bottle	cooker/canchero	florero/flaring vase	grater	jar/bottle: body fragment	jar/olla	kero/straight sided florero	lid	other	oval cup (no handle)	undetermined vessel	Group 1 Total	base: flat	"base: narrow, flat, heeled"	base: ring	handle: stirrup	handle: strap	lug/pierced lug	Group 2 total
0	N/A (none)	20	18	4	28	7	17	143	1	24	9	1	5	277	1	1	11	55	2	0	70
	No Imagery (Group 0)	**20**	**18**	**4**	**28**	**7**	**17**	**143**	**1**	**24**	**9**	**1**	**5**	**277**	**1**	**1**	**11**	**55**	**2**	**0**	**70**
1	Angry Moche Man	0	21	0	0	0	0	1	0	0	0	0	0	22	0	0	0	0	0	0	0
	Cacheton face	0	0	0	0	0	0	0	0	0	0	0	0	0	0	0	0	0	0	0	0
	Split-lip face	0	0	0	0	0	0	0	0	0	0	0	0	0	0	0	0	0	0	0	0
	Man with no lips	0	0	0	0	0	0	2	0	0	0	0	0	2	0	0	0	0	0	0	0
	Smiling face	0	2	0	0	0	0	0	0	0	0	0	0	2	0	0	0	0	0	0	0
	Wrinkle Face	0	0	0	0	0	9	6	0	0	0	0	0	15	0	0	0	0	0	0	0
	Other face	0	4	0	0	0	1	11	1	0	1	0	0	18	0	0	0	0	0	0	0
	Musician	0	0	0	0	0	0	0	0	0	0	0	0	0	0	0	0	0	0	0	0
	Costume/Headdress	0	0	0	0	0	0	3	0	0	0	0	0	3	0	0	0	0	0	0	0
	Female: clothed	0	0	0	0	0	0	0	0	0	0	0	0	0	0	0	0	0	0	0	0
	Female: nude	0	0	0	0	0	0	0	0	0	0	0	0	0	0	0	0	0	0	0	0
	Male: prisoner	0	0	0	0	0	0	1	0	0	0	0	0	1	0	0	0	0	0	0	0
	Male: warrior	0	0	0	0	0	0	1	0	0	0	0	0	1	0	0	0	0	0	0	0
	body part: face/head	0	0	0	0	0	3	6	0	0	1	0	0	10	0	0	0	0	0	0	0
	body part: arm/hand/torso	0	0	0	0	0	4	1	0	0	0	0	0	5	0	0	0	0	0	0	0
	body part: leg/foot/lower body	0	0	0	0	0	1	3	0	0	1	0	0	5	0	0	0	0	0	0	0
	body part: unspecified	0	0	0	0	0	2	1	0	0	0	0	0	3	0	0	0	0	0	0	0
	misc. other human	0	0	0	0	0	5	3	0	0	6	0	0	14	0	0	0	0	0	0	0
	Humans (Group 1)	**0**	**27**	**0**	**0**	**0**	**25**	**39**	**1**	**0**	**9**	**0**	**0**	**101**	**0**	**0**	**0**	**0**	**0**	**0**	**0**
2	Bird (except Owl)	0	0	0	1	0	1	0	0	0	0	0	0	2	0	0	0	0	0	0	0
	Crab	0	0	0	0	0	3	0	0	0	0	0	0	3	0	0	0	0	0	0	0
	Feline	0	0	0	0	0	1	3	0	0	0	0	0	4	0	0	0	0	0	0	0
	Fox Snarling	0	0	0	0	0	0	1	0	0	0	0	0	1	0	0	0	0	0	0	0
	Fanged Fox/Lizard	0	0	0	0	0	0	2	0	0	0	0	0	2	0	0	0	0	0	0	0
	Frog	0	0	0	0	0	0	0	0	0	0	0	0	0	0	0	0	0	0	0	0
	Hand Modeled Animal	0	0	0	0	0	0	1	0	0	10	0	0	11	0	0	0	0	0	1	1
	Lizard	1	0	0	0	0	3	2	0	0	0	0	0	6	0	0	0	0	0	0	0
	Monkey	0	0	0	0	0	0	0	0	0	1	0	0	1	0	0	0	0	0	0	0
	Owl/Fanged Owl	0	1	0	0	0	1	1	0	0	2	0	0	5	0	0	0	0	0	0	0
	Snake	0	0	0	1	0	2	0	1	0	3	0	0	7	0	0	0	0	0	0	0
	Undetermined animal	0	0	0	0	0	4	3	0	0	1	0	0	8	0	0	0	0	0	0	0
	Animals (Group 2)	**1**	**1**	**0**	**2**	**0**	**15**	**13**	**1**	**0**	**17**	**0**	**0**	**50**	**0**	**0**	**0**	**0**	**0**	**1**	**1**
3	dots	1	0	0	8	0	5	1	0	0	0	0	0	15	0	0	0	0	0	0	0
	escalonados	3	4	0	25	0	1	3	0	0	0	0	0	36	0	0	0	0	0	0	0
	Step fret/snake ("la liza")	0	0	0	0	0	0	0	2	0	0	0	0	2	0	0	0	0	0	0	0
	lines	0	0	0	0	0	8	4	1	0	0	0	0	13	0	0	0	0	0	0	0
	mixture or other motif	1	0	0	7	0	9	6	0	1	0	1	0	25	0	0	0	0	0	0	0
	rolling waves	0	0	0	1	0	0	2	7	0	0	0	0	10	0	0	0	0	0	0	0
	scallops	0	0	0	22	0	0	1	0	0	0	0	0	23	0	0	0	0	0	0	0
	stripes	1	0	0	6	0	3	20	0	0	0	0	0	30	0	0	0	0	2	0	2
	Vegetable or Plant	0	0	0	0	0	3	1	0	0	0	0	0	4	0	0	0	0	0	0	0
	Water Snake - repeating	0	0	0	3	0	0	0	0	0	0	0	0	3	0	0	0	0	0	0	0
	Repeat Motifs (Group 3)	**6**	**4**	**0**	**72**	**0**	**29**	**38**	**10**	**1**	**0**	**1**	**0**	**161**	**0**	**0**	**0**	**0**	**2**	**0**	**2**
4	Dance of the Dead	0	9	0	0	0	0	0	0	0	0	0	0	9	0	0	0	0	0	0	0
	Deer/Deer Hunt	1	0	0	0	0	2	0	0	0	6	0	0	9	0	0	0	0	0	0	0
	Fishing/Sea monster	0	0	0	1	0	1	0	0	0	0	0	0	2	0	0	0	0	0	0	0
	Flower/Marsh/Heron	0	0	0	6	0	0	0	0	0	0	0	0	6	0	0	0	0	0	0	0
	Ribbon Dance	0	0	0	0	0	0	0	0	0	0	0	0	0	0	0	0	0	0	0	0
	Other Complex Scene	0	3	0	0	0	4	0	1	0	0	0	0	8	0	0	0	0	0	0	0
	Scenes (Group 4)	**1**	**12**	**0**	**7**	**0**	**7**	**0**	**1**	**0**	**6**	**0**	**0**	**34**	**0**	**0**	**0**	**0**	**0**	**0**	**0**
5	Other	0	1	0	0	0	8	11	2	0	13	0	0	35	0	0	0	0	0	0	0
	Unrecognized Motif	0	1	0	0	0	45	3	1	0	2	0	1	53	0	0	0	0	0	0	0
	Misc. Imagery (Group 5)	**0**	**2**	**0**	**0**	**0**	**53**	**14**	**3**	**0**	**15**	**0**	**1**	**88**	**0**	**0**	**0**	**0**	**0**	**0**	**0**
	Grand Total	**28**	**64**	**4**	**109**	**7**	**146**	**247**	**17**	**25**	**50**	**8**	**6**	**711**	**1**	**1**	**11**	**57**	**2**	**1**	**73**
	% of total	10.47%	3.35%	0.21%	5.71%	0.37%	7.65%	12.94%	0.89%	1.31%	2.62%	0.42%	0.31%	37.24%	0.05%	0.05%	0.58%	2.99%	0.10%	0.05%	3.82%
	total with imagery	8	46	0	81	0	129	104	16	1	41	7	1	434	0	0	0	2	0	1	3
	% of total with imagery	0.54%	3.12%	0.00%	5.50%	0.00%	8.75%	7.06%	1.09%	0.07%	2.78%	0.47%	0.07%	29.44%	0.00%	0.00%	0.00%	0.14%	0.00%	0.07%	0.20%

Appendix A

Chart showing cross-tabulation of Form and Image frequency.

Figures Group 3			Musical Group 4					Specialty forms Group 5							Applique Group 6			Mold Group 7				
figurine: hollow	figurine: solid	Group 3 total	rattle handle	rattle pod (chamber)	trumpet	whistle	Group 4 total	bead	miniature vessel	spindle whorl	spoon	turnette	Group 5 total	jar neck applique	modeled applique element	Group 6 total	mold: whole or fragment	Group 7 total	Grand Total	% of total with iconography (1474ac)	% of subgroup
0	0	0	4	5	2	0	11	2	6	21	23	13	65	1	0	1	11	11	435	n/a	n/a
0	0	0	4	5	2	0	11	2	6	21	23	13	65	1	0	1	11	11	435	n/a	n/a
0	0	0	0	0	0	0	0	0	0	0	0	0	0	0	0	0	9	9	31	2.10%	4.11%
0	0	0	0	0	0	0	0	0	0	0	0	0	0	10	1	11	0	0	11	0.75%	1.46%
0	0	0	0	0	0	0	0	0	0	0	0	0	0	3	1	4	0	0	4	0.27%	0.53%
0	0	0	0	0	0	0	0	0	0	0	0	0	0	2	0	2	1	1	5	0.34%	0.66%
0	0	0	0	0	0	0	0	0	0	0	0	0	0	2	0	2	0	0	4	0.27%	0.53%
0	0	0	0	0	0	0	0	0	0	0	0	0	0	1	1	2	5	5	22	1.49%	2.91%
27	11	38	0	1	0	0	1	0	0	0	0	0	0	15	7	22	40	40	119	8.07%	15.76%
1	8	9	0	0	0	1	1	0	0	0	0	0	0	0	0	0	7	7	17	1.15%	2.25%
7	14	21	0	0	0	2	2	0	0	0	0	0	0	0	2	2	5	5	33	2.24%	4.37%
34	57	91	0	0	0	0	0	1	0	0	0	0	1	0	0	0	14	14	106	7.19%	14.04%
5	32	37	0	0	0	0	0	3	0	0	0	0	3	0	0	0	5	5	45	3.05%	5.96%
0	0	0	0	0	0	0	0	0	0	0	0	0	0	0	0	0	1	1	2	0.14%	0.26%
9	17	26	0	0	0	2	2	1	0	0	0	0	1	0	1	1	4	4	35	2.37%	4.64%
31	22	53	0	0	0	0	0	5	0	0	0	0	5	1	0	1	21	21	90	6.11%	11.92%
3	3	6	0	0	0	0	0	0	0	0	0	0	0	0	2	2	8	8	21	1.42%	2.78%
16	7	23	0	0	0	0	0	0	0	0	0	0	0	0	0	0	8	8	36	2.44%	4.77%
75	7	82	0	0	0	0	0	0	0	0	0	0	0	0	0	0	5	5	90	6.11%	11.92%
5	24	29	0	0	0	0	0	6	0	0	0	0	6	2	0	2	33	33	84	5.70%	11.13%
213	202	415	0	1	0	5	6	16	0	0	0	0	16	36	15	51	166	166	755	51.22%	100.00%
0	0	0	0	0	0	0	0	0	0	0	2	0	2	0	4	4	13	13	21	1.42%	9.50%
0	0	0	0	0	0	0	0	0	0	0	0	0	0	0	0	0	1	1	4	0.27%	1.81%
0	0	0	0	0	0	0	0	1	0	0	0	0	1	6	10	16	4	4	25	1.70%	11.31%
0	0	0	0	0	0	0	0	0	0	0	0	0	0	6	10	16	1	1	18	1.22%	8.14%
0	0	0	0	0	0	0	0	0	0	0	0	0	0	14	8	22	4	4	28	1.90%	12.67%
0	0	0	0	0	0	0	0	0	0	0	0	0	0	0	1	1	2	2	3	0.20%	1.36%
0	0	0	0	0	0	0	0	0	0	0	0	1	1	0	2	2	1	1	16	1.09%	7.24%
0	0	0	0	0	0	0	0	0	0	0	0	0	0	0	3	3	4	4	13	0.88%	5.88%
0	0	0	0	0	0	1	1	0	0	0	0	0	0	3	4	7	2	2	11	0.75%	4.98%
0	2	2	0	0	0	0	0	1	0	0	0	0	1	9	6	15	7	7	30	2.04%	13.57%
0	0	0	1	3	0	0	4	0	0	0	0	0	0	0	5	5	6	6	22	1.49%	9.95%
0	0	0	0	0	0	0	0	0	0	0	0	0	0	0	7	7	15	15	30	2.04%	13.57%
0	2	2	1	3	0	1	5	2	0	0	3	0	5	38	60	98	60	60	221	14.99%	100.00%
0	0	0	0	0	0	0	0	0	0	0	0	0	0	0	0	0	0	0	15	1.02%	6.94%
0	0	0	0	0	0	0	0	0	0	0	0	0	0	0	0	0	3	3	39	2.65%	18.06%
0	0	0	0	3	0	0	3	0	0	0	0	0	0	0	0	0	5	5	10	0.68%	4.63%
0	0	0	0	0	0	0	0	0	0	0	0	0	0	0	0	0	0	0	13	0.88%	6.02%
0	0	0	0	0	0	0	0	0	1	0	0	0	1	0	1	1	5	5	32	2.17%	14.81%
0	0	0	0	0	0	0	0	0	0	0	0	0	0	0	0	0	0	0	10	0.68%	4.63%
0	0	0	0	0	0	0	0	0	0	0	0	0	0	0	0	0	1	1	24	1.63%	11.11%
0	0	0	0	0	0	0	0	0	0	0	0	0	0	0	0	0	0	0	32	2.17%	14.81%
0	0	0	0	3	0	0	3	16	0	0	0	0	16	0	1	1	14	14	38	2.58%	17.59%
0	0	0	0	0	0	0	0	0	0	0	0	0	0	0	0	0	0	0	3	0.20%	1.39%
0	0	0	0	6	0	0	6	16	1	0	0	0	17	0	2	2	28	28	216	14.65%	100.00%
0	0	0	0	0	0	0	0	0	0	0	0	0	0	0	0	0	1	1	10	0.68%	16.95%
0	0	0	0	0	0	0	0	0	1	0	0	0	1	0	3	3	11	11	24	1.63%	40.68%
0	0	0	0	0	0	0	0	0	0	0	0	0	0	0	0	0	2	2	4	0.27%	6.78%
0	0	0	0	0	0	0	0	0	0	0	0	0	0	0	0	0	0	0	6	0.41%	10.17%
0	0	0	0	0	2	0	2	0	0	0	0	0	0	0	0	0	0	0	2	0.14%	3.39%
0	0	0	0	0	0	0	0	0	0	0	0	0	0	0	0	0	5	5	13	0.88%	22.03%
0	0	0	0	0	2	0	2	1	0	0	0	0	1	0	3	3	19	19	59	4.00%	100.00%
1	0	1	0	0	3	0	3	1	0	0	0	0	1	12	15	27	16	16	83	5.63%	37.22%
1	0	1	0	0	0	1	1	1	2	0	0	0	3	6	6	12	70	70	140	9.50%	62.78%
2	0	2	0	0	3	1	4	2	2	0	0	0	4	18	21	39	86	86	223	15.13%	100.00%
215	204	419	5	15	5	9	34	39	9	21	26	13	108	93	101	194	370	370	1909	100%	
11.26%	10.69%	21.95%	0.26%	0.79%	0.26%	0.47%	1.78%	2.04%	0.47%	1.10%	1.36%	0.68%	5.66%	4.87%	5.29%	10.16%	19.38%	19.38%	100.00%		
215	204	419	1	10	3	9	23	37	3	0	3	0	43	92	101	193	359	359	1474		
14.59%	13.84%	28.43%	0.07%	0.68%	0.20%	0.61%	1.56%	2.51%	0.20%	0.00%	0.20%	0.00%	2.92%	6.24%	6.85%	13.09%	24.36%	24.36%	100.00%		

APPENDIX B

MUCHIC PHONETICS

Fernando de la Carrera's notation of the Muchic language's different sounds presents a challenge to the modern scholar. Because the language is now extinct, there is considerable controversy over how the spoken language might have sounded. Carrera's orthography is ambiguous in this regard. The tables place the results of seven interpretations side by side, in an effort to clarify Muchic phonetics, signaling points of agreement and difference among scholars, including me (Tables B.1 and B.2). In chronological order, they are (1) Fernando de la Carrera, *Arte de la Lengua Yunga* ([1644] 1939); (2) E. W. Middendorf, *Das Muchik öder die Chimu-Sprache* (1892); (3) John P. Harrington, "Yunka, Language of the Peruvian Coastal Culture" (1945); (4) Louisa R. Stark, "Mayan Affinities with Yunga of Peru" (1968); (5) Antonio and Consuelo Tovar, *Católogo de las Lenguas de America del Sur* (1984); (6) Alfredo Torero, "Deslindes Linguisticos en la Costa Norte Peruana" (1986); (7) Rodolfo Cerrón-Palomino, *Lengua de Naymlap* (1995); and (8) Margaret A. Jackson (with grateful acknowledgment of the guidance and contribution of Dr. Pamela Munro, University of California, Los Angeles, Department of Linguistics).

Table B.1. Muchic Vowel Sounds

Carrera [1644] 1939	Middendorf 1892	Harrington 1945	Stark 1968	Tovar and Tovar 1984	Torero 1986	Cerrón-Palomino 1995	Jackson
a short or long[1]	a	a short or long	a	a	a	a, a:	a short or long
e short or long	e	short e	e	e	e	e	e
i short or long	i	i short or long	i	i	i	i, i:	i short or long
o short or long	o	o short or long	o	o	o	o, o:	o short or long
u short or long	u	u short or long	u	u	u	u, u:	u short or long
æ[2]	ä, ů	short ä,[3] short ü	ø	ɨ	æ, œ	ö	æ
n/a	ai[4]	diphthong ai	aⁱ	n/a	n/a	n/a	n/a
n/a	oi[4]	diphthong oi	oⁱ	n/a	n/a	n/a	n/a
n/a	ei[4]	diphthong ei	ⁱe, eⁱ	n/a	n/a	n/a	n/a
n/a	œi[4]	diphthong ui	øⁱ	n/a	n/a	n/a	n/a

[1] Carrera tells us that vowels can be pronounced either short or long. He identifies short vowels with an accent mark (´) and long vowels with a circumflex (^); however, in his text, his use of these marks is inconsistent.

[2] Carrera describes this sixth vowel as being like a Latin diphthong that appears in Altieri's edition as æ. Carrera informs us that "no se puede escribir su sonido, y aunque tiene de e y fin de u, de manera que son dos vocales en una" ([1644] 1939:11).

[3] Harrington describes the short ä as being more like æ than œ.

[4] Middendorf, Harrington, and Stark interpret these vowels as diphthongs when they occur together, whereas other sources do not. Carrera does occasionally spell words using these vowel combinations, but he does not identify them as diphthongs.

Table B.2. Muchic Consonant Sounds

Consonant Type	Carrera [1644] 1939	Middendorf 1892	Harrington 1945	Stark 1968	Tovar and Tovar 1984	Torero 1986	Cerrón-Palomino 1995	Jackson
Stops	p	p	p	p	p	p	p bilabial	p
	t	t	th	t	t	t	t dento-alveolar	t
	c, qu	k	k	k	k	k non-palatal	k velar	k
	d	d	d	¢ (d)[1]	d	d	d dento-alveolar sounded	d
Affricates	ch	ch	tc [č]	č	č	č	č	č
	cɥ described as c + inverted h; final h prounounced forcefully	c'h, ch	tch [čh] aspirated	ç	č? (authors unsure)	kʸ velar palatalized	tʸ alveo-palatal	čh
Fricatives	f	f, v	f	f	f	f	f	f
	x described as more like Portuguese x than Spanish x	š, sch, j	c	x	s	š palatal	š alveo-palatal	š
	tzh described as tzha, not cha	ts	tsh [tsh]	¢[2]	š	ts non-palatal	ts dento-alveolar	ts
	ç	s	ts	š	ç fricative	s non-palatal	s dento-alveolar	s
	çi[3]	none	ts + i	none	ç aspirated	sʸ palatal	none	none
	z	s	none	š	none	none	s dento-alveolar	s
	s	s	s	s [z]	s	ś	ŝ pre-palatal fricative	s
	ss very long SS when at beginning or end of word	ss	s	s	ss (unknown purpose)	ś non-palatal	ŝ pre-palatal fricative	s: length depends on context
	j occurs in words borrowed from Spanish	j	X	none	none	none	y	X

Table B.2. Muchic Consonant Sounds (continued)

Consonant Type	Carrera [1644] 1939	Middendorf 1892	Harrington 1945	Stark 1968	Tovar and Tovar 1984	Torero 1986	Cerrón-Palomino 1995	Jackson
Laterals	xll described as x + l pronounced with rolled tongue	š, j	c + ly author divides these sounds into x + ll	š	xll possible silent lateral	ɫ palatal	çʳ velar	ɫ voiceless lateral fricative
	l	l	x^4	l	l	l non-palatal	l dento-alveolar	l
	ll	ll	ly	l	none	ɫ palatal	l palatal	ly
Nasals	m	m	m	m	m	m	m bilabial	m
	n	n	n	n	n	n non-palatal	n dento-alveolar	n
	ñ	ñ	ny	ñ	ñ	ñ palatal	ñ palatal	nʸ
	ng	ng	ŋ	ŋ	ŋ	ng a contextual variant of n	ŋ velar	ŋ
Vibrants	r	r	r	r	r	r	r dento-alveolar	ř
	rr author says both letters are pronounced	r	rr trilled or doubled at beginning or end of word	r	rr trilled as in Spanish	rr uvular, multiple	r dento-alveolar	r
Glide	y	y	y	y	none	l non-palatal	y palatal	y

[1] Stark (1968:10) interprets Carrera's use of the letter *d* as a voiced dental stop but uses the ¢ symbol to indicate it. Since *d* is the usual symbol for a voiced dental stop, this is somewhat puzzling.

[2] Stark (1968:11) claims that both Carrera's *tzh* and Middendorf's *ts* are voiceless affricated dental stops, and she uses the ¢ symbol to indicate them.

[3] Carrera gives no particular information about this letter combination, although it is almost always used at the beginning of words. It does not appear that Carrera considered it a distinct sound. And, although several subsequent scholars comment on it, Torero is the only one to assign it a separate value.

[4] The Greek *chi* is written in place of *l* by Harrington; he gives no explanation for his choice of this symbol.

Linguistic Classification

Linguistic affinities can suggest the presence of other kinds of cultural affinities; however, within the sphere of South American languages, the linguistic classifications of Yunga and Muchic are unresolved. Most agree that Muchic was a dialect of a larger family, but there are disagreements as to what other languages the larger family included and what the larger family should be called. Earlier scholars proposed linguistic affinities with Quechua, leading investigators to search for cultural affinities between the coast and the central sierras.[1] However, most scholars now classify Yunga languages as either an isolate group, or include them with those of southern Ecuador, a finding that invites investigations of coastal associations northward.

Čestmír Loukotka's very influential study of South American languages classifies Muchic as a member of the Chimu language family.[2] In his analysis, the geographic distribution of the Chimu language group ranges from southern Ecuador, southward along the coast, to approximately Paramonga. Loukotka divided the Chimu family into Northern languages, primarily north of Piura and into Ecuador, and Southern languages, called variously "Chimu or Yunga or Chincha or Quignam or Muchic or Mochica."[3] Loukotka saw the Chimu family as part of a larger category that he called the North Central Division of Andean Tribes.[4]

Tovar and Tovar also group the Yunga languages with those of southern Ecuador, calling the family Yunga-Puruhá.[5] The authors' classificatory scheme is based on a combination of both linguistic and geographic groupings. Like Loukotka, they classify the northern coastal languages as an independent language family.[6] The designation of "Yunca-Puruhá" stems from Jijón y Caamaño's exhaustive investigation of Ecuadorian languages.[7] In it, he places Muchic as a southern member of the Yunca-Puruhá group. Jijón y Caamaño asserts that Yunca-Puruhá was not an isolated family and should be included among the larger phylum, Macro-Chibcha.[8]

Joseph Greenberg, intent on demonstrating that many hundreds (or even thousands) of indigenous American languages originated from a primary source that he calls "Amerind," reiterates Paul Rivet's suggestion of a connection between the Chibchan and Paezan families.[9] Citing Max Uhle for his information on Chibchan and Paul Rivet for his information on Paezan, Greenberg includes Loukotka's Chimu family within the Paezan subgroup of Chibchan-Paezan.[10]

In summation, it seems likely that the Muchic language was a member of a larger linguistic family having several related branches along the coast of northern Peru and southern Ecuador. These would include a northern group (Puruhá, Cañari, Manteña); a southern group (correlative to Loukotka's Southern Chimu family) that included Eten, Muchic, and Quignam (Yunga), ranging from approximately Morrope in the north to Paramonga in the south; and an Atalan group that included Huancavilca and possibly Tallan (Catacaos, Tallan, Sec, Sechura, Chira, Colan, Piura), hence the name Yunca-Puruhá. Although relationships among the main branches of Yunca-Puruhá are tentative at best, most scholars have dropped the idea of a Quechua connection almost entirely. A possible connection between Yunga and isolated Andean languages such as Uru-Chiripaya does exist; however, most recent scholarship associates Yunga with Macro-Chibcha or Chibchan-Paezan phyla.[11] The presence of interrelated languages in the coastal areas of Ecuador and northern Peru fits well with archaeological and historic data, combining to suggest that this area formed a cultural unit.

NOTES

CHAPTER ONE

1. The cultural complex and style were originally articulated by Uhle (1991), Larco Hoyle (1938), Kroeber (1944), and Rowe (1962).

2. Early Moche ceramic style overlaps temporally other north coastal traditions such as Gallinazo, Salinar, and Vicus. Some of the earliest artistic correspondences are found in Cupisnique and Chavín art, dating as early as 1200 B.C.; see Boone 1996; Makowski et al. 1994.

3. Iconographic studies include Castillo 1989; Donnan 1976, 1978; Hocquenghem 1987; Lavallée 1970; Yakovleff 1932; Yakovleff and Herrera 1934. On funeral practices, see Alva and Donnan 1993; Bennett 1939; Donnan and Mackey 1978; Kaulicke 2000; Millones and Lemlij 1996. On commodity exchange, see Lothrop 1932; Marcos 1978. Studies on craft technology include Collier 1959; Shimada 1998. On political structures, see Bawden 1996; Chapdelaine 2004; Haas et al. 1987.

4. Kroeber 1925, 1926, 1944; Larco Hoyle 1948, 1966; Rowe 1961, 1967b; Uhle 1991; Willey 1953.

5. Uceda and Mujica 1994, 2003.

6. The degree of phonetic correspondence coded into the knots of Inca khipus is a subject of great controversy and fascinating research; for more on this, see Quilter and Urton 2002.

7. On writing, see Boone and Mignolo 1994; Houston 2004; Postgate et al. 1995; Quilter and Urton 2002; Sampson 1985; Schmandt-Besserat 1996; Urton 2003. Mnemonics are addressed in Carruthers 1990; Küchler and Melion 1991; Noë and Thompson 2002. For sign and image studies, see Elkins 1999; Mitchell 1986.

8. Coe 1992:13.

9. Urton's (2003:28) definition is a modification of one put forward by Elizabeth Boone, who regards writing as "the communication of relatively specific ideas in a conventional manner by means of permanent visible marks" (Boone and Mignolo 1994:15). See also Sampson 1985:26–27.

10. Elkins 1999:82–91; see further discussion in chapter 4.

11. Houston 2004:234–35, citing Collon 1990 on Near Eastern seals.
12. My thanks go to Gary Urton for this point (pers. comm., October 2005).
13. Houston 2004:224–25, citing Basso 1989:428.
14. Jackson 2000; Russell et al. 1994, 1998.
15. Jackson 2000; Russell and Jackson 2001.
16. Excavations were begun at the Cerro Mayal workshop in 1992 under the direction of Glenn Russell, Banks Leonard, and Jesus Briceño, after the site's initial discovery in 1989. For ceramic sequence, see Larco Hoyle 1948:28–36.
17. Calibrated dates are from Russell et al. 1998:82–84.
18. An *icon* is described as a sign possessing the character of that which makes it significant (the more imagistic of the three), *indexes* show something about things because of their close connection to them, and *symbols* are associated with their meanings through conventionalized usage (growing from icons or mixed signs and characterized by varying degrees of codification). See Peirce's "Logic as Semiotic: The Theory of Signs" (1985); see also Peirce's "What Is a Sign?" (1992).
19. Saussure 1983.

CHAPTER TWO

1. Bawden 1996:191–98; Castillo and Donnan 1994:161; Chapdelaine 2004; Quilter 2001:30; Quilter and Castillo forthcoming.
2. Castillo and Donnan 1994:156, figure 98.
3. These intertwined oases are sometimes thought of as forming a "horizontal economy" (Bawden 1996:45–47, citing Rostworowski 1975, 1977).
4. Bawden 1996:47.
5. Topic and Topic 1987.
6. William Duncan Strong's "Finding the Tomb of a Warrior-God" (1947) makes one of the first such references. See also Schaedel's "The City and the Origin of the State in America" for references to Moche as a "military theocracy" (1972:16, 23).
7. Donnan and Castillo 1994; Hocquenghem and Lyon 1980.
8. Bawden 1996:78; Netherly 1977, 1990; Rostworowski 1975, 1977, 1981.
9. The term *allyu* refers here to lineage structures of individual families, those who all claim descent from a common ancestor, as well as for group lineages associated with specific geographic territories; see Harrison 1989; Netherly 1977:162.
10. Rostworowski 1961; see also Cabello Valboa 1951.
11. Rostworowski 1961. *Curaca* is a highland term for lord or elite leader; such leaders could enjoy widely differing levels of ranked status and privilege. According to Larco Hoyle (1940:132), on the North Coast, middle-level curacas were called "Alaec" and the highest Moche rulers were titled "Cie-quich."

12. Jackson 2000; Moseley 1992:168; Russell and Jackson 2001.
13. Political consolidation in the Chicama Valley coalesced during the Gallinazo and Salinar phases; see Leonard and Russell 1992. Such a consolidation could be seen as an important factor in the rise of Moche political domination and expansion north. See Fogel 1993 on the development of the Gallinazo polity.
14. Larco Hoyle 1945:1. Larco's conclusion is supported by his observation that Moche ceramic Phases I and II occurred almost exclusively in the Chicama and Moche valleys.
15. Castillo and Donnan 1994:151.
16. Calancha, bk. 1, ch. 37 ([1638] 1974–81:535).
17. Arriaga [1641] 1968:11, 63.
18. Chimor is alternatively referred to in different colonial sources as Chimu and Chimo. Other examples of political intermarriage are described in Susan Ramirez's analysis of political succession in the Chicama Valley. For example, Pichan, the lord of Malabrigo during the reign of the Inca Huayna Capac, is said to have been married to the aunt of the lord of the neighboring polity, Licapa (Ramirez 1995a:249). A second example from the Chicama Valley has it that Don Juan de Mora, the lord of the sixteenth-century polity that Netherly (1984) calls First Moiety (Chicama polity north of river), was married to the daughter of Don Pedro Mache, the lord of what Netherly calls Second Moiety (Chicama polity south of river), a marriage that would have appropriately been between members of equal status rank (attributed to Zevallos Quiñones, in Ramirez 1995a: figure 2).
19. Larco Hoyle 1938:49, citing Jose Toribio Polo [1648] 1896.
20. Larco Hoyle 1938:49.
21. Charles Darwin, for example, witnessed an immense earthquake and tidal waves while visiting Valdivia, Chile, in 1835. Concurrent with the eruption of volcanoes in the region, the earthquake caused the sea to recede entirely from the port of Talcahuano. Water later returned in the form of huge tidal waves, severely damaging the coastal town and causing the shoreline to uplift by several feet; see Darwin 1839. See also Moseley 1992 on periodic El Niño–Southern Oscillation events.
22. On Chavín predecessors and ethnohistoric sources, see Burger 1992; Cieza de Leon [1553] 1959; Doyle 1988. See Quilter's (2001:21–45) discussion of Moche's archaistic tendencies reminiscent of Chavín.
23. Bawden 1996:63–65, citing Calancha [1638] 1974–81, Means 1931, and Netherly 1984.
24. Burger 1992.
25. On Mountain Sacrifice, for example, see Benson 1972; Bourget 1994b:88. On the Dance of the Dead, see Hocquenghem 1987:93.
26. On the Warrior Narrative, see Donnan and McClelland 1999:69–72. On the Sacrifice Scene, see Alva and Donnan 1993. This was originally called the Presentation Scene; see Donnan 1976, 1978:158–73.

27. Although some images appear to depict individuals with long hair, suggesting female gender, the majority of skeletal remains associated with sacrificial victims are male; see Bourget 2001.
28. This Sacrifice Scene (also called the Presentation Scene) is a fineline painting on a Moche stirrup-spout bottle in the Staatliches Museum für Völkerhunde, Munich, collection.
29. For more on the ulluchu fruit, see Wassen 1985–86.
30. Several authors have addressed this issue, with little consensus; see, for example, De Bock 2003; Donnan and Castillo 1994; Franco and Vilela 2003:392, 400; Hocquenghem 1987; Morales 2003:435.
31. See Bourget 1997 and Verano 2001 for descriptions of sacrificial victims discovered at the Huaca de La Luna in the Moche Valley.
32. See Bourget 2001:94; Donnan 2004a:113–39.
33. Donnan 1988.
34. Alva and Donnan 1993.
35. Donnan and Castillo 1994.
36. Several scholars discuss the mounting evidence in favor of a shared religion throughout the entire Moche region; see, for example, Donnan 2004b; Jackson 2000:37–42; Morales 2003.
37. Castillo and Donnan (1994) point out that this pattern is somewhat less evident in the northern Moche area (e.g., Jequetepeque, Zaña, Lambayeque, and Piura valleys).
38. Bawden 1996:245.
39. Modern agriculture has obliterated most of these smaller edifices; see, for example, Shippee and Johnson's air photos of Huaca Rosada in the Chicama Valley (in Kosok 1965).
40. Leonard and Russell (1992:32) observe that in the Chicama Valley, this pattern changed during the terminal Moche/Middle Horizon period, noting that apart from Mocollope and the El Brujo complex, the valley's largest pyramids were built in the center of the lower valley during this period using techniques that signal large-scale single-phase construction episodes.
41. Schaedel (1967) states that almost all the walls at Pañamarca show signs of having been painted, and many were carefully plastered and painted red and yellow; see also Bennett 1939:17, cited in Bonavia 1985:49. Franco et al. (1994:165–66) describe early phases of construction at Huaca Cao Viejo (El Brujo complex) as having painted walls, some yellow, some red, in addition to a complex program of murals. Uceda is cited in Bonavia 1985:72–73 as having seen traces of red on the Huaca del Sol, as well as significant amounts of plaster and paint in association with the extensive murals at Huaca de La Luna (Uceda et al. 1997). Huaca Rosario in the Chicama Valley was at least partially plastered and painted pale yellow (my observation; see also Leonard and Russell 1992).
42. On the "Decapitator" or, in Spanish, "Degollador," see Cordy-Collins 1992; Uceda et al. 1994. On "Ai-Apaec," see Larco Hoyle 1940.

43. See Zighelboim 1995.
44. Uceda et al. 1997:19–21.
45. From what can be seen of the earlier murals, in many cases equivalent or related subject matter was depicted. This point is tentative, however, and significant differences in style, level of abstraction, and color range show that important changes over time did occur.
46. Uceda 2001.
47. Uceda and Morales 1996:263; Uceda et al. 1994:271.
48. Bourget (1994a:83, 182–84, 2006:52) asserts that the character evokes aquatic symbolism, reading the spirals as octopus tentacles and casting the character as a maritime counterpart to the Spider. See also the discussion of Sipán's Tomb 3 Octopus in Alva and Donnan 1993:193; Topic 1982:279.
49. On the monolith at Kuntur Wasi, see Campana and Morales 1997:15; Cordy-Collins 1992.
50. For example, this appears on the headdress of the Anthropomorphic Feline discovered in Tomb 3 at Sipán (Alva and Donnan 1993: figure 204).
51. Respectively, Cordy-Collins 1992, Larco Hoyle 1966, Lavallée 1970, Benson 1972, and Morales 2003. Other names include the "Supernatural Warrior with Serpent Belt" (Donnan 1978), "el mellizo de cinturones de serpientes" (Hocquenghem 1987), the "Personage with Serpents" (Castillo 1989), the "Fanged Deity" (Benson 1972), the "Deity of the Mountain" (Uceda 2001), and the "Primordial Deity" (Campana and Morales 1997:27–29).
52. See Donnan 1982 for a discussion of dance in Moche art.
53. Cordy-Collins 1992:215–17.
54. Ricardo Morales, pers. comm., December 2005.
55. For discussion of the Moon Animal, see Mackey and Vogel 2003.
56. Mackey and Hastings 1982. See Morales 2003:460, figure 14.13, for drawings of the platform sequence.
57. Mackey and Hastings 1982: figure 9a–b. See Morales 2003:458 for Chavín/Cupisnique findings.
58. Uceda 2006.
59. Montoya 1997:63–65.
60. See the photo in Uceda and Tufinio 2003:194 (lamina 20.2b).
61. Verano et al. 2008:254.
62. Bourget 1997:55, 2001:90–91; Tufinio 2004; Verano 2004; Verano et al. 2008.
63. Verano 2001:117–21.
64. Bourget 2001:89–100.
65. Galvez and Briceño 2001:149; see also Franco et al. 1994; Galvez et al. 2003.
66. Franco et al. 1994:171, plates 4 and 6.

67. Galvez and Briceño 2001:152, citing Verano and Anderson 1996:151; see also Verano et al. 1999.
68. Alva and Donnan 1993; Donnan and Cock 1986.
69. See Franco and Vilela 2003 for a detailed description of the imagery.
70. Franco et al. 1994:179.
71. Franco and Vilela 2003:392–418.
72. Franco et al. 1999; see also Gutierrez 1999.
73. Mujica 2007:116. See the photo in *National Geographic* 206, no. 1 (July 2004:104–5).
74. See Galvez and Briceño 2001:154 (photo 25).
75. Schaedel 1967:109.
76. See Schaedel's (1967:112, figure 13) reconstruction drawing.
77. On the Ribbon Dance, see Donnan 1982. On baile con soga, see Jiménez Borja 1938, 1951. See also Hocquenghem 1987:122 on the Warrior Dance and Muelle 1936 on the Rope Dance.
78. Hocquenghem 1987:122–23; Molina 1959:82–83.
79. Bonavia 1961, 1985.
80. Donnan 1978; Donnan and Castillo 1994; Hocquenghem and Lyon 1980. The reader is referred to the illustrations in Bonavia 1985: figures 39–51.
81. Donnan 1976:166–67.
82. See Bourget 2006 for additional discussion of this topic.
83. See, for example, Donnan 1975; Morales 2003:436–40.
84. Morales 2003:428.
85. Cordy-Collins 1977; Donnan and McClelland 1999; Hocquenghem 1987.
86. Berezkin 1981; Bourget 2006; Gölte 1994; Hocquenghem 1987; Kaulicke 2000; Lieske 1992; Makowski 1996.
87. Donnan and Mackey 1978 (burials M-IV 18 through M-IV 23).
88. Donnan and Mackey 1978 (burials M-IV 3 through M-IV 11); see also Chapdelaine 2001; Chapdelaine et al. 1997; Strong 1947; Tello 1924; Topic 1977; Uceda and Armas 1997, 1998.
89. Alva 1988:536; Donnan and Mackey 1978.
90. On, for example, the Moche Burial Theme, see Donnan and McClelland 1999. On wooden maquettes discovered in 1995 at the Huaca de La Luna, see Jackson 2004; Uceda et al. 1997.
91. Bourget (2006:58–61, 213) highlights one known example of funerary assemblages equivalent from one tomb to another, those of Priestesses of San José de Moro.
92. This is sometimes called a "false jar neck" (Donnan and McClelland 1999).
93. Carr 1995; Chapdelaine 2001:77.
94. See, for example, burial M-IV 6; see Alva and Donnan 1993: figure 128; Donnan and Mackey 1978.

95. See, for example, at the Huaca de La Luna; see Bourget 2001:96; Montoya 1997:63–65.
96. Donnan and Mackey 1978:209.
97. Donnan and Castillo 1992, 1994; also see Bourget 2001:95 and Bourget and Newman 1998 on the antiserum testing of ceramics.
98. See also Jackson 2000; Russell and Jackson 2001.
99. Donnan 1982; Hocquenghem 1987:122; Jiménez Borja 1938, 1951; Muelle 1936.
100. On the Valdivia culture, see Myers and Brace 2003.
101. Cummins 2003; Di Capua 1994; Lathrap 1973; Stahl 1986.
102. Allen 1988:59, 201; Vaughn 2004:81.
103. Jackson 2004.
104. Dransart 1995.
105. Anónimo [1590] 1968:156; Betanzos [1557] 1996:46, 110; Ceruti 2004:116–19, citing Albornoz [1583] 1984; Cobo [1653] 1990:46; Murúa [1590] 1946:257; Polo de Ondegardo [1571] 1916:194.
106. Bray 2003; Lau 2002; Moore 1989; Vaughn 2004.
107. Vaughn 2004:81.
108. Boas 1966; Piddocke 1965.
109. Cummins 2003.
110. Netherly 1984; see also Ramirez 1996.
111. Netherly 1984:231.
112. See Castillo and Donnan 1994 and Ramirez 1995a for in-depth discussion of the history and historiography of Moche polities.
113. Rostworowski 1975, 1977.
114. Netherly 1984:231.
115. Quilter 2001:41.

CHAPTER THREE

1. Leonard and Russell 1992.
2. Russell et al. 1998.
3. Cerro Mayal was first excavated in 1992 by Russell, Leonard, and Briceño, and the details of the excavation have been published in greater detail elsewhere; see, for example, Russell et al. 1994, 1998.
4. Russell et al. 1994, 1998.
5. Jackson 2000; Russell and Jackson 2001.
6. Attarian 1996.
7. Christopher Attarian, pers. comm., 2004, based on work with Tom Wake of the University of California, Los Angeles, zooarchaeology lab.
8. See Jackson 2000; Russell and Jackson 2001.

9. *Pottery* refers to all clay wares that are not porcelain, including earthenware and stoneware (Savage and Newman 1985:231). The term *modeling* has different connotations. For example, it can mean the process of shaping an original piece of ceramic ware by hand (Donnan 1992:14). Synonymous with "hand building," this refers to a method of constructing ceramic items using slabs, coils, or other bits of clay joined and formed by hand. However, in some cases, authors refer to sculpted vessels or extremely high-relief objects as having "modeled" elements, even though in many cases those elements were mold made. To avoid confusion, in this study terms like *sculptural*, *sculpted*, and *sculpting* are used to refer to objects produced in three dimensions or extremely high relief, regardless of forming technique (Savage and Newman 1985:195). The words *modeled* and *modeling* are here reserved for those elements made exclusively by hand (e.g., without use of a mold). Terms like *molded* and *molding* refer to the processes of pressing clay into molds to make the parts of individual objects. The process of "throwing" refers to forming pieces on a potter's wheel; a ball of clay is rapidly turned on a rotating wheel head, while the potter forms the piece by exerting pressure on the spinning clay (Cohen and Hess 1993:81; Norton 1956:307). And "casting" is the process of forming objects in closed molds from a slurry of liquid clay ("slip"). Also commonly called "slip casting," this process yields finished products once the slip solidifies and hardens (Norton 1956:303).

10. Unless specifically described as entirely mold made, an object that includes "molded elements" is not necessarily entirely mold made.

11. Colors correlate to the *Munsell Soil Color Charts* as follows: brown = 2.5 YR 3/2 and 2.5 YR 3/4; red = 10 R 4/6, 2.5 YR 4/6, and 2.5 YR 4/8; orange = 2.5 YR 6/6 and 2.5 YR 6/8; white/cream = 10 YR 8/2, 10 YR 8/3, 10 YR 8/4, and 7.5 YR 8/4. Munsell color correlations give the reader an idea of the basic range of color; however, within each color category additional subtle variations of hue exist. See Munsell Color Company, Inc. 1975.

12. Larco Hoyle 1948.

13. Although evidence is inconclusive, floreros may have been at least partially mold made. Analysis of floreros from the Lower Chicama Valley shows that they most often occur in one of two distinct diameters, suggesting the existence of some mechanism of standardization.

14. Attarian 1996, 2003; Jackson 2000; Russell et al. 1994, 1998.

15. Strong and Evans 1952.

16. The statistical numbers of the iconographic sample do not represent an absolute tally of all decorated sherds from Cerro Mayal. Those that were too small to characterize or those with only a single spot or line of paint were not selected. All such fragments were, however, analyzed as part of the project's larger data tally.

17. Jackson 2000:95; see also De Bock (2003:313), who describes the motif as *escalera y ola* (step and wave), an icon referring specifically to sacrificial temples such as the Huaca de La Luna.

18. See, for example, Donnan's (1997:58) comments concerning an analogy between jars with ropes and prisoners with ropes.
19. For photos of additional variants of each image type, see Jackson 2000.
20. The Fanged Lizard character was identified as a stylized Fanged Fox in early analyses. Luis Jaime Castillo (pers. comm., 1992) later suggested that these creatures are more correctly identified as Fanged Lizards, an identification that is adopted here.
21. See, for example, Donnan and McClelland 1999; Zighelboim 1995.
22. Leonard and Russell 1992.
23. Shimada 1994a: figure 15 illustrates the way in which ceramics may have been positioned for firing in this type of kiln.
24. A concave mold is a cavity, generally made of plaster, gypsum, clay, rubber, or metal, in which a fluid paste or other malleable substance is given a desired form (Cohen and Hess 1993:61). A convex mold is a convex form over which clay or some other malleable substance is draped (Ball and Lovoos 1965). Piece molds are multiple-part molds employed in cases where the desired form is too complex or undercut to be created through the use of a single mold; they are also referred to as "two-piece" molds or "multiple-part" molds.
25. See illustrations and descriptions in Larco Hoyle 1945:15, 31 and Donnan 1992:60–63.
26. "Luting" is the process of cementing together parts of a ceramic object with fluid clay slip, sometimes referred to as "slip gluing." The term does not imply that the separate parts were formed using any particular method (Savage and Newman 1985:183). "Sprigging" is the process of attaching parts or ornaments (separately made by *molding* or *stamping*) to the surface of the body of an object or vessel with the aid of thin slip. Sprigging implicitly includes the notion of stamped or molded decorative elements attached to the surface of the piece.
27. Savage and Newman 1985:271.
28. A stamped impression is a design impressed into the surface of soft clay with a stamp or stamps, as in the case of some makers' marks on unfired pottery or in decorative designs impressed with prepared blocks, paddles, or molds. In Middle Eastern studies stamp molds are often referred to as "seals." However, because "cylinder seals" and "makers' marks" are not applicable to this study and can lead to a confusion in terminology, I refrain from interchanging the terms *stamps* and *seals*, even though technically they refer to similar types of molds.
29. An intaglio impression is a design created by incising or carving below the surface; it is sometimes called *cavo rilievo*. It is the opposite of "cameo" or "relief," where the design is raised. An "intaglio mold" is one that impresses a (usually shallow) design into or below the surface of the vessel body; this is sometimes simply called a "stamp" (Savage and Newman 1985:158).

Relief decoration is that which projects from or is raised above the surface of the piece to a varying degree; it is also referred to as high, medium, or low relief, generally in opposition to the term *intaglio* (a design carved or impressed *below* the main surface). A "low-relief" or "raised" stamp mold refers to a concave mold that leaves a raised image on the vessel's surface (Savage and Newman 1985:243).

30. When a plastic material is pressed into a concave mold, it is critical that the mold be separable from the molded piece through a simple lifting motion. If the original model, upon which the mold is fashioned, is highly three dimensional, has overhanging areas, or has areas that are undercarved, the mold that results will have "undercutting," which will prevent the mold from being easily separable when in use.

31. Sergio Purin's (1983) X-ray analysis of several Moche fineware ceramic vessels confirms this. X-ray photos clearly show the joined seams of stirrup-spout vessels, appliqué figures, and other mold-made elements.

32. *Tableaux* refers to pictures, paintings, or scenes presented on a table or panel (Dubois 1970:234).

33. *Appliqué*, meaning "applied," in reference to ceramics connotes a separate element attached as an ornament by sprigging (Savage and Newman 1985:29).

34. Finely detailed human or anthropomorphic figures and small figural appliqués attached perpendicular to the main body of the vessel are referred to as *deck figures*.

35. During firing clay will explode as a result of heat expansion if air bubbles are trapped inside. Potters must provide vent holes in hollow wares.

36. Tello 1924.

37. Donnan (1997:58) makes this connection explicit.

38. One of these molds may have been the actual tool used to make this vessel; however, conclusive testing remains to be done.

CHAPTER FOUR

1. Houston 2004:234–35.
2. Foucault 1993; Silverstein and Urban 1996.
3. Bryson 1981.
4. Sampson 1985:39–42.
5. Coe 1992:43.
6. Sampson 1985:33.
7. Boone and Mignolo 1994:15. *Semasiographic* is formed via the Greek word *semasia* (meaning) combined with *graphic*; see also Brice 1976:29–41; Sampson 1985:29.
8. Gelb 1974. Gelb's book comes as one of a long literature on writing, whose genesis in the eighteenth century was strongly influenced by William Warburton's *The Divine Legation of Moses Demonstrated* ([1738] 1978) and by subsequent works adhering to this basic developmental model.
9. Boone and Mignolo 1994:16, citing Hill 1967.

10. Brice 1976:41.
11. Ortigues writes in *Le discours et le symbole* that

> algorithm ... does not speak, except through the intermediary of a language which furnishes not only the phonetic expression of the characters, but also the formulation of axioms permitting the determination of the value of these characters. It is true that at a pinch one could decipher unknown characters, but that always supposes an acquired knowledge, a thought already formed by the usage of speech. Therefore, in all hypotheses, mathematical symbolism is the fruit of a secondary elaboration, supposing preliminarily the usage of discourse and the possibility of conceiving explicit conventions. It is nevertheless true that mathematical algorithm will express the formal laws of symbolization, of syntactic structure, independent of particular means of expression (1962:62, 171, cited in Derrida 1976:3n1).

Systems that rely on secondary elaboration are by nature polysemic, in that they express spatial (or other) relationships within the parameters of their particular schemata, yet they require mediation to find expression in communicative modes other than visual (such as aural or socially performative modes).

12. Marcus 1992:29.
13. Marcus 1992:29.
14. See chapter 1; additionally, see Peirce 1985:4–23.
15. Peirce 1985:11.
16. Langer 1979.
17. Langer 1967:84, cited in Innis 1985:88.
18. Langer 1979:102.
19. Owen 1986.
20. Owen 1986:167–68.
21. Owen 1986:167.
22. Goodman 1976:133–52; Elkins 1999:234–35.
23. Elkins 1999:85.
24. Elkins 1999:88–89.
25. Elkins's original diagram includes only the three main categories of writing, pictures, and notation; the addition of hieroglyphs, semasiographs, emblems, and schemata subsets is based on Elkins's (1999:90–91) subsequent discussion.
26. Schmandt-Besserat 1996; see also additional discussion in chapter 5.
27. Sampson 1985:30.
28. Brice 1976:43.
29. Houston 2004:226.
30. Berlo 1983.

31. Martin 2006:95–96.
32. Jiménez Borja 1951; Kutscher 1950; Larco Hoyle 1938, 1940.
33. For example, see Lavallée 1970; Yakovleff 1932; Yakovleff and Herrera 1934, 1935.
34. Benson 1974; Bourget 1994a, 1994b, 2006; Castillo 1989, 1991; Donnan 1976, 1978; Hocquenghem 1987; Hocquenghem and Lyon 1980.
35. Martin (2006:60) lists these elements (what, who, where, when) as essential to narrative.
36. See Donnan and McClelland 1999; Hocquenghem 1987.
37. Donnan 1978:158–72.
38. Castillo 1989:30.
39. Donnan 1978:29–34.
40. Donnan (1978:33) uses the example of a duck's bill, which would usually be drawn frontally even though the rest of the bird might be shown in profile.
41. Pillsbury 2001; Uceda and Mujica 2003.
42. On script communities, see Houston 2004:240; on textual communities, see Stock 1983.

CHAPTER FIVE

I initially presented portions of this discussion at the sixty-third annual meeting of the Society for American Archaeology under the title "Moche Iconography and Visual Notation at Cerro Mayal, Peru," Seattle, 1998; see also Jackson 2000, 2002.

1. The term is most often seen in connection with descriptions of Chavín and Cupisnique period artwork (Rowe 1967a).
2. For more on Fox Messengers, see Benson, ed. 1972:48–51; Donnan 1978:74–76. Birds and owls were thought of as messengers from the spirit world, as evidenced by the care and redundancy with which Father Fernando de la Carrera questioned the Indians about their beliefs and idolatrous practices. As part of confession, they were specifically asked, "Ecapæcoz xllom pæcna pæn fæpiçær, ñañissapçæn, pucu, fiñ, pocpoc, licapæcoz mœcha, macɥæc, pong, echallo?" Translated in its most literal form this means, "Do you think for certain [believe] in your dreams, in bird, owl, bird of foretelling [omens], bird of foretelling [omens], are you in the habit of [accustomed to] worship, sacred place/object of worship [*huaca*/idol], [special] stone, or other thing?" Phrased more colloquially this would be, "Do you believe in your dreams, in birds, in owls, in bird omens? Do you worship huacas, idols, stones, or other things?" (Carrera [1644] 1939:75, supplementary vocabulary from 68–74; my translation).
3. Rowe 1967a:78–79. Moche corollaries can be seen in various painted images with linear elements terminating in "snake" heads (belts, ropes, hair braids, rainbows, etc.) and in mural imagery. Here I am thinking

of the standing figure at Huaca de La Luna whose arms terminate in curvilinear elements with bird head motifs (Mackey and Hastings 1982), as well as the "Personaje Menor" in the Decapitator mural cycle described by Uceda et al. (1994; Uceda et al. 1998: figure 6; see also Campana and Morales 1997). Though *kenning* denotes the standard use of a descriptive phrase in place of the ordinary name for something, it is a type of periphrasis closely related to metonymy, synecdoche, and the use of salient descriptive features of the referenced object as a substitute for naming. Although there is some amount of controversy in various disciplines concerning these terms, kenning is a Norse literary trope most often associated with the Anglo-Saxon epic *Beowulf* and other Old Germanic language oral traditions (Abrams 1993:69).

4. See Jackson 2000: figure 2.10 for Cerro Mayal depictions of both males and females holding rattles who wear various kinds of attire.

5. Carrera writes,

> *Fœp*, es el sueño, y es nombre sustantivo, y junto con la particula *eiñ*, que es parte del verbo sustantivo, dice: *fœpeiñ*, que en rigor dice: yo soy sueño; y entienden los indios este romance, como de verbo, yo sueño; *caxll*, significa los orines, y junto con el verbo, *œz* dirá *caxllœz*, que dice en rigor, tu eres orines, y entiende el romance, como de verbo, tu orinas
> [*Fœp* is dream, and is a name/noun substantive, and together with the particle *eiñ*, which is part of the verb substantive, says *fœpeiñ*, that strictly speaking says: I am dream; and the Indians understand this romance (fiction) as a verb, I dream; *caxll* means urine, and together with the verb *œz* would say *caxllœz*, which strictly speaking says, you are urine, and they understand the romance as a verb, you urinate] [(1644) 1939:52–53; my translation].

The distinction between *sueño*, "to dream," and *sueño*, "the act of sleeping," is based on comparative language sources (Schumacher de Peña 1991:51).

6. In Muchic, the word *pregnant* was listed by Lehmann as *kûñaŋ* and by Middendorf as *kûin* (cited in Schumacher de Peña 1991:48). The term for "child" was listed by Larco as *iñin* (cited by Altieri, in Carrera [1644] 1939:xvi), inviting speculation about a linguistic relationship between pregnancy and children.

7. See Benson 1972:138.

8. Zuidema 1982:446; see also Berrin 1997: plate 77.

9. On the Huaca de La Luna workshop, see Armas et al. 1993; Uceda et al. 1997. On the Huaca Sialupe workshop, see Shimada and Wagner 2001.

10. The Huaca de La Luna workshop was in production at the end of Moche Phase III through Phase IV (Uceda and Armas 1997 :104); Cerro Mayal carbon 14 dates from Moche Phase IV to the beginning of Phase V (Russell et al. 1998:82); Shimada and Wagner (2001) date Middle Sicán as roughly A.D. 900–1100.

11. See, for example, Berrin 1997:154.

12. See also Bawden 1994 on the Moche V workshop at Galindo.
13. Shimada and Wagner (2007:189) hypothesize that the marks may relate to specific individuals.
14. Rush et al. 1986.
15. Houston 2004:234–35, 239–40.
16. Stock 1983, 1990; see also what Simon Martin (2006:59) refers to as "interpretive communities."
17. Martin 2006:58.
18. Stock 1983:91.
19. Houston 2004:240.
20. Schmandt-Besserat 1978, 1996.

CHAPTER SIX

1. Larco Hoyle 2001, 1:165. Urton (1998:415–16) notes that, for the Incas, accounting and calculation seem to have been separate functions, with khipus being the devices that recorded information and small stones used "on the ground" to apply mathematical operations.
2. Cerrón-Palomino 1995:179. See Altieri's foreword and introduction (Carrera [1644] 1939:xx–xxii). Altieri asserts that Yunga was spoken throughout much of Ecuador, as far south as Lima or even Chile, parts of lowland Bolivia, and northern Argentina.
3. Carrera [1644] 1939:6.
4. Cerrón-Palomino 1995; Loukotka 1968; Middendorf 1892; Stark 1968; Torero 1986; Zevallos Quiñones 1948b.
5. Carrera describes the Corregimiento de Trujillo, including the towns of Santiago(?), Madalena de Cao (Chicama Valley), and Chocope (Chicama) and the entire Chicama Valley and Paixan (Paijan, Chicama); the Corregimiento de Zaña, including San Pedro de Lloc (Jequetepeque Valley), Xequetepeque, Chepen (Jequetepeque), Guadalupe, San Augustin, Eten, Chiclaieop (Chiclayo), San Miguel, Santa Lucia (Zaña), Reque, Omœnffœ fœc, Firru ñap (Fereñape), Moccyumi, Lambayeque, Tucume, Yllimo, Pacora, Morrupe, and Iaianca; the Corregimiento de Piura, including Motupe, Salas, Copis (Olmos), Guacabamba, and Frias; and the Corregimiento de Cajamarca, including Santa Cruz, Ñepos, San Miguel, and San Paulo.
6. Altieri, in Carrera [1644] 1939:xix.
7. Bishop Martinez Compañon's chart is reproduced by Zevallos Quiñones (1948b) and Cerrón-Palomino (1995).
8. Paul Rivet (1949) created a linguistic family called Yünka, which he suggests included Mochica as one single "dialect." According to Rivet,

the area where Yünka was spoken included the valleys of Morrope, Etén, Chimu, Mochica, Chincha, and Chanco (Chancay?).

9. Only one brief example of Quignam is known today, written in 1607 by Oré in "Rituale, seu peruanum . . ." (1607), reprinted in Rivet 1949 and Cerrón-Palomino 1995.

10. Calancha, bk. 3, chs. 2–3 ([1638] 1974–81, 4:1235).

11. Carrera [1644] 1939:7.

12. The reader is referred to maps 1–2 illustrated in Cerrón-Palomino 1995.

13. For discussion related to a Muchic variant reportedly spoken among beachside fishing communities, referred to as La Lengua Pescadora, see Ramirez 1995a.

14. See Middendorf 1892; Rowe 1967b; Uhle 1922.

15. Bastian 1878; Brüning 1989; Kosok 1965; Larco Hoyle 1940; Lehmann 1991; Villareal 1921; Zevallos Quiñones 1946. See also Jose Antonio Salas's *Diccionario Mochica–Castillano, Castillano–Mochica* (2002) for a recent recompilation of word lists.

16. Stark 1968:6.

17. Cerrón-Palomino 1995; Torero 1986.

18. My synthetic analysis, plus the following: Cerrón-Palomino 1995; Harrington 1945; Middendorf 1892; Stark 1968; Torero 1986; Tovar and Tovar 1984.

19. Cerrón-Palomino 1995:125.

20. Stark (1968:27) gives the following examples: *ox* = fire, *xa* = water, *tes* = heel, *atput* = two, and *mentop* = full; see also Cerrón-Palomino (1995:126–27), who notes that the preceding syllabic canon appears to be contradicted by Middendorf's notation of words having three or more intervocalic consonants. Cerrón-Palomino (1995:127) suggests that these were actually syncopated versions of larger words. But as Cerrón-Palomino (1995:127–28) notes, Carrera's text is unclear as to whether these medially occurring vowel clusters should be considered as separate vowels or (as Middendorf suggests) as diphthongs.

21. Cerrón-Palomino 1995:141–50; he mentions that consonants shift only when a second nominative is formed from a derived noun, or in the formation of a gerund, or in marking the passive.

22. Carrera ([1644] 1939:33) gives, for example, a conjugation for the verb "to bring": *meteiñ* (I bring), *metaz* (you bring), *metang* (he/she/it brings), *meteix* (we bring), *metazchi* (you all bring), *metænang* (they/those bring). See also Carrera [1644] 1939:51.

23. Carrera ([1644] 1939:15–16, 69) uses Latin and Muchic possessive adjectives to illustrate this point:

pater meus (Latin) = pater (father) meus (my)

mæiñ efêio (Muchic) = mæiñ (my) ef/êio (father/possessive marker)

24. Carrera ([1644] 1939:14–15) writes that each noun has two nominative forms, one for general use where there is no propriety or seniority and a second form to indicate direct possession, as in the following example:

quixmicæro	cɥilpiss
quixmic/æro	cɥilpi/ss
old man+possessive	manta+possessive
(the old man's manta)	

Carrera ([1644] 1939:13–19) also states that a genitive suffix can be one of three basic types, depending on the spelling of the root word. The selection of genitive type also appears to be determined by the grammatical use of the phrase in which it occurs. One example would be as follows:

Mocɥilpi	ang	quixmicæro.
Mo/cɥilpi	ang	quixmic/æro.
(this/manta	is	the old man/'s).

25. Carrera ([1644] 1939:69) gives examples of body parts with the genitive ending -eio: ñitereio (buttocks), poleio (heart); see also Carrera [1644] 1939:80–81.

26. Carrera's ([1644] 1939:69) examples of kinship relationships also include genitive endings: uxllureio (cousin or younger sister), ponéio (sister-in-law of man or woman), yquisseio (father-in-law, mother-in-law, brother- or sister-in-law of man).

27. Carrera ([1644] 1939:74) gives an example of a positional adverb: locɥ (eye) +æc (in) = Locɥæc (in the eye); see the additional list of positional adverbs in Carrera [1644] 1939:61–62.

28. Carrera [1644] 1939:19.

29. Carrera ([1644] 1939:14) notes that a plural is created with the suffix +æn, as in mecherræc (woman) +æn = mecherræcæn (women).

30. An example of reduplication from Carrera ([1644] 1939:80–81) is as follows: Locɥ locɥ eio (eye/eye/genitive marker) = eyes (plural).

31. Carrera [1644] 1939:19, 27.

32. Stark (1968:47) gives the following example of sentence order:

čox	ak	kukuli	fahsøk
boy	sees	dove nest	in
S +	V +	D.O. +	Locative

33. Benveniste 1985:234.

34. Kubler 1967:5.

35. Kubler 1967:5.

36. Taube 2000:15.

37. Urton and Brezine (2005:1067) identify a similar tendency toward reduplication of signs as likely place signifiers in the khipus of Puruchuco. Additionally, Urton (1998:426) proposes examples of syntactic junctures where indicators of verbs in Andean khipus will likely occur.

38. Donnan 1978:8.
39. Portrait heads are a noteworthy exception.
40. Donnan and McClelland 1999:59, 104, 176–77.
41. Mixtec records indicate Mixtec culture history as early as A.D. 940. Speculation on any connection between the cultures of the Oaxaca/Pacific coast region and the North Coast of Peru is not the aim of this study, even though some level of interchange surely occurred at various points during history.
42. Extended periods of long-distance exchange surely did occur along the western coasts of Mexico and South America, yet the details of any such exchange are beyond the scope of the present study.
43. Smith 1973a, 1973b; much of what follows here is indebted to her analysis.
44. Smith (1973a:21) explains that when a conquest was represented and only the ruler (and other key figures) was shown, it was assumed that the ruler had a contingent of troops, but they were not included; there are no generic "soldiers."
45. For example, *yucu dzaa* = yucu (hill, substantive) + dzaa (bird, qualifying element); Smith 1973a:36.
46. See Donnan 1978:79–83 for a lengthier discussion of architectural forms and decoration in Moche art; see also Bawden 1996:72 for a discussion of the social symbolism of pyramid architecture.
47. Donnan and McClelland 1999:59.
48. De Bock (2003:313) proposes that step-fret icons with spiral motifs on top signal a specific type of stepped pyramids, those that were the site of sacrificial temples; see also chapter 2, on temples and *huacas*.
49. See, for example, the splendid golden crescent headdress found in the Tomb of the Warrior Priest at Sipán (Alva 1988). Donnan (1978:79, figures 135–36) points out the similarity of architectural ornament and headdress worn by certain individuals.
50. Donnan 1978:73–76, figures 116–23; Donnan and McClelland 1999:60.
51. In the Moche example, Donnan (1978:79) notes that this type of structure would have had a split overlapping gable roof.
52. Although there is some suggestion that in the Andes particular textile designs correlated to specific geographic locations, none is evident in the present example; see Zuidema 1982:446.
53. Actual maces, or *porras*, were generally solid, yet examples of hollow ceramic mace heads used as architectural adornments have been recovered in the Moche and Chicama valleys (Donnan 1978:83, figure 138), as well as at the Huaca de La Luna (Uceda et al. 1998).
54. Pending future investigation, a range of symbols recently identified by Donnan and McClelland (1999) may soon allow this list to expand.
55. Smith (1973b:40), in connection with the Mixtec word *ñuu* (town), discusses this concept, as, for example, the English word *city* can be used either to describe a geographic unit (the city of Dallas) or as part of a proper name (New York City).

56. Zevallos Quiñones 1948b, 1993a, 1993b, 1994.
57. The following examples give some idea of Carrera's usage:

> Ex. 1) *macyæc* (noun), *macycæro* (genitive form):
> el idolo de huaca
> the huaca,   the huaca's idol ([1644] 1939:68)

> Ex. 2) *licapæcoz mæcha macyæc*:
> soleis hacer adoracion a los idolos
> are you accustomed to worship at the huaca: you usually
> make worship to the idols ([1644] 1939:71)

> Ex. 3) *Ecapæcoz xllom pæcna pæn fæpiçær,*
> *ñañissapçæn, pucu, fiñ,*
> Do you think for certain (believe) in your dreams,
> in bird, owl, bird of foretelling (omens),
>
> *pocpoc,   licapæcoz mæcha,*
> bird of foretelling (omens), are you in the
> habit of (accustomed to) worship,
>
> *macyæc,   pong, echallo?*
> sacred place/object of worship (huaca/idol),
> (special) stone, or other thing?
>
> ([1644] 1939:75, vocabulary from 68–74)

58. My translation, from "la palabra mochadero es el nombre vulgar con que los Indio nombran a sus adoratorios" (Calancha, bk. 4, ch. 2 ([1638] 1974–81, 5:1800]).
59. For example, *curandero* is a person who cures, and *matadero* is a place where killing occurs.
60. Sampson 1985:145–47.
61. Sampson 1985:148.
62. Lehmann 1991. Spellings vary depending on source, highlighting the desperate need for intensive linguistic correlation between sources. Carrera wrote "sun" as *xllang*, Middendorf wrote "sun" as *jiang* and "crab" as *iang*, Villareal translated "sun" as *shiam*, and Bastian translated "sun" as *cheang* (Schumacher de Peña 1991:29).
63. The entire passage, quoting Lehmann, is as follows:

> A mi pregunta, porqué las dos palabras sonaban igual, la anciana me contestó literalmente: "porque el cangrejo tiene la corona del mismo rey del sol." Mas tarde, Francisco Cumpa, mi acompañante, me regaló un tal carapacho de cangrejo. En otros, se me aseguró, el dibujo es más claro. El bosquejo adjunto, esquemático, representa el dibujo que se ve claro en el carapacho del cangrejo. Esta información es importante para explicar varias representaciones en los huacos de Trujillo. El dios-cangrejo parece significar entonces un dios-sol, que solía se dibujado a

menudo luchando con otros personajes [To my question, why do the two words sound the same, the old woman answered literally: "because the crab has the same crown as the king of the sun." Later, Francisco Cumpa, my companion, presented me with a crab shell. On others, he assured me, the design is more clear. The attached sketch, schematic, represents the design that is clearly seen in the crab shell. This information is important to explain various representations in the *huacos* (ceramic vessels) of Trujillo. The crab-god appears to signify a sun-god, which is often drawn fighting with other personages] [in Schumacher de Peña 1991:29; my translation].

64. Berrin 1997:151, figure 92.
65. Donnan 1978:29–41.

CHAPTER SEVEN

1. Castillo 1989:30; Donnan 1978:158–72.
2. Langer 1979.
3. Early scholars of narratology refer to this as an Ur-narrative, the core elements of a society's foreknowledge on which all other culturally determined signs must build; see Martin 2006:62, citing Todorov 1969.
4. Donnan 1978:158–72.
5. Castillo 1991; Donnan 1988.
6. Donnan and McClelland 1999.
7. Exceptions are perhaps the filling of background space with small dots or circles seen in Late Moche fineline paintings from San José de Moro (McClelland et al. 2007:20), which seem to signal "ground" in a fairly generic way.
8. Barthes 1977:93.
9. Martin uses the version of the Sacrifice Scene found on a Moche stirrup-spout bottle in the Staatliches Museum für Völkerkunde, Munich, collection, almost certainly originally from San José de Moro.
10. Martin 2006:70.
11. Barthes 1977:86, citing Benveniste 1971:32.
12. Barthes 1977:86.
13. Donnan and McClelland 1999:59. See also Larco Hoyle 1938:77–91 for discussion of regional flora as locator elements. Larco Hoyle (1938:97–103) identifies fish and animals as follows: seventeen kinds of mammals, thirty-seven bird species, seven reptile types, twenty-three types of insects and mollusks, and sixteen kinds of fish.
14. Donnan 1978:73.
15. Carrera [1644] 1939:52.
16. See chapter 5, note 5.

17. In his discussion of the Deer Hunt, Moche blood sacrifice, and jars with ropes in *Spirit of Ancient Peru*, Donnan (1997:58) makes this connection explicit; see also chapter 3.
18. This connection was first noted by Donnan (1978:178).
19. Martin 2006:76.
20. See chapter 4; also see Boone and Mignolo 1994:16; Derrida 1976:3; Martin 2006:76–78.
21. Martin 2006:80. See also Kubler 1967.
22. Bonavia 1985; Donnan and McClelland 1999; Hocquenghem 1987; Krickeberg 1928; Lieske 1992; Lyon 1981; Makowski 2005; McClelland et al. 2007; Quilter 1990, 1997.
23. *Huarochiri Manuscript*, ch. 4 (Urioste 1983; originally compiled by Avila, ca. 1598).
24. Krickeberg 1928; Kroeber 1930; on *Popol Vuh*, see Tedlock 1985.
25. Lyon 1981, 1989; Makowski 2005:33.
26. McClelland et al. 2007:117, 178; Quilter 1997.
27. Donnan 1997:50–59.

CHAPTER EIGHT

1. Stock 1983, 1990; see chapter 5.
2. This type of substitution has been described by John Rowe as "kenning," referring to an Old Norse literary trope most often associated with the Anglo-Saxon epic *Beowulf* and other Old Germanic language oral traditions (Abrams 1993:69). He describes them as comparisons made through the substitution of descriptive phrases whose connection to the original words is known only by familiarity with convention ("her nest of snakes"), versus similes, which are direct comparisons ("her hair is like snakes"), and metaphors, which are implied comparisons ("her snaky hair" [Rowe and Menzel 1967:78–79]). Kenning is closely related to metonymy, which occurs when the literal term for one thing is applied to another, with which it is closely associated because of contiguity in common experience ("crown" or "scepter" stand for "king"), and synecdoche, which refers to a part of something that is used to signify the whole ("ten hands" in place of "ten workmen" [Abrams 1993:68–69]).
3. E. P. Benson, catalog entry in Berrin 1997:164; Donnan 2004a:16–18.
4. Jackson 2004:318.

APPENDIX B

1. For example, Rivero and Tschudi (1851) identified Yunga as an isolated Andean language, having a probable Quechua relationship. J. Alden Mason, in *The Handbook of South American Indians* (1950), echoes the idea that Carrera's Yunga language is similar to Quechua, as does

J. P. Harrington (1945). Yet it is worth mentioning that Jijón y Caamaño's (1940–47) work along with Rivet's findings published in 1949 appear to represent a turning point in linguistic studies of the region and a recognition that Yunga languages are not very much like Quechua at all, the most significant differences being in the languages' basic vowel and consonant sounds.

2. Loukotka 1968. See also Meillet and Cohen 1924.

3. Loukotka 1968:261–62. Northern languages, listed as Ayahuaca, Calva, Tumbi, Lapuna, Colonche, Chanduy, Tacame, Congon, Coaque, Manabi, Huancavilca, Cañari, and Puruhá, are described in greater detail by Loukotka (1968:262–63).

The fact that he has provided so many alternative names for the Southern languages is indicative of the confusion in the literature surrounding the language's nomenclature. Loukotka goes on to name the family's variant dialects as Chimu, Eten, Mochica, Casma, and Paramonga. Chimu was once spoken around the modern city of Trujillo but is now extinct. "Eten" was spoken in the villages of Etén and Monsefu in the department of Lambayeque. Mochica was once spoken on the coast of the department of Libertad. Casma was once spoken on the river of the same name, department of Ancash, and Paramonga was once spoken on the Fortaleza River, department of Ancash.

4. Other "Andean Tribes" are Atacama, Aymara, Catacao, Chibcha, Choco, Diaguit, Huarape, Humahuaca, Jirajara, Lule, Mapuche, Puquina, Quechua, Sechura, Timote, Uru, and Yurimangui. Loukotka also indicates a long stretch of central Peruvian coastline (which includes Ica, Nazca, Lima, Rimac, and Supe) as unclassified. Additionally, the Sechura area near the Ecuadorian border had two independent, nonrelated languages (or stocks, as Loukotka calls them), called Sechura (or Sec) and Catacaos, which coexisted with the larger Chimu language groups distributed to the north, south, and west (Loukotka 1968:261–62).

5. These are essentially the same languages that Loukotka called "Chimu" (Tovar and Tovar 1984:168–70).

6. The Tovars' work differs slightly from Loukotka's in its geographic assignments, stating that the Yunga languages in the Trujillo and Jequetepeque region included Mochica, Chimu, and Quignam. They include Puruhá, Cañari, and Manteña as northern Yunga languages in Ecuador.

7. Jijón y Caamaño 1940–47.

8. In regard to a possible affinity with Quechua, it should be pointed out that Jijón y Caamaño's text has an overtly nationalist agenda, reflecting the bitter political enmity between Peru and Ecuador that exists to this day. The extent to which he did (or did not) cross-reference Yunga and other Ecuadorian languages with Quechua/Aymara is unclear. Notwithstanding the possibility of bias, Jijón y Caamaño's study is this century's main work dealing with Muchic, and his conclusions are widely cited. An independent study by Alfredo Torero seems to support his conclusions. Torero compared word lists for seven North Coast languages

and Quechua (IIb variety) recorded at the time of Spanish conquest by Martinez Compañon. His results show virtually no word correlations with Quechua.

9. Greenberg 1987:38; Rivet 1949. Also see Greenberg's ch. 1, "Principles of Genetic Classification" (1987:1–37).

   In South America, Greenberg divides Amerind into nine major subgroups using linguistic genetic relationships based on restricted comparisons of vocabulary items. These are Macro-Ge, Macro-Panoan, Macro-Carib, Equatorial, Macro-Tucanoan, Andean, Chibchan-Paezan, Hokan, Penutian, and unclassified (Greenberg 1987:389). The Sechura, Catacao, Choluna, Culli, and Leco languages that Loukotka called independent and which the Tovars tentatively placed with Yunga-Puruhá, Greenberg places together to create what he calls "the Northern Andean subgroup." Greenberg (1987:99–100) provides word etymologies for these in support of his classification.

10. Greenberg 1987:106–7.

11. For more on this, see Cerrón-Palomino 1995:49; Stark 1968. The Uru-Chiripaya connection figures strongly in Stark's analysis of possible linguistic relationships between Yunga and Maya languages.

BIBLIOGRAPHY

Abrams, M. H. *A Glossary of Literary Terms*. Fort Worth: Harcourt Brace College Publishers, 1993.

Abu-Lughod, Janet. *Before European Hegemony*. Oxford: Oxford University Press, 1989.

Adams, Hazard, and Leroy Searle, eds. *Critical Theory since 1965*. Tallahassee: Florida State University Press, 1986.

Adorno, Rolena. "The Depiction of Self and Other in Colonial Peru." *Art Journal* 49, no. 2 (1990): 110–18.

Albornoz, Cristóbal de. *La Instrucción para descubrir todas las Guacas del Pirú y sus smayos y haziendas*. 1583. Edited by Pierre Duviols. Paris: Musée de l'homme, 1967.

Allen, Catherine J. *The Hold Life Has: Coca and Cultural Identity in an Andean Community*. Washington, DC: Smithsonian Institution Press, 1988.

Altman, Patricia B. *Ceramics: Form and Technique*. Los Angeles: Museum and Laboratories of Ethnic Arts and Technology, 1970.

Alva, Walter. "Discovering the New World's Richest Unlooted Tomb." *National Geographic* 174, no. 4 (October 1988): 510–49.

———. "Splendors of the Moche, New Royal Tomb Unearthed." *National Geographic* 177, no. 6 (June 1990): 2–15.

Alva, Walter, and Christopher B. Donnan. *Royal Tombs of Sipan*. Los Angeles: Fowler Museum of Cultural History, University of California, 1993.

Anders, Martha B. "Producción cerámica del horizonte medio temprano en Maymi, Valle de Pisco, Perú." In *Tecnología y organización de la producción de cerámica prehispanica en los Andes*, edited by Izumi Shimada. Lima: Pontifica Universidad Católica del Perú, 1994.

Anónimo (Blas Valera). "Relación de las costumbres antiguas de los naturales del Pirú." 1590. In *Crónicas peruanas de interés indigena, Biblioteca de autores españoles*, vol. 209, edited by Francisco Esteve. Madrid: Ediciones Atlas, 1968.

Armas Asmad, J., V. Chamorro Castillo, and G. Jara Flores. "Investigaciones Arqueológicas en el Complejo Huaca del Sol y la Luna: Talleres Alfareros de la Sociedad Moche." Informe de Practicas Pre-Profesionales de Arqueología. Facultad de Ciencias Sociales, Universidad Nacional de Trujillo, 1993.

Arriaga, Pablo Joseph de. *Extirpation of Idolatry in Peru*. 1641. Edited by Clark L. Keating. Lexington: University of Kentucky Press, 1968.

Arsenault, Daniel. "El Personaje del Pie Amputado en la Cultura Mochica del Peru: Un Ensayo sobre la Arqueología del Poder." *Latin American Antiquity* 4, no. 3 (1993): 225–45.

Attarian, Christopher. "Plant Foods and Ceramic Production: A Case Study of Mochica Ceramic Production Specialists in the Chicama Valley, Peru." Master's thesis, Department of Anthropology, University of California, Los Angeles, 1996.

———. "Pre-Hispanic Urbanism and Community Expression in the Chicama Valley, Peru." Ph.D. diss., Department of Anthropology, University of California, Los Angeles, 2003.

Austin, William M., ed. *Papers on Linguistics in Honor of Leon Dostert*. The Hague: Mouton, 1967.

Aveni, Anthony. "Non-Western Notational Frameworks and the Role of Anthropology in Our Understanding of Literacy." In *Toward a New Understanding of Literacy*, edited by Merald E. Wrolstad and Dennis F. Fisher. New York: Praeger, 1986.

Balfet, Helene, Marie-France Fauvet-Berthelot, and Susana Monzon. *Lexique Plurilingue pour la Description des Poteries*. Paris: Centre National de la Recherche Scientifique, 1988.

Ball, F. Carlton, and Janice Lovoos. *Making Pottery without a Wheel*. New York: Reinhold Publishing Co., 1965.

Barthes, Roland. "Introduction to the Structural Elements of Narrative." In *Image—Music—Text*, translated by Stephen Heath. New York: Hill and Wang, 1977.

———. *Elements of Semiology*. 1964. New York: Noonday Press, 1992.

Basso, Keith H. "The Ethnography of Writing." In *Explorations in the Ethnography of Speaking*, edited by Richard Bauman and Joel Sherzer. Cambridge: Cambridge University Press, 1989.

Bastian, Adolf. *Die culturländer des alten America*. Berlin: Weidmannsche buchhandlung, 1878.

Bastien, Joseph W. *Mountain of the Condor*. American Ethnological Society, Monograph 64. Prospect Heights, IL: Waveland Press, 1985.

Bawden, Garth. "Galindo: A Study in Cultural Transition during the Middle Horizon." In *Chan Chan: Andean Desert City*, edited by Michael Moseley and Kent Day. Albuquerque: University of New Mexico Press, 1982.

———. "Nuevas formas de ceramica Moche V procedentes de Galindo, valle de Moche, Peru." In *Moche: Propuestas y Perspectivas*, edited by Santiago Uceda and Elias Mujica. Lima: Universidad Nacional de La Libertad, 1994.

———. *Moche*. Cambridge: Blackwell Publishers, 1996.

Bennett, Wendell C. "Archaeology of Peru's North Coast." In *Anthropology Papers of the American Museum of Natural History*, vol. 37, pt. 1. New York: Museum of Natural History, 1939.

———. *The Gallinazo Group, Viru Valley, Peru*. Yale University Publications in Anthropology, no. 43. New Haven: Yale University, 1950.

Bennyhoff, James A. "The Viru Valley Sequence: A Critical Review." *American Antiquity* 17 (1952): 231–49.

Benson, Elizabeth P. *The Mochica*. New York: Praeger Publishers, 1972.

———, ed. *The Cult of the Feline Conference*. Washington, DC: Dumbarton Oaks Research Library and Collections, 1972.

———. "A Man and a Feline in Mochica Art." In *Studies in Pre-Colombian Art and Archaeology*, no. 14. Washington, DC: Dumbarton Oaks, 1974.

———. *Death and the Afterlife in Pre-Columbian America*. Washington, DC: Dumbarton Oaks, 1975.

———. "The World of Moche." In *The Ancient Americas: Art from Sacred Landscapes*, edited by Richard Townsend. Chicago: Art Institute of Chicago, 1992.

———. "Art, Agriculture, Warfare and the Guano Islands." In *Andean Art: Visual Expression and Its Relation to Andean Beliefs and Values*, edited by Penny Dransart. Hampshire: Avebury Press, 1995.

Benson, Elizabeth P., and William Conklin. *Museums of the Andes*. Tokyo: Newsweek, Inc., 1981.

Benveniste, Emile. *Problems in General Linguistics*. 1966. Translated by Mary Meek. Coral Gables: University of Miami Press, 1971.

———. "The Semiology of Language." Reprint. In *Semiotics*, edited by Robert Innis. Bloomington: Indiana University Press, 1985.

Berezkin, Yuri E. "An Identification of Anthropomorphic Mythological Personages in Moche Representations." *Ñawpa Pacha* 18 (1981): 1–26. Berkeley.

Bergh, Susan E. "Death and Renewal in Moche Phallic-Spouted Vessels." *RES: Anthropology and Aesthetics* (Cambridge, MA) 24 (1993): 78–94.

Berlo, Janet C. "Conceptual Categories for the Study of Texts and Images in Mesoamerica." In *Text and Image in Pre-Columbian Art*, edited by Janet Berlo. BAR International Series 180. Oxford: BAR Press, 1983.

———. "Early Writing in Central Mexico: *In Tlilli, In Tlapalli* before AD 1000." In *Mesoamerica after the Decline of Teotihuacan*, edited by R. Diehl and J. Berlo. Washington, DC: Dumbarton Oaks, 1989.

Berrin, Kathleen, ed. *The Spirit of Ancient Peru*. New York: Thames and Hudson; and San Francisco: Fine Arts Museum of San Francisco, 1997.

Berrin, Kathleen, and Esther Pasztory. *Teotihuacan: Art from the City of the Gods*. New York: Thames and Hudson; and San Francisco: Fine Arts Museums of San Francisco, 1994.

Betanzos, Juan de. *Narratives of the Incas*. 1557. Austin: University of Texas Press, 1996.

Binford, Lewis R. "Mortuary Practices: Their Study and Their Potential." In *An Archaeological Perspective*. Studies in Archaeology Series. New York: Seminar Press, 1972.

Bird, Junius. "Preceramic Art from Huaca Prieta, Chicama Valley." *Ñawpa Pacha* 1 (1963): 29–34.

———. "Preceramic Cultures in Chicama and Viru." 1948. Reprint. In *Peruvian Archaeology: Selected Readings*, edited John H. Rowe and Dorothy Menzel. Palo Alto: Peek Publications, 1967. First published in *American Antiquity* 13, no. 4.

Boas, Franz. *Kwakiutl Ethnography*. Chicago: University of Chicago Press, 1966.

Bonavia, Ducio. "A Mochica Painting at Pañamarca." *American Antiquity* 26, no. 4 (April 1961): 540–43.

———. *Mural Painting in Ancient Peru*. Bloomington: University of Indiana Press, 1985.

Boone, Elizabeth H. "Writing and Recorded Knowledge in Pre-Columbian America." In *Records without Words. Dumbarton Oaks, March 1991. Papers from Dumbarton Oaks Conference, March 1991, "Art and Writing: Recording Knowledge in Pre-Columbian America."* Washington, DC: Dumbarton Oaks, 1992.

———, ed. *Andean Art at Dumbarton Oaks*, vols. 1–2. Washington, DC: Dumbarton Oaks, 1996.

———. *Stories in Red and Black: Pictorial Histories of the Aztecs and Mixtecs*. Austin: University of Texas Press, 2000.

Boone, Elizabeth H., and Walter D. Mignolo. *Writing without Words*. Durham: Duke University Press, 1994.

Bourget, Steve. "Bestiare sacre et flore magique: Ecologie rituelle de l'iconographie de la culture Mochica, cote nord du Perou." Ph.D. diss., Department d'anthropologie, Universite de Montreal, 1994a.

———. "Los Sacerdotes a la Sombra del Cerro Blanco y del Arco Bicefalo." *Revista de Museo de Arqueología, Antropología, e Historia* 5 (1994b): 81–125. Trujillo.

———. "Las Excavaciones en la Plaza 3A de la Huaca de La Luna." In *Investigaciones en la Huaca de la Luna 1995*, edited by Santiago Uceda, Elias Mujica, and Ricardo Morales. Trujillo: Universidad Nacional de La Libertad, 1997.

———. "Rituals of Sacrifice: Its Practice at Huaca de la Luna and Its Representation in Moche Iconography." In *Moche Art and Archaeology in Ancient Peru*, edited by Joanne Pillsbury. Washington, DC: Center for Advanced Study of the Visual Arts, National Gallery of Art, 2001.

———. *Sex, Death, and Sacrifice in Moche Religion and Visual Culture*. Austin: University of Texas Press, 2006.

Bourget, Steve, and Margaret E. Newman. "A Toast to the Ancestors: Ritual Warfare and Sacrificial Blood in Moche Culture." *Baessler Archiv N.F.* 46 (1998): 85–106. Berlin.

Bower, Gordon H. "Analysis of a Mnemonic Device." *American Scientist* 58, no. 5 (September–October 1970): 496–510.

Bray, Tamara. "Inka Pottery as Culinary Equipment: Food, Feasting, and Gender in Imperial State Design." *Latin American Antiquity* 14 (2003): 3–28.

Brice, W. C. "The Principles of Non-phonetic Writing." In *Writing without Letters*, edited by W. Haas. Manchester: University of Manchester Press, 1976.

Brotherston, Gordon. *Book of the Fourth World*. Cambridge: Cambridge University Press, 1992.

Brumfiel, Elizabeth M., and Timothy K. Earle. *Specialization, Exchange, and Complex Societies*. Cambridge: Cambridge University Press, 1987.

Bruning, Enrique. *Estudios monograficos del departamento de Lambayeque*. Chiclayo: Fasciculo II-Olmos, 1922.

———. *Lambeyeque Estudios Monograficos*. 1928. Chiclayo: SICAN, 1989.

Bryson, Norman. *Word and Image: French Painting of the Ancien Regime*. Cambridge: Cambridge University Press, 1981.

———. *Vision and Painting*. New Haven: Yale University Press, 1983.

Buchwald, Otto von. "Migraciones sudamericanas." *Boletín de la Sociedad Ecuatoriana de Estudios Historicos Americanos* 1 (1918): 227–36. Quito.

Burger, Richard L. *The Prehistoric Occupation of Chavin de Huantar*. University of California Publications in Anthropology, vol. 14. Berkeley: University of California Press, 1984.

———. *Chavin and the Origins of Andean Civilization*. London: Thames and Hudson, 1992.

Burkhart, Louise. *The Slippery Earth: Nahua–Christian Moral Dialog in 16th Century Mexico*. Tucson: University of Arizona Press, 1989.

Cabello Valboa, Miguel. *Miscelanea Antarctica*. Lima: Universidad Nacional Mayor de San Marcos, 1951.

Calancha, Antonio de la. *Coronica Moralizada de la Provincia del Peru*. 1638. 6 vols. Transcribed and edited by Ignacio Prado Pastor. Lima: Universidad Nacional Mayor de San Marcos, 1974–81.

Camille, Michael. "Seeing and Reading: Some Visual Implications of Medieval Literacy and Illiteracy." *Art History* 8, no. 1 (1985): 26–49.

Campana, Cristobal, and Ricardo Morales. *Historia de una Deidad Mochica.* Lima: A and B, S.A., 1997.

Campbell, James Edward. *Pottery and Ceramics.* Art and Architecture Information Guide Series, vol. 7. Detroit: Gale Research Company, 1978.

Carmichael, Patrick H. "Nasca Ceramics: Production and Social Context." In *Andean Ceramics: Technology, Organization, and Approaches,* edited by Izumi Shimada. MASCA Research Papers in Science and Archaeology, Supplement to Vol. 15. Philadelphia: Museum Applied Science Center for Archaeology, University of Pennsylvania Museum of Archaeology and Anthropology, 1998.

Carr, Christopher. "Mortuary Practices: Their Social, Philosophical-Religious, Circumstantial, and Physical Determinants." *Journal of Archaeological Method and Theory* 2, no. 2 (1995): 105–200.

Carrera, Fernando de la. *Arte de la lengua yunga.* 1644. Edited by Ramades A. Altieri. Tucman, Argentina: Instituto de Antropologia, 1939.

Carruthers, Mary J. *The Book of Memory.* Cambridge: Cambridge University Press, 1990.

Castillo, Luis Jaime. *Personajes miticos, escenas y narraciones en la iconografia mochica.* Lima: Pontifica Universidad Católica del Perú, Fondo Editorial, 1989.

———. "Narrations in Moche Iconography." Master's thesis, Department of Anthropology, University of California, Los Angeles, 1991.

Castillo, Luis Jaime, and Christopher Donnan. "Los Mochicas de Norte y los Mochicas del Sur." In *Vicús,* edited by Krzystof Makowski, Christopher B. Donnan, and Ivan Amaro Bullon. Lima: Banco de Credito, 1994.

Castriota, David. *Artistic Strategies and the Rhetoric of Power.* Carbondale: Southern Illinois University Press, 1986.

Cerrón-Palomino, Rodolfo. *Lengua de Naymlap (Reconstruccion y Obsolescencia de Mochica).* Lima: Pontifica Universidad Católica del Perú, Fondo Editorial, 1995.

Ceruti, Constanza. "Human Bodies as Objects of Dedication at Inca Mountain Shrines." *World Archaeology* 36, no. 1 (2004): 103–22.

Chapdelaine, Claude. "The Growing Power of a Moche Urban Class." In *Moche Art and Archaeology in Ancient Peru,* edited by Joanne Pillsbury. Washington, DC: Center for Advanced Study of the Visual Arts, National Gallery of Art, 2001.

———. "The Moche Occupation of the Lower Santa Valley and the Nature of the Southern Moche State." Paper presented at the 69th annual meeting of the Society for American Archaeology, at the session "Southern Moche: Understanding the First Expansionist State on the North Coast of Peru," Montreal, April 1, 2004. http://www.anthro.umontreal.ca/colloques/2004/SAA04.

Chapdelaine, Claude, Santiago Uceda, Maria Montoya, C. Jauregui, and Ch. Uceds. "Los Complejos arquitectonicos urbanos de Moche." In *Investigaciones en la Huaca de la Luna 1995*, edited by Santiago Uceda, Elias Mujica, and Ricardo Morales. Facultad de Ciencias Sociales. Trujillo: Universidad Nacional de La Libertad, 1997.

Cieza de Leon, Pedro de. *Conquest of Peru*. 1553. Translated by Harriet de Onis and V. W. von Hagen. Norman: University of Oklahoma, 1959.

Cobo, Bernabe. *History of the Inca Empire*. 1653. Translated by Roland Hamilton. Austin: University of Texas Press, 1973.

———. *Inca Religion and Customs*. 1653. Austin: University of Texas Press, 1990.

Coe, Michael D. *Breaking the Maya Code*. New York: Thames and Hudson, 1992.

Cohen, David Harris, and Catherine Hess. *Looking at European Ceramics*. Los Angeles: J. Paul Getty Museum, 1993.

Collier, Donald. "Cultural Chronology and Change as Reflected in the Ceramics of the Viru Valley, Peru." In *Fieldiana: Anthropology*, vol. 46. Chicago: Field Museum of Natural History, 1955.

———. "Pottery Stamping and Molding on the North Coast of Peru." In *Actas del 33rd Congreso Internacional de Americanistas*, 2. San Jose, Costa Rica: Congreso Internacional de Americanistas, 1959.

Collon, Dominique. *Interpreting the Past: Near Eastern Seals*. London: British Museum Press, 1990.

Conkey, Margaret, and Christine Hasdorf. *The Uses of Style in Archaeology*. Cambridge: Cambridge University Press, 1990.

Conrad, G. W., and A. Demerest. *Religion and Empire: The Dynamics of Aztec and Inca Expansionism*. Cambridge, MA: Harvard University Press, 1984.

Cook, Anita. "Art and Time in the Evolution of Andean State Expansionism." Ph.D. diss., New York State University, Binghamton, 1985.

———. *Wari y Tiwanaku: Entre el estilo y la imagen*. Lima: Pontifica Universidad Católica del Perú, Fondo Editorial, 1994.

Cordy-Collins, Alana, ed. *Pre-Columbian Art Selected Readings*. Palo Alto: Peek Publications, 1977.

———. "Archaism or Tradition?: The Decapitation Theme in Cupisnique and Moche Iconography." *Latin American Antiquity* 3, no. 3 (1992): 206–20.

Cummins, Thomas B. "Abstraction to Narration: *Kero* Imagery of Peru and the Colonial Alteration of Native Identity." Ph.D. diss., Department of Art History, University of California, Los Angeles, 1988.

———. "The Style and Technology of Prehispanic Ecuadorian Figurines." Paper presented at the College Art Association meetings, Washington, DC, 1991.

———. "La Tradicion de Figurinas de la Costa Ecuatoriana: Estilo Tecnologico y el Uso de Moldes." In *Tecnologia y Organizacion de la Produccion de Ceramica Prehispanica en los Andes*, edited by Izumi Shimada. Lima: Pontifica Universidad Católica del Perú, 1994.

———. *Toasts with the Inca: Andean Abstraction and Colonial Images on Quero Vessels*. Ann Arbor: University of Michigan Press, 2002.

———. "Nature as Culture's Representation: A Change of Focus in Late Formative Iconography." In *Archaeology of Formative Ecuador*, edited by J. Scott Raymond and Richard Burger. Washington, DC: Dumbarton Oaks, 2003.

Cummins, Thomas, and Holme Olaf. "Ecuadorian Pre-Hispanic Art." Postdoctoral manuscript, Massachusetts Institute of Technology, Boston, 1989.

Cushion, J. P., and W. B. Honey. *Handbook of Pottery and Porcelain Marks*. London: Faber and Faber, 1956.

Darwin, Charles. *Narrative of the Surveying Voyages of His Majesty's Ships Adventure and Beagle, Between the Years 1826 and 1836 . . .*, vol. 3. London: Henry Colburn, 1839.

De Bock, Edward K. "Templo de la escalera y ola y la hora del sacrificio humano." In *Moche: Hacia el final del milenio*, vol. 1, edited by Santiago Uceda and Elias Mujica. Lima: Universidad Nacional de Trujillo and Pontificia Universidad Católica del Perú, 2003.

De Boer, Warren. "Figuring Figurines: The Case of the Chachi, Ecuador." In *Recent Advances in the Archaeology of the Northern Andes: In Memory of Gerardo Reichel-Dolmatoff*, edited by Augusto Oyuela-Caycedo and J. Scott Raymond. Los Angeles: University of California–Los Angeles Institute of Archeology Press, 1998.

DeFrancis, John. *Visible Speech: The Diverse Oneness of Writing Systems*. Honolulu: University of Hawaii Press, 1989.

Derrida, Jaques. *Of Grammatology*. Translated by Gayatri Chakravorty Spivak. Baltimore: Johns Hopkins University Press, 1976.

———. "Structure, Sign and Play in the Discourse of the Human Sciences." In *Critical Theory since 1965*, edited by Hazard Adams and Leroy Searle. Tallahassee: Florida State University Press, 1986.

Di Capua, Constanza. "Valdivia Figurines and Puberty Rituals." *Andean Past* 4 (1994): 229–79.

Dobres, Marcia-Ann, and John E. Robb, eds. *Agency in Archaeology*. London: Routledge Press, 2000.

Donnan, Christopher B. "An Ancient Peruvian Architectural Model." *The Masterkey* 49(1): 20–29.

———. *Moche Art and Iconography*. University of California–Los Angeles Latin American Center. Los Angeles: University of California Press, 1976.

———. *Moche Art of Peru: Pre-Columbian Symbolic Communication*. Museum of Cultural History. Los Angeles: University of California Press, 1978.

———. "Dance in Moche Art." *Ñawpa Pacha*, no. 20 (1982): 97–120. Berkeley.

———. "Unraveling the Mystery of the Warrior-Priest." *National Geographic* 174, no. 4 (1988): 550–55.

———. "Masterworks of Art Reveal a Remarkable Pre-Inca World." *National Geographic* 177, no. 6 (1990): 17–33.

———. *Ceramics of Ancient Peru*. Los Angeles: University of California–Los Angeles Fowler Museum, 1992.

———. "Deer Hunting and Combat." In *The Spirit of Ancient Peru*, edited by Kathleen Berrin. San Francisco: Fine Arts Museum of San Francisco, Thames and Hudson, 1997.

———. *Moche Portraits from Ancient Peru*. Austin: University of Texas Press, 2004a.

———. "Moche State Religion: A Unifying Force in Moche Political Organization." Paper presented at the Dumbarton Oaks, Pontificia Universidad Católica del Perú, and Museo Larco Herrera symposium "New Perspectives on Moche Political Organization," Lima, August 2004b.

Donnan, Christopher, and Luis Jaime Castillo. "Finding the Tomb of a Moche Priestess." *Archaeology* 45, no. 6 (1992): 38–42.

———. "Excavaciones de tumbas de sacerdotisas Moche en San Jose de Moro, Jequetepeque." In *Moche: Propuestas y Perspectivas*, edited by Santiago Uceda and Elias Mujica. Lima: Universidad Nacional de La Libertad, 1994.

Donnan, Christopher B., and Gillermo Cock. *Pacatnamu Papers*. Los Angeles: Museum of Cultural History, University of California Press, 1986.

Donnan, Christopher B., and Carol Mackey. *Ancient Burial Patterns of the Moche Valley, Peru*. Austin: University of Texas Press, 1978.

Donnan, Christopher B., and Donna McClelland. *Moche Fineline Painting: Its Evolution and Its Artists*. Los Angeles: University of California–Los Angeles Fowler Museum of Cultural History, 1999.

Doyle, Mary E. "Ancestor Cult and Burial Ritual in the Seventeenth and Eighteenth Century, Central Peru." Ph.D. diss., University of California, Los Angeles, 1988.

Doyle, Michael. *Empires*. Ithaca, NY: Cornell University Press, 1986.

Dransart, Penny. *Elemental Meanings: Symbolic Expression in Inka Miniature Figurines*. London: Institute of Latin American Studies, 1995.

Dubois, Marguerite-Marie. *Larousse's French–English Dictionary*. New York: Washington Square Press, 1970.

Duviols, Pierre. *Cultura Andina y Represion (Extirpation of Idolatry in Cajatambo, Peru)*. Achivos de Historia Andina, no. 5. Cuzco: Centro de Estudios Rurales Andinos, 1987.

Earle, Timothy K. "Comment on Evolution of Specialized Pottery Production: A Trial Model, by P. M. Rice." *Current Anthropology* 22 (1981): 219–40.

———. "Specialization and the Production of Wealth: Hawaiian Chiefdoms and the Inka Empire." In *Specialization, Exchange, and Complex Societies*, edited by Elizabeth M. Brumfiel and Timothy K. Earle. Cambridge: Cambridge University Press, 1987.

Edmonson, Munro S. *Lore.* New York: Holt, Rinehart and Winston, Inc., 1971.

Elkins, James. *The Domain of Images.* Ithaca, NY: Cornell University Press, 1999.

Estete, Miguel. "Noticia del Peru." 1535. In *Biblioteca Peruana*, ser. 1, vol. 1. Lima: Editores Tecnicos Asociados, 1968.

Fogel, Heidi. "Settlements in Time: A Study of Social and Political Development during the Gallinazo Occupation of the North Coast of Peru." Ph.D. diss., Yale University. Ann Arbor: University Microfilms International, 1993.

Ford, James. "Cultural Dating of Prehistoric Sites in Viru Valley, Peru." *Anthropological Papers of the American Museum of Natural History* 43, pt. 1. New York: Museum of Natural History, 1949.

Ford, James, and Gordon Willey. "Surface Survey in the Viru Valley, Peru." In *Anthropological Papers of the American Museum of Natural History* 43(1). New York, 1949.

Foucault, Michel. *The Foucalt Reader.* Edited by Paul Rabinow. Harmondsworth, UK: Penguin, 1986.

———. *The Archaeology of Knowledge* and *The Discourse on Language*. 1972. Translated by A. M. Sheridan Smith. New York: Barnes and Noble, 1993.

Franco J., Regulo, Cesar Galvez M., and Segundo Vasquez S. "Arquitectura y Decoración Mochica en la Huaca Cao Viejo, Complejo El Brujo: Resultados Preliminares." In *Moche Propuestas y Perspectivas*, edited by Santiago Uceda and Elias Mujica. Lima: Universidad Nacional de La Libertad, 1994.

———. "Los descubrimientos Arquológicos en la Huaca Cao Viejo, Complejo El Brujo." *Arkinka*, no. 5 (1996): 82–94. Lima.

———. "Desentierro ritual de una tumba Moche." *Revista Arqueológica SIAN*, año 3, no. 6 (1998): 9–18. Trujillo.

———. "Porras Mochicas del Complejo El Brujo." *Revista Arqueológica SIAN*, año 4, no. 7 (June 1999): 16–23. Trujillo.

Franco J., Regulo, and Juan Vilela. "Aproximaciones al calendario ceremonial Mochica del complejo El Brujo, valle Chicama." In *Moche: Hacia el Final del Milenio*, vol. 1, edited by Santiago Uceda and Elias Mujica. Lima: Universidad Nacional de Trujillo and Pontificia Universidad Católica del Perú, Fondo Editorial, 2003.

Franco, Regulo, Cesar Galvez, and Segundo Vasquez. "Modelo, funcion y cronologia de la Huaca Cao Viejo, complejo El Brujo." In *Moche: Hacia el Final del Milenio*, vol. 1, edited by Santiago Uceda and Elias Mujica. Lima: Universidad Nacional de Trujillo and Pontificia Universidad Católica del Perú, Fondo Editorial, 2003.

French, Pamela. "The Problems of In Situ Conservation of Mudbrick and Mud Plaster." In *In Situ Archaeological Conservation*. Malibu: Getty Conservation Institute, 1987.

Galvez M., Cesar, and Jesus Briceño R. "The Moche in the Chicama Valley." In *Moche Art and Archaeology in Ancient Peru*, edited by Joanne Pillsbury. Washington, DC: Center for Advanced Study of the Visual Arts, National Gallery of Art, 2001.

Garcilaso de la Vega, El Inca. *The Royal Commentaries of the Inca Garcilaso de la Vega*. 1609. Edited by Alain Gheerbrant. New York: Orion Books, 1961.

Gelb, Ignacio J. *A Study of Writing*. Chicago: University of Chicago Press, 1974.

Giersz, Milosz, Krzystof Makowski, and Patrycja Przadka. *El Mundo Sobrenatural Mochica*. Lima: Fondo Editorial de la Pontificia Universidad Católica del Perú, 2005.

Gledhill, John, and Barbara Bender, eds. *State and Society: The Emergence and Development of Social Hierarchy and Political Centralization*. London: Unwin Hyman, 1988.

Gölte, Jürgen. *Los Dioses de Sipan*. Lima: Instituto de Estudios Peruanos, 1993.

———. *Iconos y Narraciones*. Lima: Instituto de Estudios Peruanos, 1994.

Goodman, Nelson. *Languages of Art*. Indianapolis: Hackett, 1976.

———. *Of Mind and Other Matters*. Cambridge, MA: Harvard University Press, 1984.

Goody, Jack. *The Interface between the Written and the Oral*. Cambridge: Cambridge University Press, 1987.

Greenberg, Joseph H. *Language in the Americas*. Stanford: Stanford University Press, 1987.

Grice-Hutchinson, Marjorie. *Early Economic Thought in Spain, 1177–1740*. Boston: George Allen and Unwin, 1978.

Grieder, Terence. "Interpretation of Ancient Symbols." *American Anthropologist* 77, no. 1 (1975): 849–55.

Guaman Poma de Ayala, Felipe. *La nueva cronica y buen gobierno*. 1613. 3 vols. Translated by Luis Bustios Galvez. Lima: Lima Editorial Cultura, 1956.

Gutierrez L., Belkys. "Porras: Simbologia y estatus en los rituals Moche." *Revista Arqueologica SIAN*, año 4, no. 7 (June 1999): 9–15. Trujillo.

Haas, Jonathan, Shelia Pozorski, and Thomas Pozorski, eds. *The Origins and Development of the Andean State*. Cambridge: Cambridge University Press, 1987.

Haas, W., ed. *Writing without Letters*. Manchester: Manchester University Press, 1976.

Hamer, Frank, and Janet Hamer. *The Potter's Dictionary of Materials and Techniques*. London: A and C Black, Ltd., 1986.

Hanks, William F., and Don S. Rice. *Word and Image in Maya Culture: Explorations in Language, Writing, and Representation*. Salt Lake City: University of Utah Press, 1989.

Harbsmeier, Michael. "Invention of Writing." In *State and Society: The Emergence and Development of Social Hierarchy and Political Centralization*, edited by John Gledhill and Barbara Bender. London: Unwin Hyman, 1988.

Harrington, John P. "Yunka, Language of the Peruvian Coastal Culture." *International Journal of American Linguistics* 11, no. 1 (1945): 24–30.

Harrison, Regina. *Signs, Songs, and Memory in the Andes*. Austin: University of Texas Press, 1989.

Hill, Archibald. "The Typology of Writing Systems." In *Papers on Linguistics in Honor of Leon Dostert*, edited by W. M. Austin. The Hague: Mouton, 1967.

Hobsbawm, Eric, and Terence Ranger, eds. *The Invention of Tradition*. Cambridge: Cambridge University Press, 1983.

Hocquenghem, Anne Marie. *Iconografica Mochica*. Lima: Pontifica Universidad Católica del Perú, Fondo Editorial, 1987.

Hocquenghem, Anne Marie, and P. Lyon. "A Class of Anthropomorphic Supernatural Females in Moche Iconography." *Ñawpa Pacha*, no. 18 (1980): 27–50. Berkeley.

Hodder, Ian. *Symbols in Action: Ethnoarchaeological Studies of Material Culture*. New York: Cambridge University Press, 1982.

———. "Agency and Individuals in Long-Term Processes." In *Agency in Archaeology*, edited by Marcia-Anne Dobres and Hohn E. Robb. London: Routledge Press, 2000.

Hodder, Ian, and Clive Orton. *Spatial Analysis in Archaeology*. London: Cambridge University Press, 1976.

Hodges, Henry. *In Situ Archaeological Conservation*. Malibu: Getty Conservation Institute, 1987.

Horkheimer, Hans. *Vistas arqueológicas del noroeste del Perú*. Trujillo: Instituto Arqueológico de la Universidad Nacional de Trujillo, Libreria y Imprenta Moreno, 1944.

Houston, Stephen D. "The Archaeology of Communication Technologies." *Annual Review of Anthropology* 33 (2004): 223–50.

Hull, G. *Changing Work, Changing Workers: Critical Perspectives on Language, Literacy and Skills*. Albany: State University of New York Press, 1997.

Huntington, Richard, and Peter Metcalf. *Celebrations of Death*. Cambridge: Cambridge University Press, 1979.

Innis, Robert E., ed. *Semiotics: An Introductory Anthology*. Bloomington: Indiana University Press, 1985.

Jackson, Margaret A. "Mold Use at Cerro Mayal, Chicama Valley, Peru." Paper presented at the 33rd Annual Meetings of the Institute for Andean Studies, Berkeley, 1993.

———. "Moche Iconography and Visual Notation at Cerro Mayal, Peru." Paper presented at the 63rd annual Society of American Archaeology meetings, at the session "Beyond Temples and Tombs: Recent Work in Moche Studies," Seattle, 1998.

———. "Notation and Narrative in Moche Iconography, Cerro Mayal, Perú." Ph.D. diss., Department of Art History, University of California, Los Angeles, 2000.

———. "Proto-writing in Moche Pottery at Cerro Mayal, Perú." In *Andean Archaeology II*, edited by Helaine Silverman and William H. Isbell. New York: Plenum Publishers, 2002.

———. "The Chimú Sculptures of Huacas Tacaynamo and El Dragón, Moche Valley, Perú." *Latin American Antiquity* 15, no. 3 (September 2004): 298–322.

Jijón y Caamaño, Jacinto. *El Ecuador interandino y occidental antes de la conquista castellana*, 4 vols. Quito: Editorial Ecuatoriana, 1940–47.

Jiménez Borja, Arturo. *Moche*. Lima: Editorial Lumen, S.A., 1938.

———. "Instrumentos musicales peruanos." In *Revista de Museo Nacional* 19–20. Lima, 1951.

Jones, G. D., and R. Kautz, eds. *The Transition to Statehood in the New World*. New York: Cambridge University Press, 1981.

Jones, Julie. "Mochica Works of Art in Metal." In *Pre-Columbian Metallurgy of South America*, edited by E. P. Benson. Washington, DC: Dumbarton Oaks, 1979.

Kaeppler, Adrienne L. "Memory and Knowledge in the Production of Dance." In *Images of Memory*, edited by S. Küchler and W. Melion. Washington, DC: Smithsonian Institution Press, 1991.

Kaulicke, Peter. *Memoria y Muerte en el Perú Antiguo*. Lima: Pontificia Universidad Católica del Perú, Fondo Editorial, 2000.

Keatinge, R. *Peruvian Prehistory*. Cambridge: Cambridge University Press, 1988.

Kosok, Paul. *Life, Land, and Water in Ancient Peru*. New York: Long Island University Press, 1965.

Krickeberg, Walter. "Mexicanishe-Peruanische Parallelen. Ein Ueberblick und ine Ergänzung." In *Festschrift: Publication D'Hommage offerte au P. W. Schmidt*, edited by Wilhelm Koppers. Vienna: Mechithiaristen-Congregations-Buchdruckerei, 1928.

Kroeber, Alfred L. "The Uhle Pottery Collections from Moche." In *University of California Publications in American Archaeology and Ethnography*, vol. 21, nos. 5–6. Berkeley: University of California, 1925.

———. "Archaeological Explorations in Peru, Part 1: Ancient Pottery from Trujillo." In *Anthropology Memoirs*, vol. 2, no. 1. Chicago: Field Museum of Natural History, 1926.

———. "Archaeological Explorations in Peru, Part 2: The Northern Coast." In *Anthropology Memoirs*, vol. 2, no. 2. Chicago: Field Museum of Natural History, 1930.

———. *Peruvian Archaeology in 1942*. Viking Fund Publications in Anthropology, no. 4. New York: Viking Fund, 1944.

———. "Proto-Lima: A Middle Period Culture of Peru." In *Fieldiana*, vol. 44. Chicago: Natural History Museum, 1954.

———. *Style and Civilizations*. Ithaca, NY: Cornell University Press, 1957.

Kubler, George. "Toward Absolute Time: Guano Archeology." In *A Reappraisal of Peruvian Archaeology*, edited by W. Bennett. Memoirs of the Society for American Archaeology and Institute for Andean Research, no. 4. Washington, DC: Society for American Archaeology and Institute for Andean Research, 1948.

———. *The Art and Architecture of Ancient America*. Baltimore: Penguin Books, 1962a.

———. *The Shape of Time*. New Haven: Yale University Press, 1962b.

———. "The Iconography and Art of Teotihuacan." In *Studies in Pre-Columbian Art and Architecture*, no. 4. Washington, DC: Dumbarton Oaks, 1967.

———. "Period, Style, and Meaning in Ancient American Art." *New Literary History: A Journal of Theory and Interpretation from the University of Virginia* 1, no. 2 (1970): 127–44.

———. "Science and Humanism among Americanists." In *The Iconography of Middle American Sculpture*, by Ignacio Bernal and Elizabeth K. Easby. New York: Metropolitan Museum of Art, 1973.

Küchler, Susanne, and Walter Melion, eds. *Images of Memory: On Remembering and Representation*. Washington, DC: Smithsonian Institution Press, 1991.

Kus, James S. "Selected Aspects of Irrigated Agriculture in the Chimu Heartland, Peru." Ph.D. diss., University of California, Los Angeles, 1972.

Kutscher, Gerdt. *Chimu, eine altindianische Hochhkultur*. Berlin: Verlag Gebr. Mann, 1950.

———. *Nord-peruanische Gefafsmalereien de Moche-Stils*. Munich: Verlag C. H. Beck, 1983.

LaGamma, Alisa. "A Visual Sonata at Teotihuacan." *Ancient Mesoamerica* 2, no. 2 (Fall 1991): 275–84. Cambridge.

Langer, Susanne K. *Mind: An Essay on Human Feeling.* Baltimore: Johns Hopkins University Press, 1967.

———. "Discursive and Presentational Forms." 1942. In *Philosophy in a New Key.* Cambridge, MA: Harvard University Press, 1979.

Langley, James C. "The Forms and Usage of Notation at Teotihuacan." *Ancient Mesoamerica* 2, no. 2 (Fall 1991): 285–98. Cambridge.

Lapiner, Alan. *Pre-Columbian Art of South America.* New York: Abrams, 1976.

Lara, Jesus, ed. *Diccionario Qheshwa-Castellano.* La Paz: Los Amigos del Libro Impresores, 1978.

Larco Hoyle, Rafael. *Los Mochicas*, vol. 1. Museo Rafael Larco Herrera. Lima: La Cronica y Varedades, S.A., 1938.

———. *Los Mochicas*, vol. 2. Museo Rafael Larco Herrera. Lima: Rimac, S.A., 1940.

———. "La escritura Mochica sobre pallares." *Revista Geografica Americana* 9, no. 107 (August 1942). Buenos Aires.

———. *La escritura peruana sobre pallares.* Año 11, vol. 20, nos. 122–23. Buenos Aires: Ediciones de la Revista Geografica Americana, 1943.

———. *Los Mochicas (Pre-Chimu, de Uhle y Early Chimu de Kroeber).* Buenos Aires: Sociedad Geografica Americana, 1945.

———. *Cronología Arqueologica del Norte del Peru.* Museo Rafael Larco Herrera. Buenos Aires: Sociedad Geográfica Americana, 1948.

———. *"Checan" (Ama en Moche).* Geneva: Nagel Publishing, 1965.

———. *Peru.* Translated by James Hogarth. Archaeologica Mundi Series. New York: World Publishing Company, 1966.

———. *Los Mochicas*, vols. 1–2. 1938–39. Reprint. Lima: Museo Larco, 2001.

Larcom, Joan. "The Invention of Convention." *Mankind* 13 (1982): 330–37.

Lathrap, Donald. "Gifts of the Cayman." In *Variation in Anthropology.* Urbana: Illinois Archaeological Survey, 1973.

Lau, George. "Feasting and Ancestor Veneration at Chinchawas, North Highlands of Ancash, Peru." *Latin American Antiquity* 13 (2002): 279–304.

Lavalle, Jose Antonio. *Moche.* Culturas Precolombinas Series. Lima: Banco de Credito del Peru, 1985.

Lavallée, Danielle. *Les representations dans le ceramique Mochica.* Memoire de Maitrise, Universite de Paris IV, Memoires de l'Institut d'Ethnologie-IV. Paris: Musee de l'Homme, 1970.

Lehmann, Walter. "Vocabulario Mochica." In *El vocabulario mochica de Walter Lehmann (1929) comparado con otras fuentes lexicas*, edited by Gertrud Schumacher de Peña. Lima: Universidad Nacional Mayor de San Marcos, 1991.

Leonard, Banks L. "Moche through Late Horizon Settlement Patterns, Chicama Valley, Peru." Paper presented at the 55th annual meeting of the Society for American Archaeology, Las Vegas, 1990.

Leonard, Banks L., and Glenn S. Russell. "The Mocollope Site Complex, Chicama Valley, Peru." Paper presented at the 30th annual meeting of the Institute of Andean Studies, Berkeley, 1990.

———. "Informe Preliminar: Proyecto de Reconocimiento Arqueologico del Chicama, Resultados de la Primera Temporada de Campo, 1989." Report submitted to the Instituto Nacional de Cultura, Trujillo, 1992.

Leventhal, Richard, and Alan Kolata. *Civilization in the Ancient Americas*. Cambridge, MA: University of New Mexico Press and Peabody Museum, Harvard University, 1983.

Lévi-Strauss, Claude. *Totemism*. Translated by Rodney Needham. Boston: Beacon Press, 1963.

———. *Structural Anthropology*. Translated by Claire Jacobson and Brooke Grundfest Schoepf. New York: Basic Books, 1963–76.

———. *The Way of the Masks*. Translated by Sylvia Modelski. Seattle: University of Washington Press, 1982.

Lieske, Bärbel. *Mythische Bilderzählungen in den Gefässmalereien der altperuanischen Moche-Kultur*. Bonn: Holos, 1992.

Lizárraga, Reginaldo de. *Descripcion breve del Peru*. 1591. Madrid: Biblioteca de Autores Españoles, 216, 1919.

Locke, Leland. *The Ancient* Quipu *or Peruvian Knot Record*. New York: American Museum of Natural History, 1923.

Lopez Serano, Matilde. *Drawings of XVIII Trujillo by Martinez Campiñon*. Barcelona: Editorial Patrimonio Nacional, 1976.

Lothrop, Samuel K. "Aboriginal Navigation Off the West Coast of South America." *Journal of the Royal Anthropological Institute* 62 (1932): 229–56.

———. *Inca Treasure as Depicted by Spanish Historians*. Los Angeles: Southwest Museum, 1938.

Loukotka, Čestmír. *Classification of South American Indian Languages*. Edited by Johannes Wilbert. Los Angeles: Latin American Center, University of California, 1968.

Lumbreras, Luis. *The Peoples and Cultures of Ancient Peru*. Translated by Betty Meggers. Washington, DC: Smithsonian Institution Press, 1974.

Lyon, Patricia J. "Arqueología y mitología: La escena de 'los objetos animados' y el tema de 'el alzamiento de los objetos.'" *Scripta Ethnologica* 6 (1981): 103–8.

———. "Archaeology and Mythology, II: A Reconsideration of the Animated Objects Theme in Moche Art." *Cultures in Conflict: Current Archaeological Perspectives*, no. 20 (1989): 62–68.

Mackey, Carol, and Charles Hastings. "Moche Murals from the Huaca de La Luna." In *Pre-Columbian Art Selected Readings*, edited by Alana Cordy-Collins. Palo Alto: Peek Publications, 1982.

Mackey, Carol, and Melissa Vogel. "La Luna sobre los Andes: Una revision del animal lunar." In *Moche: Hacia el Final del Milenio*, vol. 1, edited by Santiago Uceda and Elias Mujica. Lima: Universidad Nacional de Trujillo and Pontificia Universidad Católica del Perú, Fondo Editorial, 2003.

Makowski, Krzysztof. "Los seres radiantes, el águila y el búho." In *Imágenes y mitos. Ensayos sobre las artes figurativas en los andes prehispanicos*, edited by Krzystof Makowski, Ivan Amaro Bullon, and Max Hernandez. Lima: Australis, Fondo Editorial Sidea, 1996.

———. "Hacia la reconstrucción del panteón Moche: Tipos, personalidades iconográficas, narraciones." In *El Mundo Sobrenatural Mochica*, edited by Milosz Giersz, Krzystof Makowski, and Patrycja Przadka. Lima: Fondo Editorial de la Pontificia Universidad Católica del Perú, 2005.

Makowski, Krzysztof, Chirstopher B. Doonan, and Ivan Amaro Bullon. *Vicús*. Lima: Banco de Credito, 1994.

Marcos, Jorge G. "Cruising to Acapulco and Back with the Thorny Oyster Set: A Model for a Lineal Exchange System." *Journal of the Steward Anthropological Society* 9 (1978): 99–132. Urbana-Champagne.

Marcus, Joyce. *Mesoamerican Writing Systems: Propaganda, Myth, and History in Four Ancient Civilizations*. Princeton: Princeton University Press, 1992.

Martin, Simon. "On Pre-Columbian Narrative." In *A Pre-Columbian World*, edited by J. Quilter and M. Miller. Washington, DC: Dumbarton Oaks, 2006.

Martinez Compañon y Bujanda, Baltasar Jaime. *Trujillo del Peru a fines del siglo XVIII, dibujos y acuarelas que mando hacer el obispo*. 1785. Madrid: Edicion de Jesus Dominguez Bordona, 1936.

Mason, John Alden. *The Languages of South American Indians. Handbook of South American Indians*, vol. 6. Washington, DC: Smithsonian Institution, 1950.

McClelland, Donna, Donald McClelland, and Christopher B. Donnan. *Moche Fineline Painting from San José de Moro*. Los Angeles: Cotsen Institute of Archaeology at University of California–Los Angeles, 2007.

Means, Philip A. *Ancient Civilizations of the Andes*. New York: Charles Scribner's Sons, 1931.

Meillet, A., and Marcel Cohen. *Les langues de monde*. Paris: Edouard Champion, 1924.

Melion, Walter, and Susanne Küchler, eds. *Images of Memory*. Washington, DC: Smithsonian Institution Press, 1991.

Menzel, Dorothy. "Style and Time in the Middle Horizon." *Ñawpa Pacha* 2 (1964): 1–106.

———. *The Archaeology of Ancient Peru and the Work of Max Uhle.* Lowie Museum of Anthropology. Berkeley: University of California Press, 1977.

Middendorf, Ernst W. *Das Muchik öder die Chimu-Sprache.* Leipzig: F. A. Brockhaus, 1892.

———. *Peru: Beobachtungen und Studien über das Land und seine Bewohner während eines 25 Jährigen Aufenthalts.* 3 vols. Berlin: R. Oppenheim, 1893–95.

Mignolo, Walter. *The Darker Side of the Renaissance: Literacy, Territoriality, and Colonization.* Ann Arbor: University of Michigan Press, 1995.

Miller, Arthur. *The Mural Painting of Teotihuacan.* Washington, DC: Dumbarton Oaks, 1973.

Millon, Clara. "A Reexamination of the Teotihuacan Tassel Headdress Insignia." In *Feathered Serpents and Flowering Trees.* San Francisco: Fine Arts Museum of San Francisco, 1988.

Millones, Luis, and Moises Lemlij, eds. *Al Final del Camino.* Lima: Fondo Editorial SIDEA, 1996.

Mitchell, W. J. T. *The Language of Images.* Chicago: University of Chicago Press, 1980.

———. *Iconology: Image, Text, Ideology.* Chicago: University of Chicago Press, 1986.

———. *Picture Theory.* Chicago: University of Chicago Press, 1994.

Molina, Cristobal de. "Replacion de las favulas y ritos de los Incas." 1573. In *Los pequenos grandes libros de historia americana,* ser. 1, vol. 4, edited by Francisco A. Loayza. Lima: D. Miranda, 1943.

———. *Ritos y Fabulas de los Incas.* Buenos Aires: Ed. Futuro, 1959.

Montoya, Maria. "Excavaciones en la Plaza 3b en la Huaca de La Luna." In *Investigaciones en la Huaca de la Luna 1995,* edited by Santiago Uceda, Elias Mujica, and Ricardo Morales. Trujillo: Universidad Nacional de La Libertad, 1997.

Moore, Jerry D. "Pre-Hispanic Beer in Coastal Peru: Technology and Social Context in Prehistoric Production." *American Anthropologist* 91 (1989): 682–95.

———. *Architecture and Power in the Ancient Andes.* Cambridge: Cambridge University Press, 1996.

Morales G., Ricardo. "Pintura Mural Moche: Technica y Conservación." Conservation techniques at Huaca Coton, Trujillo, 1981a.

———. "Pinturas Murales de La Huaca Coton." Report to the Instituto Nacional de Cultura on Mural Restoration at Huaca Coton, Guadalupe, Trujillo, 1981b.

———. "Iconografía litúrgica y contexto arquitectonico en Huaca de la Luna, valle de Moche." In *Moche: Hacia el Final del Milenio*, vol. 1, edited by Santiago Uceda and Elias Mujica. Lima: Universidad Nacional de Trujillo and Pontificia Universidad Católica del Perú, Fondo Editorial, 2003.

Moseley, Michael. "Patterns of Settlement and Preservation in the Viru and Moche Valleys." In *Prehistoric Settlement Patterns*, edited by Evon Z. Vogt and Richard M. Leventhal. Albuquerque: University of New Mexico Press, 1983.

———. *The Incas and Their Ancestors: The Archaeology of Peru*. London: Thames and Hudson, 1992.

Moseley, Michael, and Alana Cordy-Collins. *The Northern Dynasties: Kingship and Statecraft in Chimor*. Dumbarton Oaks Symposium, October 1985. Washington, DC: Dumbarton Oaks, 1991.

Moseley, Michael, and Kent Day. "Chan Chan, Peru's Ancient City of Kings." *National Geographic* 143 (1973): 318–45.

———, eds. *Chan Chan: Andean Desert City*. Albuquerque: University of New Mexico Press, 1982.

Muelle, Jorge C. "Chalchalcha (Un analisis de los dibujos muchik)." *Revista del Museo Nacional* 5, no. 1 (1936): 65–88. Lima.

Mujica Barreda, Elias, ed. *El Brujo*. Lima: Fundación Wiese, 2007.

Munsell Color Company, Inc. *Munsell Soil Color Charts*. Baltimore: Munsell Color Company, Inc., 1975.

Murra, John. "Cloth and Its Functions in the Inca State." *American Anthropologist* 64, no. 4 (1962): 710–28.

Murra, John V., and Craig Morris. "Dynastic Oral Tradition, Administrative Records and Archaeology in the Andes." *World Archaeology* 7, no. 3 (1976): 269–79.

Murúa, Fray Martin de. *Historia del Orígen y Geneaología Real de los Reyes Incas del Perú*, vol. 2. 1590. Madrid: Biblioteca Missionalia Hispanica, 1946.

Myers, Thomas, and Karrie Porter Brace. "Face Painting and Clothing of a Capuli Coquero." *Journal of Latin American Lore* 21 (2003): 2.

Nelson, Robert, and Richard Shiff. *Critical Terms for Art History*. Chicago: University of Chicago Press, 1996.

Netherly, Patricia. "Local Level Lords on the North Coast of Peru." Ph.D. diss., Department of Anthropology, Cornell University, Ithaca, NY, 1977.

———. "The Management of Late Andean Irrigation Systems on the North Coast of Peru." *American Antiquity* 49 (1984): 227–54.

———. "From Event to Process: The Recovery of Late Andean Organizational Structure by Means of Spanish Colonial Written Records." In *Peruvian Prehistory*, edited by R. W. Keatinge. Cambridge: Cambridge University Press, 1988.

———. "Out of Many, One: The Organization of Rule in North Coast Polities." In *The Northern Dynasties*, edited by Michael Moseley and Alana Cordy-Collins. Washington, DC: Dumbarton Oaks, 1990.

Nicholson, Henry B. "Preclassic Mesoamerican Iconography from the Perspective of the Post Classic: Problems in Interpretational Analysis." In *Origins of Religious Art and Iconography in Preclassic Mesoamerica*, edited by Henry B. Nicholson. Los Angeles: University of California–Los Angeles Latin American Center Publications, 1976.

Noë, Alva, and Evan Thompson, eds. *Vision and Mind*. Cambridge, MA: MIT Press, 2002.

Norton, F. H. *Ceramics for the Artist Potter*. Cambridge: Addison-Wesley Publishing Co., 1956.

Ong, Walter J. *Orality and Literacy: The Technologizing of the Word*. London: Mathuen, 1982.

Oré, Geronimo de. "Rituale, seu peruanum. . . ." 1607. In *Langues Puquina. Textes puquina contenus dans le Rituale seu Manuale Peruanum de Geronimo de Ore, public a Naples en 1607*, Raoul de La Grasserie and Luis Jeronimo de Ore. Leipzig: K. F. Koeler, 1894.

Ortigues, Edmond. *Le discours et le symbole*. Paris: Editions Aubier Montaigne, 1962.

O'Sullivan, Tim, John Hartley, Sanny Saunders, and John Fiske. *Key Concepts in Communication*. New York: Methuen and Co., 1983.

Owen, C. L. "Technology, Literacy and Graphic Systems." In *Toward a New Understanding of Literacy*, edited by Merald E. Wrolstad and Dennis F. Fisher. New York: Praeger, 1986.

Panofsky, Erwin. "Iconography and Iconology: An Introduction to the Study of Renaissance Art." In *Studies in Iconology*. New York: Doubleday, 1955a.

———. *Meaning in the Visual Arts: Papers in and on Art History*. Garden City, NY: Double Day, 1955b.

———. *Renaissance and Renascences in Western Art*. Stockholm: Almquist and Wiksells, 1960.

Pasztory, Esther. "Still Invisible." *RES* 19–20 (1990): 105–35.

———. "Strategies of Organization in Teotihuacan Art." *Ancient Mesoamerica* 2, no. 2 (Fall 1991): 247–48. Cambridge.

Peacock, D. P. S. *Pottery in the Roman World: An Ethnoarchaeological Approach*. London: Longman, 1982.

Peirce, Charles Sanders. "Logic as Semiotic: The Theory of Signs." 1931. Reprint. In *Semiotics*, edited by Robert E. Innis. Bloomington: Indiana University Press, 1985.

———. "What Is a Sign?" 1894. Reprint. In *The Essential Peirce*, vol. 2, edited by Nathan Houser and Christian Kloesel. Bloomington: Indiana University Press, 1992.

Piddocke, Stuart. "The Potlatch System of the Southern Kwakiutl: A New Perspective." *Southwestern Journal of Anthropology* 21 (1965): 244–64.

Pillsbury, Joanne, ed. *Moche Art and Archaeology in Ancient Peru.* Washington, DC: Center for Advanced Study of the Visual Arts, National Gallery of Art, 2001.

Pirenne, Henri. *Economics and Social History of Medieval Europe.* New York: Harcourt, Brace, Jovanovich, 1937.

Polo de Ondegardo, Juan. *Informaciones Acerca de la Religión y Gobierno de los Incas.* 1571. Colección de libros y documentos referentes a la Historia de Perú, vol. 3. Lima: Sanmartí and Cia, 1916.

Postgate, Nicholas, Tao Wang, and Toby Wilkinson. "The Evidence for Early Writing: Utilitarian or Ceremonial?" *Antiquity* 69 (1995): 458–80.

Pottier, Bernard, ed. *America Latina en sus Lenguas Indigenas.* Caracas: UNESCO, 1983.

Proulx, Donald A. *An Archaeological Survey of the Nepeña Valley, Peru.* Department of Anthropology Research Report, no. 2. Amherst: University of Massachusetts, 1968.

Purin, Sergio. "Utilization des Rayons-X pour l'observacion des traces de fabrication sur cinq vases Mochicas." *Bulletin des Musées Royaux d'Art et d'Histoire* 54, no. 2 (1983): 5–20. Brussels.

Quilter, Jeffrey. "The Moche Revolt of the Objects." *Latin American Antiquity* 1, no. 1 (1990): 42–65.

———. "The Narrative Approach to Moche Iconography." *Latin American Antiquity* 8, no. 2 (1997): 113–33.

———. "Moche Mimesis: Continuity and Change in Public Art in Early Peru." In *Moche Art and Archaeology in Ancient Peru*, edited by Joanne Pillsbury. Washington, DC: Center for Advanced Study of the Visual Arts, National Gallery of Art, 2001.

Quilter, Jeffrey, and Luis Jaime Castillo, eds. *New Perspectives on Moche Political Organization. Studies in Pre-Columbian Art and Archaeology.* Washington, DC: Dumbarton Oaks Research Library and Collections (forthcoming).

Quilter, Jeffrey, and Gary Urton, eds. *Narrative Threads: Accounting and Recording in Andean Khipu.* Austin: University of Texas Press, 2002.

Rabinowitz, Joel. "La Lengua Pescadora: The Lost Dialect of Chimu Fishermen." In *Latin American Studies Program*, edited by Daniel Sandweiss. New York: Cornell University, 1983.

Ralph, E. K., H. N. Michael, and M. C. Han. "Radiocarbon Dates and Reality." *MASCA Newsletter* 9, no. 1 (1973): 1–19.

Ramirez, Susan E. "De Pescadores y Agricultores: Una historia local de la gente del Valle de Chicama antes de 1565." *Bulletin de l'Institut Français de'Etudes Andines* 24, no. 2 (1995a): 245–79.

———. "An Oral History of the Valley of Chicama, circa 1524–1565." *Journal of the Steward Anthropological Society* 23, nos. 1–2 (1995b): 299–343.

———. *The World Upside Down: Cross-Cultural Contact and Conflict in Sixteenth-Century Peru*. Stanford: Stanford University Press, 1996.

Ramos Cabredo, Josefina. "Ensayo de un vocabulario de la lengua Tallan o Tallanca." In *Cuadernos de Estudio, Instituto de Investigaciones Historicas de la Ponitfica Universidad Catolica de Peru*, vol. 4, no. 3, annex C. Lima: Pontificia Universidad Católica del Perú, 1950.

Rivero y Ustáriz, Mariano Eduardo, and Johann Jacob von Tschudi. *Antigüedades peruanas*. Vienna: Imprenta de la Corte y del Estado, 1851.

Rivet, Paul. "Les langues de l'ancien diocese de Trujillo." *Journal de la Societe des Americanistes* 38 (1949): 1–51. Paris.

Rostworowski, Maria. *Curacas y Sucesiones: Costa Norte*. Lima: Imprenta Minerva, 1961.

———. "Pescadores, artesanos y mercaderes costeños en el Peru prehispanico." *Revista del Museo Nacional* 41 (1975): 320. Lima.

———. "Coastal Fishermen, Merchants, and Artisans in Pre-Hispanic Peru." In *The Sea in the Pre-Columbian World*, edited by E. Benson. Washington, DC: Dumbarton Oaks Research Library and Collection, 1977.

———. *Recursos naturales renovables y pesca, siglos XVI y XVII*. Lima: Instituto de Estudios Peruanos, 1981.

Rowe, John H. "Inca Culture at the Time of the Spanish Conquest." In *Handbook of South American Indians*, vol. 2, edited by Julian Steward. Washington, DC: Smithsonian Institute, 1946.

———. "The Kingdom of Chimor." *Acta Americana* 6 (1948): 26–59.

———. "Stratigraphy and Seriation." *American Antiquity* 26 (1961): 324–30.

———. "Form and Meaning in Chavin Art." In *Peruvian Archaeology: Selected Readings*, edited John H. Rowe and Dorothy Menzel. Berkeley: Peek Publications, 1967a.

———. "Stages and Periods in Archaeological Interpretation." 1962. Reprint. In *Peruvian Archaeology: Selected Readings*, edited John H. Rowe and Dorothy Menzel. Berkeley: Peek Publications, 1967b. First published in *Southwestern Journal of Anthropology* 18, no. 1.

Rowe, John H., and Dorothy Menzel, eds. *Peruvian Archaeology: Selected Readings*. Palo Alto: Peek Publications, 1967.

Rush, R. T., A. J. Moe, and R. L. Storlie. *Occupational Literacy Education*. Newark, DE: International Reading Association, 1986.

Russell, Glenn S. "Preceramic through Moche Settlement Pattern Change in the Chicama Valley, Peru." Paper presented at the 55th annual meeting of the Society for American Archaeology, Las Vegas, 1990.

Russell, Glenn, Christopher Attarian, and Rosario Becerra Urtega. "Informe Parcial: Excavaciones en Mocollope, Valle de Chicama, Perœ, temporada de excavaciones (Junio–Agosto, 1998)." Report on file, Instituto Nacional de Cultura, Trujillo, 1999.

Russell, Glenn, and Margaret Jackson. "Patronage and Political Economy at Cerro Mayal, Peru." In *Moche Art and Archaeology in Ancient Peru*, edited by J. Pillsbury. Washington, DC: Center for Advanced Study of the Visual Arts, National Gallery of Art, 2001.

Russell, Glenn, Banks L. Leonard, and Jesus Briceño R. "Produccion de Ceramica a Gran Escala en el Valle de Chicama, Peru: El Taller de Cerro Mayal." In *Tecnología y Organización de la Producción de Cerámica Prehispanica en los Andes*, edited by Izumi Shimada. Lima: Pontifica Universidad Católica del Perú, 1994.

———. "The Cerro Mayal Workshop: Addressing Issues of Craft Specialization in Moche Society." In *Andean Ceramics: Technology, Organization, and Approaches*, edited by Izumi Shimada. MASCA Research Papers in Science and Archaeology, Supplement to Vol. 15. Philadelphia: Museum Applied Science Center for Archaeology, University of Pennsylvania Museum of Archaeology and Anthropology, 1998.

Salas, Jose Antonio. *Diccionario Mochica–Castillano, Castillano–Mochica*. Lima: Universidad de San Martin de Porres, 2002.

Sampson, Geoffrey. *Writing Systems: A Linguistic Introduction*. Stanford: Stanford University Press, 1985.

Sancho de la Hoz, Pedro. "Relacion para SM de lo sucedido en la conquista y pacificacion de la Nueva Castilla y de la calidad de la tierra." 1543. In *Biblioteca Peruana*, ser. 1, vol. 1. Lima: Editores Tecnicos Asociados, 1968.

Sarmiento de Gamboa, Pedro. *Historia de los Incas*. 1572. Buenos Aires: Biblioteca Emece, 1947.

Saussure, Ferdinand de. *Course in General Linguistics*. 1959. Edited by Charles Bally and Albert Sechehaye. London: Duckworth, 1983.

Savage, George, and Harold Newman. *An Illustrated Dictionary of Ceramics*. London: Thames and Hudson, 1985.

Sawyer, Alan R. *Mastercraftsmen of Ancient Peru*. New York: Guggenheim Museum, 1968.

Schaedel, Richard P. "Mochica Murals at Pañamarca." 1951. Reprint. In *Peruvian Archaeology: Selected Readings*, edited by John H. Rowe and Dorothy Menzel. Palo Alto: Peek Publications, 1967. First published in *Archaeology* 4, no. 3: 145–54.

———. "The City and the Origin of the State in America." In *Urbanizacion y proceso social en America*. Lima: Instituto de Estudios Peruanos, 1972.

Schapiro, Meyer. "On Some Problems in the Semiotics of Visual Art: Field and Vehicle in Image-Signs." In *Semiotics*, edited by Robert E. Innis. Bloomington: University of Indiana Press, 1985.

Schele, Linda, and Mary Ellen Miller. *The Blood of Kings*. Fort Worth: Kimbell Art Museum, 1986.

Schmandt-Besserat, Denise. "The Earliest Precursors of Writing." *Scientific American* 238 (1978): 50–59.

———. *How Writing Came About*. Austin: University of Texas Press, 1996.

Schumacher de Peña, Gertrud, ed. *El Vocabulario Mochica de Walter Lehmann (1929) comparado con otras fuentes lexicas*. Lima: Universidad Nacional Mayor de San Marcos, 1991.

Seler, Eduard. "Archaologische Reise in Sud-und Mittel-Amerika." In *Zeitschrift für Ethnologie*, 44. Berlin: Jahrgang, Heft 1, 1912.

Sharon Douglas. "The San Pedro Cactus in Peruvian Folk Healing." In *Flesh of the Gods: The Ritual Use of Hallucinogens*, edited by Peter Furst. New York: Praeger, 1972.

———. "The Symbol System of a North Peruvian Shaman." Ph.D. diss., Department of Anthropology, University of California, Los Angeles, 1974.

———. "The Inca Warachikuy Initiations." In *Enculturation in Latin America*, vol. 37, edited by J. Wilbert. Los Angeles: University of California–Los Angeles Latin American Studies, 1976.

Sharon, Douglas, and Christopher Donnan. "Shamanism in Moche Iconography." In *Ethnoarchaeology*. Monograph 3. Los Angeles: University of California, 1974.

Shimada, Izumi. "La producción de cerámica en Mórrope, Perú: Productividad, especialización y espacio vistos como recursos." In *Tecnología y Organización de la Producción de Cerámica Prehispanica en los Andes*, edited by Izumi Shimada. Lima: Pontifica Universidad Católica del Perú, 1994a.

———. *Pampa Grande and the Mochica Culture*. Austin: University of Texas Press, 1994b.

———, ed. *Tecnología y Organización de la Producción de Cerámica Prehispanica en los Andes*. Lima: Pontifica Universidad Católica del Perú, 1994.

———, ed. *Andean Ceramics: Technology, Organization, and Approaches*. MASCA Research Papers in Science and Archaeology, Supplement to Vol. 15. Philadelphia: Museum Applied Science Center for Archaeology, University of Pennsylvania Museum of Archaeology and Anthropology, 1998.

Shimada, Izumi, and U. Wagner. "Peruvian Black Pottery Production and Metalworking: A Middle Sican Craft Workshop at Huaca Sialupe." *MRS Bulletin* 26, no. 1 (2001): 25–30.

———. "A Holistic Approach to Pre-Hispanic Craft Production." In *Archaeological Anthropology*, edited by J. Skibo, M. Graves, and M. Stark. Tucson: University of Arizona Press, 2007.

Silverstein, Michael, and Greg Urban, eds. *Natural Histories of Discourse*. Chicago: University of Chicago Press, 1996.

Smith, Mary Elizabeth. *Picture Writing from Ancient Southern Mexico: Mixtec Place Signs and Maps*. Norman: University of Oklahoma Press, 1973a.

———. "The Relationship between Mixtec Manuscript Painting and Language." In *Mesoamerican Writing Systems*, edited by Elizabeth Benson. Washington, DC: Dumbarton Oaks, 1973b.

Smith, Terry. "Modes of Production." In *Critical Terms for Art History*, edited by Robert Nelson and Richard Shiff. Chicago: University of Chicago Press, 1996.

Squier, Ephraim George. *Peru: Incidents of Travel and Exploration in the Land of the Incas*. 1877. Foreword by Gordon R. Willey. Cambridge, MA: Peabody Museum of Archaeology and Ethnology, Harvard University Press, 1973.

Stahl, Peter. "Hallucinatory Imagery and the Origin of Early South American Figurine Art." *World Archeology* 18, no. 1 (1986): 134–50.

Stanish, Charles. *Ancient Andean Political Economy*. Austin: University of Texas Press, 1992.

Stark, Louisa R. "Mayan Affinities with Yunga of Peru." Ph.D. diss., New York University, 1968.

Stock, Brian. *The Implications of Literacy*. Princeton: Princeton University Press, 1983.

———. *Listening for the Text: On the Uses of the Past*. Philadelphia: University of Pennsylvania Press, 1990.

Stoler Miller, Barbara, ed. *The Powers of Art: Patronage in Indian Culture*. Oxford: Oxford University Press, 1992.

Strong, William Duncan. "Finding the Tomb of a Warrior-God." *National Geographic* 91, no. 4 (April 1947): 453–82.

Strong, William, and Clifford Evans. "Cultural Stratigraphy in the Viru Valley, Northern Peru." *Columbia University Studies in Archaeology and Ethnology* 4 (1952): 1–373.

Strong, William D., Gordon Willey, and John Corbett. *Archaeological Studies in Peru, 1941–1942*. New York: Columbia University Press, 1943.

Tannen, Deborah. *Spoken and Written Language: Exploring Orality and Literacy*. Norwood, NJ: Ablex Publishing Corp., 1982.

Taube, Karl. "The Teotihuacan Spider Woman." *Journal of Latin American Lore* 9, no. 2 (1983): 107–89. Los Angeles.

———. "The Temple of Quetzalcoatl and the Cult of Sacred War at Teotihuacan." *Res* 21 (Spring 1992): 53–87.

———. *The Writing System of Ancient Teotihuacan*. Washington, DC: Center for Ancient American Studies, 2000.

Taylor, Gerald. *Ritos y tradiciones de Huarochiri: Manuscrito quechua de comienzos del siglo XVII*. Lima: Instituto de Estudios Peruanos, 1987.

Teale, William, and Elizabeth Sulsby. *Emergent Literacy*. Norwood, NJ: Ablex Publishing Corp., 1986.

Tedlock, Dennis. *Popul Vuh*. New York: Simon and Schuster, 1985.

Tello, Julio C. "Muchik." *Inca* 2 (1924): vii–280. Lima.

Thapar, Romila. "Patronage and the Community." In *The Powers of Art: Patronage in Indian Culture*, edited by Barbara Stoler Miller. Delhi: Oxford University Press, 1992.

Tilley, Christopher. "Foucault: Toward an Archaeology of Archaeology." In *Reading Material Culture: Structuralism, Hermenentics, and Post-structuralism*, edited by Christopher Tilley. Cambridge: Basil Blackwell, 1990.

Todorov, Tzvetan. "Structural Analysis of Narrative." *Novel* 1, no. 3 (1969): 70–76.

Topic, John, and Teresa Topic. "The Archaeological Investigation of Andean Militarism: Some Cautionary Observations." In *The Origins and Development of the Andean State*, edited by J. Haas, T. Pozorski, and S. Pozorski. Cambridge: Cambridge University Press, 1987.

Topic, Teresa Lange. "Excavations at Moche." Ph.D. diss., Department of Anthropology, Harvard University, Cambridge, MA, 1977.

———. "The Early Intermediate Period and Its Legacy." In *Chan Chan: Andean Desert City*, edited by Michael Moseley and Kent Day. Albuquerque: University of New Mexico Press, 1982.

Torero, Alfredo. "Delindes Linguisticos en la Costa Norte Peruana." *Revista Andina* 4, no. 2 (December 1986): 523–48. Lima.

Toribio Polo, Jose. *Memorias de los virreyes del Peru, marques de Mancera y conde de Salvatierra*. 1648. Lima: Imprenta del estado, 1896.

Tovar, Antonio, and Consuelo Larrucea de Tovar. *Católogo de las Lenguas de America del Sur*. Madrid: Editorial Gredos, S.A., 1984.

Tufinio, Moises. "Excavaciones en la Plaza 3c de la Huaca de la Luna." In *Investigaciones en la Huaca de la Luna 1999*, edited by Santiago Uceda, Elias Mujica, and Ricardo Morales. Facultad de Ciencias Sociales. Trujillo: Universidad Nacional de La Libertad, 2004.

Tufte, Edward R. *Envisioning Information*. Cheshire, UK: Graphics Press, 1990.

Turner, V. W. *Dramas, Fields and Metaphors, Symbolic Action in Human Society*. Ithaca, NY: Cornell University Press, 1974.

Ubbelode-Doering, Heinrich. *Old Peruvian Art*. New York: E. Weyhe, 1936.

———. *The Art of Ancient Peru*. New York: Praeger Publishers, 1952.

Uceda, Santiago. "Investigations at Huaca de la Luna, Moche Valley: An Example of Moche Religious Architecture." In *Moche Art and Archaeology in Ancient Peru*, edited by J. Pillsbury. Washington, DC: Center for Advanced Study of the Visual Arts, National Gallery of Art, 2001.

———. "El nivel alto de la Plataforma 1 de Huaca de la Luna: Un espacio multifuncional." In *Investigaciones en la Huaca de la Luna 2000*, edited by Santiago Uceda, Elias Mujica, and Ricardo Morales. Facultad de Ciencias Sociales. Trujillo: Universidad Nacional de La Libertad, 2006.

Uceda, Santiago, and Jose Armas. "Los Talleres alfarenos en el centro urbano Moche." In *Investigaciones en la Huaca de la Luna 1995*, edited by Santiago Uceda, Elias Mujica, and Ricardo Morales. Facultad de Ciencias Sociales. Trujillo: Universidad Nacional de La Libertad, 1997.

———. "An Urban Pottery Workshop at the Site of Moche, North Coast of Peru." In *Andean Ceramics: Technology, Organization, and Approaches*, edited by Izumi Shimada. MASCA Research Papers in Science and Archaeology, Supplement to Vol. 15. Philadelphia: Museum Applied Science Center for Archaeology, University of Pennsylvania Museum of Archaeology and Anthropology, 1998.

Uceda, Santiago, and Jose Canziani. "Evidencias de grandes precipitaciones en diversas etapas constructivas de la Huaca de La Luna, costa norte del Peru." *Bulletin de l'Institut Fancais d'Etudes Andines* 22, no. 1 (1993): 313–43. Lima.

Uceda, Santiago, and Ricardo Morales. "La Huaca de La Luna/The Huaca de La Luna." In *Trujillo Precolombino*, edited by J. A. Lavalle. Lima: Odebrecht Foundation, 1996.

Uceda, Santiago, Ricardo Morales G., Jose Canziani A., and Maria Montoya V. "Investigaciones sobre la arquitectura y relieves policromos en la Huaca de la Luna, Valle de Moche." In *Moche: Propuestas y Perspectivas*, edited by Santiago Uceda and Elias Mujica. Lima: Universidad Nacional de La Libertad–Trujillo, 1994.

Uceda, Santiago, and Elias Mujica, eds. *Moche: Propuestas y Perspectivas*. Lima: Universidad Nacional de La Libertad, 1994.

———, eds. *Moche: Hacia el Final del Milenio*, vols. 1–2. Lima: Universidad Nacional de Trujillo and Pontificia Universidad Católica del Perú, Fondo Editorial, 2003.

Uceda, Santiago, Elias Mujica, and Ricardo Morales, eds. *Investigaciones en la Huaca de la Luna 1995*. Facultad de Ciencias Sociales. Trujillo: Universidad Nacional de La Libertad, 1997.

———. *Investigaciones en la Huaca de la Luna 1995–1996*. Facultad de Ciencias Sociales. Trujillo: Universidad Nacional de La Libertad, 1998.

———. *Investigaciones en la Huaca de la Luna 1997*. Facultad de Ciencias Sociales. Trujillo: Universidad Nacional de La Libertad, 2000.

Uceda, Santiago, and Moises Tufinio. "El Complejo arquitectonico religioso Moche de Huaca de la Luna: Una aproximacion a su dinamica ocupacional." In *Moche: Hacia el Final del Milenio*, vol. 2, edited by Santiago Uceda and Elias Mujica. Lima: Universidad Nacional de Trujillo and Pontificia Universidad Católica del Perú, Fondo Editorial, 2003.

Uhle, Max. *Fundamentos etnicos y arqueologia de Arica y Tacna*. Quito: Imprenta de la Universidad Central, 1922.

———. *Pachacamac and Pachacamc Archaeology*. 1903. Reprint. Edited by Izumi Shimada. Monograph 62. Philadelphia: University Museum of Archaeology and Anthropology, 1991.

Urcid, Javier. *Zapotec Writing: Knowledge, Power and Memory in Ancient Oaxaca*. Department of Anthropology, Brandeis University, 2005. On the Foundation for the Advancement of Mesoamerican Studies, Inc., website: http://www.famsi.org/zapotecwriting/zapotec_text.pdf.

Urioste, G. L. *Hijos de Pariya Qaqa: La tradicion oral de Waru Chiri (mitologia y costumbres)*. 2 vols. Latin American Studies Series, no. 6, v. 11. Syracuse: Maxwell School of Citizenship and Public Affairs, 1983.

Urton, Gary. "From Knots to Narratives: Reconstructing the Art of Historical Record-Keeping in the Andes from Spanish Transcriptions of Inka Khipus." *Ethnohistory* 45, no. 3 (1998): 409–38.

———. *Signs of the Inka* Khipu: *Binary Coding in the Andean Knotted-String Records*. Austin: University of Texas Press, 2003.

Urton, Gary, and Carrie J. Brezine. "*Khipu* Accounting in Ancient Peru." *Science* 309 (2005): 1065–67.

Vasquez de Espinosa, Antonio. *Compendio y descripcion de las Indias Occidentales*. Washington, DC: Smithsonian Institution, 1948.

Vaughn, Kevin J. "Households, Crafts, and Feasting in the Ancient Andes: The Village Context of Early Nasca Craft Consumption." *Latin American Antiquity* 15, no. 1 (March 2004): 61–88.

Verano, John. "A Mass Burial of Mutilated Individuals at Pacatnamu." In *Pacatnamu Papers*, edited by Christopher B. Donnan and Guillermo Cock. Los Angeles: Museum of Cultural History, University of California Press, 1986.

———. "War and Death in the Moche World: Osteological Evidence and Visual Discourse." In *Moche Art and Archaeology in Ancient Peru*, edited by Joanne Pillsbury. Washington, DC: Center for Advanced Study of the Visual Arts, National Gallery of Art, 2001.

———. "Un analysis antropológico físico preliminar del material óseo recuperado en el área de sacrificios de la Plaza 3c de la Huaca de la Luna." In *Investigaciones en la Huaca de la Luna 1999*, edited by Santiago Uceda, Elias Mujica, and Ricardo Morales. Facultad de Ciencias Sociales. Trujillo: Universidad Nacional de La Libertad, 2004.

Verano, John, and Laurel S. Anderson. "Analisis del material osteologco." In *Informe del Programa Arqueologico complejo El Brujo, temporada 1996*. Manuscript on file, Instituto Nacional de Cultura, La Libertad, Trujillo, 1996.

Verano, John, Laurel Anderson, and Guido Lombardi. "Análisis osteológico de los resto humanos Moche hallados en la Huaca Cao Viejo por el Proyecto Arqueolçgico Complejo 'El Brujo.'" In *Investigaciones en la Huaca Cao Viejo, Valle de Chicama, Perú*, edited by Franco J. Regulo, Cesar Galvez M., and Segundo Vasquez S. Lima: Fundación Augusto N. Wiese, 1999.

Verano, John, Moises Tufinio, and Melissa Lund Valle. "Esqueletos humanos de la Plaza 3c de Huaca de la Luna." In *Investigaciones en la Huaca de la Luna 2001*, edited by Santiago Uceda, Elias Mujica, and Ricardo Morales. Facultad de Ciencias Sociales. Trujillo: Universidad Nacional de La Libertad, 2008.

Villareal, Federico. *La Lengua Yunga o Mochica*. Lima: Imprenta Peruana de E.Z. Casanova, 1921.

Wallis, Mieczyslaw. "Medieval Art as a Language." In *Actes du cinquieme Congres international d'esthetique, Amsterdam 1964*. Amsterdam: La Haye, Mouton and Co., 1968.

Warburton, William. *The Divine Legation of Moses Demonstrated*. 1738. New York: Garland Publishers, 1978.

Wassen, S. Henry. *Ulluchu in Moche Iconography and Blood Ceremonies: The Search for Identification*. Göteborg: Etnografiska Museum Arstryck Annals, 1985–86.

———. "El 'ulluchu' en la iconografía y ceremonias de sangre Moche: La busqueda de su identificacíon." *Boletín del Museo Chileno de Arte Precolomino* 3 (1989): 25–45. Santiago.

Wasserman-San Blas, Bruno John. *Ceramics del antiguo Peru de la coleccion Wassermann-San Blas*. Buenos Aires: Casa Jacob Peuser, 1938.

Whorf, Benjamin Lee. "A Linguistic Consideration of Thinking in Primitive Communities." In *Language, Thought and Reality: Selected Writings of Benjamin Lee Whorf*, edited by John B. Carroll. Cambridge, MA: MIT Press, 1956.

Wilbert, Johannes. *The Thread of Life: Symbolism of Miniature Art from Ecuador*. Washington, DC: Dumbarton Oaks, 1974.

———, ed. *Enculturation in Latin America*, vol. 37. Los Angeles: University of California–Los Angeles Latin American Center Publications, 1976.

Wilkins, David G., and Rebecca L. Wilkins, eds. *The Search for a Patron in the Middle Ages and the Renaissance*. Medieval and Renaissance Studies, vol. 12. Lewiston, NY: Edwin Mellen Press, 1996.

Willey, Gordon. *Prehistoric Settlement Patterns in the Viru Valley, Peru*. Bureau of American Ethnology, Bulletin 155. Washington, DC: Smithsonian Institution, U.S. Government Printing Office, 1953.

———. "Mesoamerican Art and Iconography and the Integrity of the Mesoamerican Ideological System." In *The Iconography of Middle American Sculpture*. New York: Metropolitan Museum of Art, 1973.

Willey, Gordon, and Philip Phillips. *Method and Theory in American Archaeology*. Chicago: University of Chicago Press, 1958.

Williams, Raymond. *Culture*. London: Fontana, 1981.

Wilson, David. *Prehispanic Settlement Patterns in the Lower Santa Valley, Peru*. Washington, DC: Smithsonian Institution Press, 1988.

Wobst, H. Martin. "Style in Archaeology or Archaeologists in Style." In *Material Meanings: Critical Approaches to the Interpretation of Material Culture*, edited by Elizabeth S. Chilton. Salt Lake City: University of Utah Press, 1999.

Wolf, Eric R. *Europe and the People without History*. Berkeley: University of California Press, 1982.

Wrolstad, Merald E., and Dennis F. Fisher, eds. *Toward a New Understanding of Literacy*. New York: Praeger, 1986.

Xerez, Francisco, and Miguel Estete. *Conquista del Peru*. 1534. Edited by Antonio R. Rodriquez Moñino. Badajos, Spain: Casa Arqueros, 1929.

Yakovleff, E. "Las falconidas en el arte y en las creencias de los antiguos peruanos." *Revista del Museo Nacional* 1, no. 1 (1932): 33–111.

Yakovleff, Eugenio, and Fernando Herrera. "El mundo vegetal de los antiguos personas." *Revista del Museo Nacional* 3, no. 3 (1934): 243–322.

———. "El mundo vegetal de los antiguos personas." *Revista del Museo Nacional* 4, no. 1 (1935): 31–102.

Zevallos Quiñones, Jorge. "Toponimia prehispanica en las tierras yungas." In *27th Congreso Internacional de Americanistas. Lima y Mexico 1939*, 2. Lima, 1943.

———. "Un Diccionario Yunga." *Revista del Museo Nacional* 15 (1946): 163–88.

———. "Los gramaticos de la lengua yunga." *Cuadernos de Estudio* 3, no. 1 (1948a): 40–67. Lima.

———. "Primitivas lenguas de la costa." *Revista del Museo Nacional* 17 (1948b): 114–19. Lima.

———. "Onomastica prehispanica de Chachapoyas." *Lenguaje y Ciencias* 20 (1966): 27–41. Lima.

———. *Onomastica Chimu*. Trujillo: Fundacion "Alfredo Pinillos Giocochea," 1993a.

———. *Toponimia Chimu*. Trujillo: Fundacion "Alfredo Pinillos Giocochea," 1993b.

———. *Toponimia Mochica Lambayeque*. Trujillo, 1994.

Zighelboim, Ari. "Mountain Scenes of Human Sacrifice in Moche Ceramic Iconography." "Current Research in Andean Antiquity," edited by Ari Zighelboim and Carol Barnes, *Journal of the Steward Anthropological Society* 23, nos. 1–2 (1995): 153–88. Urbana.

Zuidema, R. T. "Bureaucracy and Systematic Knowledge in Andean Civilization." In *The Inca and Aztec States, 1400–1800*, edited by G. A. Collier, R. Rosaldo, and J. B. Wirth. New York: New York Academic Press, 1982.

———. "Huaman Poma and the Art of Empire: Toward an Iconography of Royal Dress." In *Transatlantic Encounters: Europeans and Andeans in the Sixteenth Century*, edited by Kenneth J. Andrien and Rolena Adorno. Berkeley: University of California Press, 1991.

INDEX

Page numbers in *italic* text refer to figures and tables.

abbreviation, in Moche imagery, 153, 154
"action markers," and verb phrases in Muchic linguistic structure, 139–41, 148
adobe brick, and markers' marks, 20, 111
Ai-Apaec, 21, 23, 37
Allen, Catherine J., 45
Altieri, Rademes, 117, 182n2
Anderson, Laurel S., 31
Angry Moche Man, 55
animals: and imagery on ritual serving vessels from Cerro Mayal, 55, *58*; and use of regional fauna as locator elements, 187n13. *See also* feline motifs; fox motifs; Moon Animals
appliqués, and production of ceramics at Cerro Mayal, 71–72, 178n33
apus (living mountain peaks), 20
archaeology: and Moche political collapse in transitional Middle Horizon, 156; and Moche religious practices, 19; and research on communication technology, 7–8. *See also* botanical remains; burials; ceramics; faunal remains; skeletal remains
archaism, and monumentalism in Moche art, 48

architecture: and function of muralism, 36; and ideological correlations between Chicama and Moche valleys, 33. *See also* monumental art
Arraignment of Prisoners, 25, 33
Arriaga, Pablo Joseph de, 16
"artistic nouns," and iconographic system of Moche imagery, 123
astronomy. *See* calendar; Pleiades constellation
Atalan language group, 167

banded mouth, as artistic convention in Peruvian coastal art, 95
Barthes, Roland, 135, 136, 142
Bastian, Adolf, 117, 186n62
Bean Warriors, *147*
Benson, Elizabeth P., 89, 131
Benveniste, Emile, 120–22, 131
Berlo, Janet C., 87–88
"bicephalic arch" icon, 22
bird motifs, 96–97, 106–7, 180n2. *See also* Bird Priest; owl motifs; Owl Warrior
Bird Priest, 19
Bonavia, Ducio, 172n41
Boone, Elizabeth H., 83, 169n9

223

botanical remains, analysis of at Cerro Mayal, 50

Bourget, Steve, 89, 173n48, 174n91

Brezine, Carrie J., 184n37

Brice, W. C., 86

Briceño, Jesus, 170n16, 175n3

Brüning, Enrique, 117

burials: of elite people in monumental structures, 21; and funerary contexts for high-quality Moche ceramics, 38–42, 174n91. *See also* Burial Theme; skeletal remains

Burial Theme, 37, 89

"Cachetón," 55

Calancha, Antonio de la, 16, 117, 129

calendar, and rituals keyed to agricultural and celestial events, 18

Carrera, Fernando de la, 100, 116, 118, 129, 139, 163–66, 180n2, 181n5–6, 182n5, 183n20, 183–84n22–27, 184n29–30, 186n57, 186n62

cascabeles (ceramic), 62, 65

Castillo, Luis Jaime, 89, 172n37, 177n20

ceramics: and architectural elements at Huaca de La Luna, 33; and changes in technology in Chimu period, 156; differentiation between images found in monumental arts and, 154–55; early Moche style and other north coastal traditions, 169n2; iconography and form types from Cerro Mayal workshop, 160–61; iconography and mold technology, 93–114, 152–53; as primary vehicle for transmission of Moche ideology, 37–47, 152; and production of imagery at workshop of Cerro Mayal, 50–76; use of terms in production and decoration of, 176n9, 177n26, 177–78n29. *See also* figurines (ceramics); molds (ceramics); *porras* (ceramic war clubs); rattles (ceramics)

Cerro Blanco, 22, 29

Cerro Mayal: frequency of iconographic types and ceramic forms from, 160–61; history of excavations at, 170n16, 175n3, 181n10; and production of ceramic imagery, 50–76; typology of inscriptions from molds or mold fragments from, 94–105

Cerro Mocollope, 50, 51, 75, 112, 172n40

Cerrón-Palomino, Rodolfo, 118, 163–66, 183n20–21

Chavín culture: and early Moche ceramic style, 169n2; and elements of figures in murals at Huaca de La Luna, 26. *See also* Cupisnique tradition

Chibchan language family, 167, 168

Chicama Valley: Moche political domination in, 171n13; and Muchic language, 117; pattern and sequence of monumental construction in, 172n40; and social organization of Moche culture, 16; and subdivision into complex pattern of moieties, 46–47

chicha (ceremonial beverage), 55

Chimu language family, 167, 189n3–5

Chinese script, as example of logographic writing system, 81

chirimoya motifs, 62, 64

class: burials and grave goods, 38–39; and feasting as display of status, 46. *See also* elites

climate, of Moche region, 14

clothing: and ceramic figurines produced at Cerro Mayal, 61, 99; and headdresses as indicators of rank and social role, 126–27, 139, 185n49. *See also* textiles

Codex Muro (Mixtec), 127–28

Coe, Michael D., 6

communication technology, research on in archaeological context, 7–8

Compañon, Bishop Martinez, 117

Complex Theme, 26–27, 32, 33, 155

configurations, of symbols in diagramming systems, 85

convention(s), and hybrid presentational syntax, 135–44

"conventional" semasiographic systems, 82–83

Cordy-Collins, Alana, 26

crab/sun/*xian* motif, 130–31, 158

Cupisnique tradition: and early Moche ceramic style, 169n2; and visual notation, 48

dance: and friezes at Huaca Cao Viejo, 31; and murals at Pañamarca, 35. *See also* Dance of the Dead; performance; Ribbon Dance (*baile con soga*)

Dance of the Dead, 65, 89

Darwin, Charles, 171n21

De Bock, Edward K., 176n17, 185n48

Decapitator motif, 21, 31, 33–34, 37, 155

Deer Hunt, 89, 147, 188n17

Deer Warriors, *147*

despachos (small figurines), 45

diagrammatic images, and iconic inscriptions on molds from Cerro Mayal, 98–105

diagramming systems, and iconographic analysis, 85

diet, and analysis of botanical and faunal remains at Cerro Mayal, 50–51. *See also* feasting

discourse and discursiveness, and analysis of Moche iconography, 80–88

Donnan, Christopher B., 89, 123, 124, 172n37, 177n18, 180n40, 185n49, 185n51, 188n17

drum cylinders (ceramic), 62, 63

economics. *See* labor; patronage

El Brujo complex. *See* Huaca Cao Viejo (El Brujo complex)

elites: and ceramics in funerary contexts, 38–39; and Moche social organization, 15; and monumental iconography, 152; and role of ideology in hierarchic social structures, 47, 155. *See also* class

Elkins, James, 85–86, 179n25

El Niño events, 18, 19, 29

embedded texts, and iconographic analysis, 87–88, 154

environment, and physical geography of Moche region, 14–15, 17

Eten language, 167, 189n3

ethnohistory, and music at ritual events, 65. *See also* Spanish (historic period chronicles)

Evans, Clifford, 53

evolutionary model, and ceramic mold inscriptions, 112–13

faces: and low-relief stamps, 69; and register marks on molds, 98; on ritual serving vessels from Cerro Mayal, 55, *57*; and textile motifs in mold inscriptions, 105

Fanged God, 24

Fanged Lizards, 55, 58, 59, 97, 177n20

faunal remains, analysis of at Cerro Mayal, 50

feasting: and generalizations about use of ceramics, 76; and ritual use of ceramics, 45, 53, 55. *See also* diet

feet, addition of to visual images as "action marker," 140

feline motifs, 29, 55, 58, *145*

fideos (ceramic), 64

figurines (ceramic): and artistic canons for profiles, 99; and correlation of form and image in ceramics from Cerro Mayal, *54*, 60–62; one-piece press molds and production of at Cerro Mayal, 71; ritual functions of, 43, *44*, 45

florero (flaring vase), *41*, 45, 52, 176n13

fox motifs, 58, 96–97

Franco J., 172n41

frog motifs, 97–98, *145*

Gelb, Ignacio J., 82, 112, 178n8
gender, of sacrificial victims at Huaca de La Luna, 29, 172n27. *See also* women
geographic features, of Moche region, 15
glottographic writing systems, 80–82, 83
grammar: and internal ordering in analysis of Moche iconography, 88–91; of Muchic language, 118–19, 121. *See also* syntax
Greenberg, Joseph H., 167, 190n9

Harrington, John P., 163–66, 189n1
Hastings, Charles, 27
hieroglyphs, and semiotic relationships in theory of signs, 84, 85
Hocquenghem, Anne Marie, 35, 89
homologous relationships, between visual and oral languages, 122–23
horizontal axis, of Moche visual narrative sequences, 135–38, 154
Houston, Stephen D., 7, 87, 111
huaca: and expression of ideology in monumental art, 19–37; and stylized icon as logographic element, 129, 158
Huaca Cao Viejo (El Brujo complex), 21, 25, 31–34, 134, 155, 172n40–41
Huaca de La Luna: and architectural juncture of ideology, pictorial representation, and ritualized performance, 21, 22–31; and ceramic mold technology, 105–10; and importance of ideological matrix, 134; and maker marks on bricks, 20; and murals, 172n41; and narratively structured murals and friezes, 155; skeletal remains of sacrifices at, 29, 90. *See also* Cerro Mayal
Huaca del Sol, 20, 172n41
Huaca Rosario, 172n41
Huaca Sialupe, and ceramic mold technology, 105–10
Huancavilca language, 167
Huarochiri Manuscript (colonial period), 146

hybrid presentational syntax, and analysis of Moche iconography, 133–49, 157
hybrid writing forms, and Mixtec notation, 124

icon(s): and hybrid presentational syntax, 135–44; and inscriptions on molds from Cerro Mayal, 98–105; Muchic language and Moche visual imagery, 120; and semiotic relationships in theory of signs, 84; use of term, 9, 10, 170n18. *See also* iconography (Moche)
"iconic" semasiographic systems, 83
iconography (Moche): and ceramic form types from Cerro Mayal workshop, 160–61; ceramic mold technology and formation of semantic units, 93–114; ceramics as primary vehicle for transmission of, 37–47; future directions in research on, 157–58; and hybrid presentational syntax, 133–49; as independent visual language, 11; issues in analysis of, 79–91; methodological approaches to study of, 7–8; and monumental architecture of Huaca de La Luna, 30–31; Muchic language and linguistic analogy to ceramics imagery, 115–31; and murals, 8–9, 155, 173n45; and relationships between ceramic motifs and forms, 50–76; review of studies on, 5–6; and use of ceramic molds for replication of pictorial signs, 76; visual culture and logic of, 151–57. *See also* icon(s); ideology; imagery
ideographs: and nature of Chinese script, 81; and semiotic relationships in theory of signs, 84
ideology: and centrality of religion in Moche art, 17; and changes in iconographic content, 156; and importance of blood sacrifice to Moche theocratic power, 19; and logic of Moche iconography, 151; and monumental art of temples and huacas, 19–37; and political function of Moche pictorial system,

155; and semiotic model for Moche iconographic system, 120
iguana motif, 59
imagery: Muchic language and visual, 120; and production of ceramic forms at workshop of Cerro Mayal, 51–65; standardization and abbreviation in, 153; vertical compression of in narrative sequences, 138–41, 153–54
Inca: and Ribbon Dance in Moche society, 35; and use of figurines, 45. See also *khipu*
indexes: and semiotic relationships in theory of signs, 84; stereotyped expression and mnemonic visualization in Moche imagery, 154; and structural commonalities in narratives, 135; use of term, 9, 10, 170n18
intaglio stamps, 69, 177n29

Jackson, Margaret A., 163–66, 181n4
jar (*olla*), 41
Jijón y Caamaño, Jacinto, 167, 189n1, 189n8
Jiménez Borja, Arturo, 89
joinery, of multiple-part ceramic compositions, 73–74, 76, 108

kawsaqkuna (living ones), 45
keros (jar), 45
khipu, and systems of phonetic writing, 6, 169n6, 182n1, 184n37
kilns, and technology of ceramic production at Cerro Mayal, 67–68
kinship, complex terminology of in Muchic language, 118–19, 184n26. *See also* marriages
knowledge, artists and specialized esoteric in Moche society, 76, 153
Kosok, Paul, 117
Kubler, George, 122–23, 143
Kutscher, Gerdt, 89

labor, and technology of ceramic production at Cerro Mayal, 76

Langer, Susanne K., 84–85, 87, 88
languages and linguistic analysis: and analysis of visual syntax, 10; and ceramic imagery, 115–31; and classification of South American language groups, 167–68, 189–90n3-9; and linguistic signs, 9–10. *See also* Muchic language; Quechua language; Quignam language; writing and writing systems
Larco Hoyle, Rafael, 16, 52, 89, 111, 115, 117, 170n11, 171n14, 181n6, 187n13
Lehmann, Walter, 117, 130–31, 181n6, 186–87n63
Leonard, Banks L., 170n16, 172n40, 175n3
"locators": in Mixtec pictorial writing systems, 124, 126; in Moche narrative sequences, 138; regional flora and fauna as, 187n13
logographic writing systems, 81, 82, 124–30, 148
Lord of Sicán, 109
Loukotka, Čestmír, 167, 189n3–5, 190n9
low-relief stamps, 69

mace heads. See *porras*
Mackey, Carol, 27
Macro-Chibcha language family, 167, 168
makers' marks, on adobe brick, 20, 111
Marcus, Joyce, 84
marriages, and political alliances of Moche culture, 16, 171n18. *See also* kinship
Marsh Scene, 37
Martin, Simon, 88, 135–36, 143, 144, 182n16, 187n9
Mason, J. Alden, 188n1
mathematical symbols, in semasiographic writing systems, 83
Maya: and linguistic relationships, 190n11; and presentational symbolism in script, 87; and similarity of Revolt of the Objects to *Popol Vuh*, 146
Mayal Mold Master, 69, 70, 74

McClelland, Donna, 124

Middendorf, Ernst W., 117, 163–66, 181n6, 183n20, 186n62

mixed writing systems, 84

Mixtec: and concepts of geographic units, 185n55; and culture history, 185n41; and linguistic analogies for visual imagery, 124–30; and Mesoamerican writing systems, 84; and standardization of figures in graphic notation, 143–44

Moche: ceramic mold technology and iconic elements as units of meaning, 93–114; and ceramics as primary vehicle for transmission of ideology, 37–47; dynamic versatility of imagery, 10–11; geographic extent of cultural influence of, 4; monumental art and ideology of, 19–37; physical environment of, 14–15; and production of ceramic imagery at Cerro Mayal, 50–76; recurrence and continuity of specific pictorial images as distinctive aspect of art, 3; and religion, 17–19; review of studies on iconography of, 5–6; social organization of, 15–16. *See also* ceramics; iconography (Moche); Muchic language

Mocollope. *See* Cerro Mocollope

molds (ceramic): iconography and technology of, 93–114, 153; and replication of pictorial signs, 76; and use of terms, 176n9–10, 177n24, 178n30; variability in from Cerro Mayal, 68–71

monumental art: differentiation between images found on ceramics and, 154–55; and expressions of Moche ideology, 19–37, 48; and logic of Moche iconography, 152

Moon Animals, 27, 28

morphemes, 80, 81

motivation, of logographic scripts, 81

Mountain Deity, 24

"Mountain Sacrifice Scene," 22

Muchic language: and analysis of visual syntax, 10; and derivative relationship between verbs and nouns, 100; and linguistic analogies for iconography in ceramics, 115–31; and linguistic classification, 167–68; and linguistic relationship between pregnancy and children, 181n6; and phonetics, 163–66; and verb phrases in visual narratives, 139–40, 149. *See also* languages and linguistic analysis

multidisciplinary approach, to Moche art and visual culture, 151

multiple-part molds, 71, 73–74, 76

Munro, Pamela, 163

murals: and expression of ideology in Moche monumental architecture, 21, 22–27, 30, 31–32, 35–37; original extent of in Moche monumental construction, 172n41; and study of Moche iconography, 8–9, 155, 173n45

Museo de Arqueología (Trujillo), 73–74

musical instruments (ceramic), 42–43, 62–65

musicians, images of in ceramics, 62, 99

narratives: and concept of Ur-narrative, 187n3; and cultural consistency, 151; and feast occasions, 46; hybrid presentational syntax in visual sequences of, 134–44; pictorial systems and structure of, 91, 154, 155. *See also* Warrior Narrative

naturalism, and degree of convention and abstraction in Moche art, 135

Near East, and development of alphabetic writing, 112–13

Netherly, Patricia, 171n18

nomenclature, and Muchic language, 116–18

Northwest Coast (North America), and potlatch tradition, 46

notational systems: and definitions of writing, 6–7; and iconographic analysis, 86; studies of ancient indigenous American, 158. *See also* semasiographic notation; writing and writing systems one-piece press molds, 71

oral/aural mode of operation, in Muchic language, 120

oral texts: and ceramic mold inscriptions, 112, 114; and collective cultural base, 151

Ortigues, Edmond, 179n11

Owen, Charles L., 85, 87

owl motifs, 55, 58, 59, 106, 180n2. *See also* bird motifs; Owl Warrior

Owl Warrior, 135, 145–46, 147

Paezan language family, 167, 168

Pañamarca (Nepeña Valley), 21, 34–35, 155, 172n41

parcialidades (moieties), in Chicama Valley, 46–47

patronage: and production of ceramics at Cerro Mayal, 50–51; and propagation of iconography by distribution of special-use ceramics, 46–47; and shared ideology of Moche pictorial system, 155

pedestal goblets, 40, *41*

Peirce, Charles Sanders, 9, 10, 84

pendants (ceramic), 43, *54*, 60, 71. *See also* figurines (ceramics)

performance: as key element in ritual experience, 25–26; musical instruments and symbolic value of, 65. *See also* dance; musicians

phonemes: and logographic writing systems, 81; and Muchic language, 121

phonetics, of Muchic language, 163–66

phonographic writing systems, 81

physical environment, of Moche culture, 14–15

pictographic writing systems, 81–82, 124

pictorial alignments, and analysis of ceramic molds, 94–97, 106, 109

pictorial units, and semantic units of ceramic mold inscriptions, 114

Pleiades constellation, 18

political organization: and complex pattern of moieties in Chicama Valley, 46–47; marriages and alliances of Moche and Chicama valleys, 16, 171n18; and Moche domination in Chicama Valley, 171n13; and shared ideology of Moche pictorial system, 155

Popol Vuh (Maya creation story), 146

porras (ceramic war clubs), 33, *34*, 106–7, 185n53. *See also* mace heads

portrait head bottle, *41*

presentational forms, and semiotic theory in analysis of pictorial communication, 84–85, 87. *See also* hybrid presentational syntax

"Presentation of Plates," *128*, *140*

Presentation Scene. *See* Sacrifice Scene

Priestess (motif), 18, 35, 145–46

priestesses: and funerary assemblages, 174n91; pedestal goblets and role in sacrificial rituals, 40

Prisoner Capture, *143*

"Prisoner Jar with Lizards," 73–74, *75*

Prisoner Procession, 155

proto-literacy, Moche art and theory of, 158

Purin, Sergio, 178n31

Quechua language, 167, 168, 188–89n1, 189–90n8

Quignam language, 10, 117, 167, 183n9

rattles (ceramic), 62, *63*, *64*, 99–100, 101–2, 181n4

Rayed Warrior Priest, 145–46, *147*, 155. *See also* Warrior Priest

rebus, concept of, 82, 130

register marks, and mold inscriptions, 97–98, 106, 109

religion: development and practice of Moche, 17–19; shared form of in Moche region, 172n36. *See also* priestesses; ritual; sacrifice; shamanism

repetition, in iconographic vocabulary, 156

Revolt of the Objects, 144–47, 155

Ribbon Dance (*baile con soga*), 35, 37, 42, 65, 89

ritual: and association of dance with ritual combat, 35; and ceramics in funerary contexts, 39–40; functions of ceramics in, 42–46; and ideology of Moche art, 17; and imagery of serving vessels, 53–59; and musical instruments, 65; practice of at Huaca de La Luna, 24–25. *See also* religion; ritual serving vessels; sacrifice

Ritual Badminton, 37

ritual serving vessels and "ritual vessel assemblage" motif, 53–59, 103, *104*, 105, *107*, *108*

Rivet, Paul, 167, 182–83n8, 189n1

road signs, as example of "iconic" semasiographic system, 83

Rowe, John H., 97, 117, 188n2

Russell, Glenn S., 170n16, 172n40, 175n3

sacrifice: as central part of Moche religious belief, 17–19; and function of muralism, 36; and skeletal remains at Huaca de La Luna, 29, 90, 172n27. *See also* Sacrifice Scene

Sacrifice Ceremony, 40

Sacrifice Scene, 17–18, 19, 25, 34, 35, 37, 89, 135–36, 146, 155, 172n28, 187n9

San José de Moro, 19, 39, 90, 187n7

Saussure, Ferdinand de, 9–10

Schaedel, Richard P., 35, 172n41

Schmandt-Besserat, Denise, 112–13

script communities: and ceramic mold inscriptions, 112, 114; and esoteric knowledge, 153

Sec language, 10, 189n4

semantic units, and ceramic mold inscriptions, 93–114

semasiographic notation, and Moche visual art, 82–83, 142–44, 149, 154, 158. *See also* notational systems

semiotics, and iconographic analysis, 84–88, 120–22

Serpent Demon, 24

shamanism: and double-chambered rattles, 102; and whistling, 73

Shimada, Izumi, 182n13

signs: Muchic language and visual imagery, 122, 124–30; semiotic relationships in theory of, 84; use of term, 9–10

Sipán, and tombs, 19, 39, 90

skeletal remains: and construction of Huaca Cao Viejo, 31; of sacrificial victims at Huaca de La Luna, 29, 90, 172n27. *See also* burials

Smith, Mary Elizabeth, 124–26, 185n44, 185n55

snake motifs, 59, 180–81n3. *See also* water serpent; Water Snake

social organization, of Moche culture: description of, 15–16; and generalizations about use of ceramics, 75–76; role of art in legitimation and maintenance of, 47–48. *See also* class; elites; kinship; patronage

Spanish (historic period chronicles): and Muchic language, 116; and use of figurines, 45. *See also* Carrera, Fernando de la; ethnohistory

spatial organization, and technology of ceramic production at Cerro Mayal, 76

spider motifs, 26, 155, 173n48

Spotted Dog, 136

Staff God (Andean), 27

stamp molds, 69, *70*, 73, 105, 177n28

standardization, and Moche imagery as cohesive iconography, 153

Standing Decapitator, 27

Stark, Louisa R., 118, 163–66, 183n20, 184n32, 190n11

step-fret *escalonado*, 55, *57*

stepped pyramid images, in Moche artwork, 55, *57*, 126–27, 129, 140, 185n48

stirrup-spout bottle, 40, *41*, 45

Stock, Brian, 112
straight-neck jars, 55
strap-handle bottle, *41, 57*
Strong, William Duncan, 53, 170n6
symbols and symbolism: and semiotic relationships in theory of signs, 84, 85, 87; and technology of ceramic production at Cerro Mayal, 76; use of term, 10, 170n18
syntax: and iconographic analysis, 84, 133–49; of Muchic language, 118–19, 121. *See also* grammar; hybrid presentational syntax

talismans (ceramics), 76
Tallan language, 167
tall-neck jar, *41*
Taube, Karl, 123, 126
technology: of ceramics production at Cerro Mayal, 66–74, 76; and changes in ceramic manufacture in Chimu period, 156
Tello, Julio C., 73
temples, monumental art of and Moche ideology, 19–37
Teotihuacán, and structural analysis of iconographic systems, 122–23, 126
text, definition of, 112. *See also* narratives; oral texts; textual communities
textiles: and ceramic mold inscriptions, 105; correlation of designs to geographic locations in Andes, 185n52. *See also* clothing
textual communities, and ceramic mold inscriptions, 111–14
tools, and production of ceramics at Cerro Mayal, *54*, 66–74
Torero, Alfredo, 118, 189–90n8
Tovar, Antonio and Consuelo Larrucea de, 163–66, 167, 189n6, 190n9
trumpets (ceramic), 42, 62, 63, 64–65
Tule Boat Theme, 37

Uhle, Max, 117, 167
Urton, Gary, 7, 169n9, 182n1, 184n37
Uru-Chiripaya language, 168
usnu (raised platform), 27

Venn diagram, of notational system, 86
Verano, John, 29, 31
verb clause, visual assemblies as, 100–101
verb phrases, and Muchic language, 139–40, 141
vertical axis, of Moche visual narrative sequences, 138–41, 153–54
Villareal, Federico, 117, 186n62

Wagner, U., 182n13
Warburton, William, 178n8
Warrior Confrontation, *137*
Warrior Narrative, 17–18, 31, 37, 89, 138–39, 146, 155
Warrior Pair, 32
Warrior Priest, 18, 19, 35, 135, 145–46. *See also* Rayed Warrior Priest
Warrior Procession, 28, 34, *52*
water serpent, 27, *28*
Water Snake, 35, 62, 64
"Waved Spiral Narrative," 146
wave motifs, 23
whistles (ceramic), 42, *43*, 62, *63*, 64–65
wind instruments (ceramic), 62, 64–65
women, and ceramic figurines produced at Cerro Mayal, 60–61. *See also* gender; priestesses
Wrinkle-Face Whistler, 55, 73, *74*, 95, *96*
writing and writing systems: definition of, 6–7, 169n9; development of alphabetic forms in Near East, 112–13; glottographic and semasiographic forms of, 80–83; and hybrid system of Mixtec notation, 124; syntax and semiotics in, 84–88. *See also* languages and linguistic analysis; notational systems

Index

231

Yunga. *See* Muchic language
Yunga-Puruhá language family, 167–68
Yünka linguistic family, 182–83n8

Zevallos-Quiñones, Jorge, 117, 129

www.ingramcontent.com/pod-product-compliance
Lightning Source LLC
Chambersburg PA
CBHW080923100426
42812CB00007B/2354